Solution Architecture Patterns for Enterprise

A Guide to Building Enterprise Software Systems

Chanaka Fernando

Apress®

Solution Architecture Patterns for Enterprise: A Guide to Building Enterprise Software Systems

Chanaka Fernando
Seeduwa, Sri Lanka

ISBN-13 (pbk): 978-1-4842-8947-1
https://doi.org/10.1007/978-1-4842-8948-8

ISBN-13 (electronic): 978-1-4842-8948-8

Managing Director, Apress Media LLC: Welmoed Spahr
Acquisitions Editor: Aditee Mirashi
Development Editor: James Markham
Coordinating Editor: Aditee Mirashi

Cover designed by eStudioCalamar

Cover image designed by Freepik (www.freepik.com)

Distributed to the book trade worldwide by Springer Science+Business Media New York, 1 New York Plaza, Suite 4600, New York, NY 10004-1562, USA. Phone 1-800-SPRINGER, fax (201) 348-4505, e-mail orders-ny@springer-sbm.com, or visit www.springeronline.com. Apress Media, LLC is a California LLC and the sole member (owner) is Springer Science + Business Media Finance Inc (SSBM Finance Inc). SSBM Finance Inc is a **Delaware** corporation.

For information on translations, please e-mail booktranslations@springernature.com; for reprint, paperback, or audio rights, please e-mail bookpermissions@springernature.com.

Apress titles may be purchased in bulk for academic, corporate, or promotional use. eBook versions and licenses are also available for most titles. For more information, reference our Print and eBook Bulk Sales web page at http://www.apress.com/bulk-sales.

Any source code or other supplementary material referenced by the author in this book is available to readers on GitHub via the book's product page, located at www.apress.com. For more detailed information, please visit http://www.apress.com/source-code.

Printed on acid-free paper

To my late mother Seelawathie De Silva. Her dedication and sacrifices made me the person I am today.

Table of Contents

About the Author

Chanaka Fernando has more than a decade of experience working in the enterprise software domain in various capacities including designing, implementing, and supporting large-scale enterprise applications and systems across different industries including healthcare, financial services, education, and telecommunication to name a few. He is also the author of the book *Designing Microservices Platforms with NATS* published in 2021. He has contributed to several open source projects as a project lead, developer, and architect while working at WSO2, which is an open source software company. Chanaka holds a bachelor's degree in engineering from the University of Moratuwa, Sri Lanka, where he specialized in electronics and telecommunication engineering.

About the Technical Reviewer

Pamod Sylvester is currently working at "WSO2" as a "Senior Lead Solutions Engineer". During his stint, he has contributed to developing enterprise integration patterns guides and spearheaded efforts carried out to implement full duplex protocols and I/O libraries for both middleware and the Ballerina programming language. Further, he has provided solutions to customers belonging to various verticals and helped them in their digital transformation journey; some of the verticals include health, finance, education, retail, and governments in different parts of the world. In addition to his occupation, he has provided tech thought leadership to various online news journals and blogs and has spoken at various summits and events.

Acknowledgments

I would like to thank my wife Subhashini for supporting me and allowing me to spend time writing this book even with her busy schedule. I would also like to thank the wonderful team at Apress and Springer who helped me immensely during the process of writing this book. Their patience and guidance let me finish this book even during a challenging time. Last but not least, I would like to thank Pamod Sylvester for technically reviewing the book and correcting my mistakes and giving some great feedback to improve the quality of the book.

Introduction

Building enterprise software systems for modern organizations requires a deep understanding of how distributed systems work as well as what applications and systems are used for the specific business domain or industry. This book provides a set of solution architecture patterns that were developed based on the experiences gained through building enterprise software systems for hundreds of different organizations across the globe. These architecture patterns are blueprints of real-world enterprise software systems used by various organizations across different business domains including healthcare, banking, education, and telecommunication to name a few. If you are working on any digital transformation project or initiative, you will find this book useful since it provides a quick reference architecture and a reference implementation to get started with your work. The architecture diagrams (patterns) along with the descriptions allow you to not only understand the concepts but also quickly build working projects to grasp the concepts deeply.

This book starts with an introduction to the concepts of enterprise software systems and solution architecture and then moves to different solution architecture patterns used in real-world enterprises that are categorized based on technology areas such as microservices, security, observability, event-driven, and cloud-native to name a few. These patterns provide generic architecture patterns that can be used across many industries. The latter parts of the book cover various industry-specific solution architecture patterns with finer details that can be used to build domain-specific software systems.

This book helps enterprise software architects and engineers to design and implement real-world enterprise software systems using the best practices and techniques adopted by organizations across the globe. It also provides software architecture blueprints to build domain-specific enterprise software systems.

CHAPTER 1

Introduction to Enterprise Software Systems

Organizations of different sizes spanning from small to medium to large multinational conglomerates use technology to expand their businesses and provide awesome customer experiences so that they can compete at the same level regardless of their size. A company operating from a remote city in South Asia can compete with a Silicon Valley–based Internet giant because of this neutral nature of the technology. The products and services that we consume in our day-to-day lives most probably have originated from different parts of the world. With the popularity of "Internet" and the advancements in the telecommunications industry, the world is becoming a one large marketplace for both consumers and producers. The global economy is primarily driven by consumer demand rather than the producer's capabilities. The competition is so high that there are hundreds or even thousands of producers available for the same consumer product or service.

Although there are different problems to be solved using technology according to the industry such as healthcare, retail, banking, manufacturing, and so on, at the end of the day, each organization tries to provide an awesome experience to their customers. This book considers the similarities and the differences of these different industries when designing and implementing solutions using technology and provides a set of technical reference architectures and examples to build great experiences to the users.

In this chapter, we are going to discuss how organizations are using technology to deliver products and services to their customers. We will be discussing the following topics in this chapter:

- What are enterprises?

- How software is used in enterprises?

- Characteristics of enterprise software systems

- Practical examples of enterprise software systems

© Chanaka Fernando 2023
C. Fernando, *Solution Architecture Patterns for Enterprise*, https://doi.org/10.1007/978-1-4842-8948-8_1

Before we chime into technical details of architecture and solutions, let us take a look at how typical organizations use technology within their business landscape.

What Are Enterprises?

The term "enterprise" historically used to denote a somewhat large business or organization. But the term has evolved with time, and today, we use it to denote an entity with one or more of the following characteristics:

- One large business corporation or a business unit within that corporation

- A government agency or one single department within the government

- A large multinational conglomerate business that spans across countries and regions

- A global alliance or organization working toward a common goal

- A small to medium size business that operates in a limited geographical context

The preceding set of characteristics covers a larger portion of enterprises that operate globally. In the context of this book, we will be discussing how technology can be used within these enterprises to achieve their business, organizational, and social aspirations.

An example of a large business corporation would be a company that produces beverages within a country or region. It is large enough to cover that entire country or region yet is not doing business outside of that territory. A government agency would be something like a health ministry that would be the governing body of healthcare for that country. There are many examples of multinational corporations such as the vehicle manufacturer Toyota and the electronics manufacturer Sony. A global alliance example would be something like UNESCO and World Health Organization (WHO). A startup technology company or a medium size business with a few branches can be considered a small to medium size business (SMB).

In a typical enterprise, there are three main components that we can identify regardless of the size and the nature of the enterprise:

1.   People

2.   Processes

3.   Technology

Figure 1-1 depicts how a typical enterprise consists of people, process, and technology in the three vertices of the rectangle, while enterprise governance controls the interactions of these components through the edges.

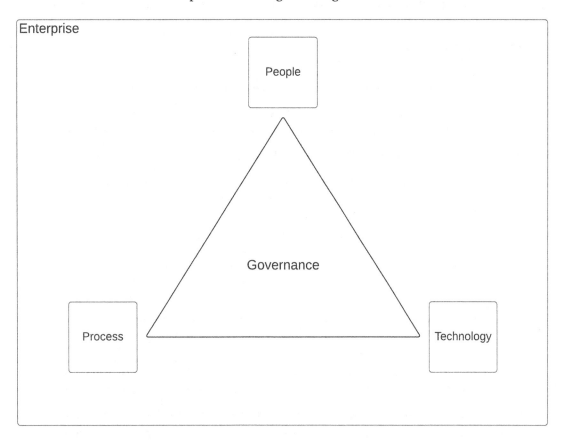

Figure 1-1. *Building blocks of an enterprise ecosystem*

People component comprises employees, customers, partners, and other human stakeholders that operate within the context of the enterprise's operations. Employees are the core of the enterprise that keeps the engine running by executing day-to-day operations and providing greater experience to the customers. Customers purchase products and/or services from the enterprise to keep it financially feasible to run the operations. Partners help the enterprise to produce and deliver products and/or services by providing raw material and other required services.

Processes define how everything is organized within the enterprise and make sure desired outputs are produced by people's actions. It streamlines different bits and pieces and defines clear steps and goals for execution. It also standardizes the operations and improves overall efficiency and quality within the enterprise.

Technology helps enterprises to improve customer experiences and overall efficiency by automating manual processes and integrating different parts of the enterprise. It also helps enterprises to reach out new customers and partners through shared ecosystems that are consumable by such external parties. We will be discussing this topic throughout this book.

The coordination between people, processes, and technology within an enterprise is called the "governance." In a practical sense, it is not much different than a "government" that overlooks a country or region. Enterprise governance helps organizations align their goals with the operational procedures of people, processes, and technology. Some of the common functions of enterprise governance include the following:

- Creation of organizational structures and hierarchies of people.

- Selection of technology for projects.

- Define standards and best practices to be followed by people.

- Introduce processes to streamline operations and continuously monitor them.

- Improve awareness in the enterprise on processes, technology, and people.

Enterprise governance is a topic on its own and it is worth a separate book, and we will touch upon the technology side of the concept throughout this book. The main intention of this book is to understand how technology or software is used within enterprise platforms with detailed architecture patterns and examples. Let us first understand how software is utilized in an enterprise ecosystem.

How Software Is Used in Enterprises?

Enterprises deal with a lot of information in their day-to-day operations. This information can be related to products, services, customers, employees, partners, or even the population that does not belong to any of the previous categories. The information changes frequently and needs to be accessed through different channels such as mobile, Web, or terminal applications such as automated teller machines (ATM), point-of-sale (POS) machines, or even Kiosk machines. It is software along with hardware that keeps all this information in storage devices and allows different channels to access it as and when required. Software allows enterprises to manage information in a much better way than the previous mode of storage, which was paper-based information storage.

Having software controlling the enterprise information, now enterprises can reap additional benefits such as the following:

- Easy discovery – Doing a search for any data point (e.g., product, customer, or employee) is much easier and faster.

- Easy to share – Sharing can be done instantly with improved security.

- Easy to secure – Information is secured at finer levels to make sure the least-privilege principle is applied.

- Easy to manage – With the scalable solutions such as cloud software, managing information has become much easier than the traditional paper-based approach.

- Easy to change (innovate) – With the software, modifying certain details of a product, service, or customer is much easier, while without software, it is almost impossible.

There can be several other advantages related to using software within enterprises. Let us keep the list lean to get started on the topic. The more we explore the enterprise software systems, the more we will be able to uncover advantages.

Let us now try to understand how software is used within enterprise platforms. Here are some of the fundamental use cases of software within enterprises:

- Store and retrieve information quickly.

- Secure information from unauthorized access.

- Expose information to third parties such as customers and partners.

- Innovate new products and services based on customer and partner interactions.

- Automate manual processes to improve efficiency and quality.

- Organize business processes and information to comply with best practices and standards.

With all the points mentioned in the preceding section, enterprises are trying to provide the best possible experience to the users, customers, or the community that belongs to that ecosystem. One might wonder why it is so hard to build robust enterprise software systems by fulfilling the previously mentioned requirements. It is not that complicated to support those requirements on a small scale. But supporting these requirements at a large scale requires a lot of planning, designing, and testing before rolling out to the end users.

It is obvious to a certain extent that usage of software helps enterprises to improve their efficiency, throughput, and the overall user experience. Let us discuss how real-world enterprises are building these software systems. This is where the concept of "Build" vs. "Buy" comes to the surface. While software provides many benefits to the enterprise, it comes with a price tag. These software systems need to be built, managed, and supported by well-trained professionals to make the investment worthy in the long run.

The first option for an enterprise to bring software into the ecosystem is to build it in-house with a few developers who are already in the team or by hiring a small team. This approach can work for not only small enterprises but also large enterprises depending on the capabilities of the development team and the nature of the software that is being built. This gives the enterprise sufficient flexibility and control over the features, timelines, and quality since everything is built in-house. Some drawbacks of this approach are management overhead, slowed innovation (since everything is built in-house), and tight dependency on SMEs.

Another option is to purchase commercial off-the-shelf (COTS) software from a third-party software vendor and install and/or configure that within the enterprise ecosystem. This sort of software may fulfill most of the needs of the enterprise given that these softwares are developed by teams who are experts on that particular domain. The enterprise does not need to spend time and resources on research and development of the product. Most of the time, these vendors provide professional services to manage and maintain the software on behalf of the enterprise so that the enterprise only needs to take care of the business requirements that need to be implemented on top of this software. One drawback of this approach is lack of control over features, timelines, and the quality of the software.

More modern approach of using enterprise software is the usage of fully managed cloud software within enterprises. This category of software is offered as "Software as a Service (SaaS)" with a vendor who offers the software controlling the development, deployment, and management of the software in a publicly accessible cloud infrastructure. The only tool that enterprise users need to access this software is a web browser in most cases. The rest of the implementation is hidden from the user, and it is a complete black box for the user. These tools have developed to such great levels that even a nontechnical user can utilize these softwares to build applications that are required for the enterprise. This kind of software offers flexible pricing options such as pay-as-you-go models so that the enterprise needs to pay only for the usage of the software rather than paying large upfront payments to other installable software. One key disadvantage of this category of enterprise software is the lack of control over features and timelines. Since these are shared services that are used by many different customers, adding a new feature may take longer than the other two options we discussed previously.

Let us take a few examples from real world enterprise software systems to understand this further.

How Software Is Used in the Healthcare Industry

Let us imagine we are building an enterprise software platform for a healthcare provider, which is a hospital located in the city. In this system, you need to store information about the following entities:

- Patients

  - Outpatient Department (OPD)

  - Long-term patients

  - Clinical patients

  - Emergency patients

- Staff
  - Doctors
  - Nurses
  - Lab technicians
  - Administration staff
  - Medical support staff
- Drugs
- Clinics
- Equipments
- Reports
- Wards
- Labs

This information needs to be stored in a database and controlled with required access controls so that whenever a consumer (doctor, nurse, patient, or admin staff) with the correct authority needs to access this information, the required information is provided without any delay. By storing this information in a computer-friendly format such as HL7 or JSON in an Electronic Medical Record (EMR) format, retrieval and sharing across multiple applications become easier. Fast Healthcare Interoperability Resources (FHIR) is a standard that allows healthcare systems to show health information in a standard format over the HTTP/REST protocol. It allows the client applications such as mobile and web clients to consume the healthcare information without worrying about the internal details of the system. That will result in a better experience to the consumer who wants to access this information. If we think about storing the same information in a manual, physical file storage, it will take some time to find out the exact detail that is required.

Once this information is stored in a standard, computer-friendly format, it becomes much easier to share this information to other stakeholders such as regional hospitals, pharmaceutical companies, research centers, and even patients via multiple channels such as mobile and web applications.

We will be discussing more on building enterprise software systems for the healthcare industry in Chapter 9, "Industry-Specific Architecture Patterns."

How Software Is Used in the Retail Industry

The retail industry is one of the few industries that turned on its head due to the use of technology. Before technology got involved in the retail industry, people loved walking inside physical stores and doing shopping for hours and hours without actually buying anything. Sometimes, they had to wait in long queues when there are seasonal offers during "Black Friday," and people barely complained about it. But it was a tedious task for the staff to maintain records of stocks, inventories, and cash registers in manual ledgers. Once the manual bookkeeping was done, it was required to go through an approval process in which a senior staff member goes through each and every invoice and tallies them with the transactions for correctness. These kinds of approval processes were cumbersome and wasted a considerable amount of time of the staff members.

Software was initially used to store information such as

- Stocks

- Inventory

- Suppliers

- Shifts

- Employees

These initial software solutions help the retail industry to improve the efficiency of the overall process and reduce the burden of keeping manual ledgers. The solutions such as business process servers helped automate the long-running approval processes so that the staff members do not need to spend extra time on manual cross-checking and paper-based approvals. Then came the online shopping websites such as Amazon and eBay, which revolutionized the retail industry. These websites not only used software for internal usage but also used it to sell products and services over the Internet.

With the increased popularity of these online shopping websites, the owners of these websites had to architect their enterprise software systems to provide real-time experiences similar to a physical store to the consumers at a global scale. These consumer demands helped software systems to become more scalable and robust and have low latency. The enterprise software systems within these retail giants became large-scale systems with hundreds or even thousands of computers running as many instances of software components in clustered environments to fulfill the consumer demands from across the globe. More and more partners are involved in the retail business in the forms of manufacturing, distribution, and last-mile delivery.

We will be discussing more and more use cases of enterprise software systems in real-world industries throughout this book. With the understanding we have gained on enterprises and usage of software systems, let us try to identify the characteristics of the enterprise software systems.

Characteristics of Enterprise Software Systems

We have discussed a few examples of how software is used in particular domains such as healthcare and retail, which are essential parts of our daily life. Even a small glitch in one of these platforms can cause a huge damage to the enterprise as well as the users. There had been many situations where a single line of malicious code had created chaos for organizations and their reputation. Due to this fact, when designing enterprise software systems, we need to be extra careful about the impact it would make on the users as well as the enterprise. The following is a list of common characteristics that need to be available in a good enterprise software system:

- Scalability

- Availability

- Latency

- Robustness

- Security

- Modularity

- Reusability

- Replaceability

- Observability

- Adaptability

It is evident in the real-world enterprise systems that not all these characteristics are optimized in every instance. But you need to consider these aspects when designing and implementing enterprise systems. In fact, there are certain characteristics such as security that impacts the latency of the overall customer experience that cannot be optimized at the same time. In such cases, we have to compromise one for the other depending on the priority of each characteristic. As an example, in a banking system, security is a higher priority than latency. The customer would be okay to spend a bit more time making the payment rather than using a less secure system that can cause significant damage to their funds. On the other hand, in a retail website, users should be able to check out the available items without much delay even without authenticating with the system.

Let us take a detailed look at each of these characteristics since we need a proper understanding of each one when we design and implement enterprise software systems.

Scalability

In the past, the growth of an enterprise took a considerable amount of time, and the enterprise teams had enough lead time to plan on scaling the applications. Most of the time, teams started a new project to scale the platform and installed new hardware and software to scale the system. But in today's world, enterprises can launch their products and services to larger audiences through the Internet, and the growth of the customer base can be instantaneous. Sometimes, you would receive ten times more traffic than what you initially estimated, and your enterprise system should be capable of scaling to these demands instantly. Otherwise, all the customers would experience service unavailability, and your reputation can go blank in a matter of minutes. Because of this reason, when you design an enterprise system, you need to understand what components need to be scaled frequently and what components need to be scaled occasionally. If you know this information, you can utilize technologies provided by infrastructure providers to automatically scale the components based on certain metrics such as CPU usage, latency, or number of users.

There are two types of scalability that we typically discuss in enterprise applications:

1. Horizontal scalability

2. Vertical scalability

In horizontal scalability, we add new components in addition to what is already running. In the case of a web server instance that is running on a virtual machine, with horizontal scalability, we will deploy additional virtual machines with the web server so that we increase the number of "instances" of application so that more requests can be served in parallel. We can scale the platform to a large extent with this approach, and there are systems that run hundreds or even thousands of instances of the same application in real-world enterprises.

In vertical scalability, we add more resources to the application so that it can perform better. We would typically increase the number of CPU cores and memory to improve the performance of the application. This approach would work well in scenarios where you need to scale the system by a small magnitude. This has its limitations in terms of how far you can scale since there are limitations on the number of CPUs and the memory that a particular computer (node) can scale up to. In addition to that, applications also start to flatten the performance improvement beyond a certain limit due to the limitations of operating systems that are running on these computers. Hence, this mode of scalability is not suitable if you have higher scalability requirements.

Availability

In the world of business, time is money. If you are offering products and services through omni-channels such as mobile, web, and telephone, your system needs to be available and accessible to the users at any given time. But in reality, the cost to support 100% availability is much higher when compared to the cost that involves providing four nines (99.99%) of availability. Hence, most of the enterprise platforms are designed in a way that its availability is expressed in number of nines (e.g., 99.9, 99.99) and the loss of availability (downtime) is considered as an opportunity loss, which can compromise the additional cost that needs to be spent to completely avoid it.

There are different systems and applications that require a certain level of minimum deployment to support high availability. In a typical stateless web application such as Tomcat or API gateway, having a two-instance deployment with both instances in an active mode would provide the high availability. A load balancer will be used to distribute the traffic coming into the web server in a round-robin fashion. When planning the capacity of the servers, it needs to be planned so that the overall capacity of both the nodes can provide two times the expected (or peak) capacity of the platform. When we do that, in the case of a single instance failure, the system will still function at 100% capacity without disrupting the availability. In a stateful application with data replication, you may need more than two instances to provide the minimum high availability.

Latency

The Internet has become so fast that consumers expect things to be available at their fingertips in a blink of an eye. But as enterprise systems designers, we need to deal with complexities such as varying systems, varying data types and formats, and even varying deployments (geographically). As an example, if a customer needs to check a particular item in an e-commerce website, that single web page provides details about product features, price, availability, related products, and even the estimated shipping cost. These different types of information come from different core systems that may be running in different data centers across the world. But the end user does not care about any of these complexities, and they expect all the details to be available instantly. Due to this reason, it is important to consider the overall latency of the platform when designing enterprise systems. You need to make sure that there are a minimum number of network interactions and data is stored in canonical format within the platform so that data transformation costs are minimal. But in some cases, we might not be able to avoid all these complexities since the application may require data from legacy systems that are hard to change.

In either case, we provide a service-level agreement (SLA) to the users mentioning the maximum (or average) latency of a particular service so that they are aware of it beforehand. The business leaders and sales teams would ask for better latency every day, and as system designers, we need to make sure that we provide the required performance without impacting the overall system stability and unnecessary cost implications. There are several technologies that can be used to improve the performance and reduce the latency such as caching that can be implemented with several approaches such as in-memory and persistence modes.

Robustness

Enterprise systems are built on top of computer networks that are destined to fail from time to time. It is really hard to design networks that do not fail. Hence, it is inevitable that enterprise systems will fail. The term "robustness" does not mean that our system should be without any failure. But it discusses how resilient our system is to these failures. As an example, a robust system would not experience cascading failures from one system to other systems. It would avoid such cascading of failures by applying techniques such as circuit breaker, which would eventually isolate the failed application from the rest of the system for a certain amount of time. After that duration, it checks the health of the failed application and reconnects that to the system.

Another common approach of building robust systems is to use techniques such as "fail-fast" so that any failure is identified fast and remedial actions are taken immediately. "Chaos engineering" is another way of designing robust systems that makes a totally different approach by randomly faltering the parts of the system intentionally to check the resiliency of the system and take measures to withstand such failures without chaos in the real world.

Security

Enterprise software systems generate a large amount of data that needs to be properly stored, processed, and distributed to the relevant stakeholders. Every time we touch enterprise data, one thing we need to make sure of is the security of data. Data needs to be secured when stored (data at rest) in data stores using techniques such as encryption so that only the intended clients can access the stored data. This functionality is provided by the applications that generate the data and the databases that store the data in storage systems such as disks.

Another aspect of enterprise security is securing data in motion. That means when the data is accessed through a network using a mobile or web application, the communication channel needs to be secured using mechanisms such as transport layer security so that an attacker who hacks into the network cannot access the data in transit. We use technologies such as Secure Sockets Layer (SSL) and Transport Layer Security (TLS) for this purpose.

The more prominent or the customer-facing aspect of enterprise security is the application-level security with authentication and authorization. If a user needs to access any information from the enterprise software system, that user needs to have the required permissions before accessing it. Authentication verifies the user and identifies that user as a valid user in the system. Authorization makes sure that the identified user has the authority to execute certain actions on enterprise data. We will be discussing this topic in detail in the upcoming chapters dedicated to enterprise security patterns.

Modularity

One of the main challenges people have to deal with when designing enterprise software systems is the complexity of the system that increases with time. In early enterprise software systems, large monolithic applications were deployed in the enterprise ecosystem, and the integration of these systems was done in a point-to-point manner with custom code written specifically for each integration. Enterprise architects then realized the challenges of maintaining such deployments and came up with the idea of Service-Oriented Architecture where each functionality required by the system is developed as separate services and integrations across services and other systems happened through standard interfaces such as REST, SOAP, or JMS to name a few. This approach helped the enterprise architects to design services with clear goals and made it easy to develop new features specifically for the required services without overhauling the entire application. This concept was then evolved into a more independent services development and deployment model with the introduction of microservice architecture and containers. It improved the overall system availability and agility by allowing individual services to maintain their own life cycle so that each service could be managed by entirely different teams with expertise on specific domains.

Having modular architecture such as SOA or microservice architecture helped the enterprise software systems to become more resilient to failures since one component failure could not impact the overall system behavior. In addition to that, it also allowed these individual modules (services) to innovate independently and bring new experiences to the customers without worrying about the readiness of the entire platform, which would otherwise delay the innovation. It also helped isolate errors and made troubleshooting easier by identifying errors related to specific components and allowed developers to quickly work on a resolution rather than going through the entire system.

Reusability

When enterprises become larger, teams become distant and start building their own siloed applications and systems to implement business functions. If such an enterprise does not have a proper governance model to overlook the different teams and align their visions with the overall enterprise goals, different teams start building the same functionality without knowing it, and in the process, these teams waste a lot of their valuable resources. That is the reason why it is important to have a proper governance model within an enterprise to make sure that teams reuse already-existing functionality, which might have been developed by other teams within the enterprise. A common approach to build such a shared platform is to use a centralized application portal where each team can publish their services into the portal and any other team can reuse the services without duplicating it.

With a reusable development model, teams can collaborate with others without going down their own siloed universes. It helps organizations to spend valuable engineering resources on critical tasks rather than using them for duplicating existing functionality. It also helps the enterprise to develop new services at a faster rate and reduce the time to market. The service developers would also get valuable feedback from other teams, which would help them to improve the service quality and the features it offers.

Replaceability

Enterprise software systems are going through continuous improvements, and replacing existing functionality with new products and vendors has become a more frequent task recently. There can be many reasons such as stability issues, performance issues, feature gaps, product support quality issues, support availability issues, and most commonly pricing challenges. Because of these reasons, we cannot guarantee that any component in the enterprise software system would last forever. Hence, we need to design the enterprise system so that any component can be replaced with the minimum impact to the overall system operations. The best approach to implement such an architecture is to use components that support standards based interfaces for integrations. As an example, if we are to select an API management platform for an enterprise, we need to make sure that the product we select supports standard API definition formats such as Swagger or OpenAPI specification so that in case we need to replace this product with another vendor, we can reuse the same API definitions to migrate APIs into the new vendor.

Having such standards-based components in the enterprise system would help us to evolve the system with time and also to avoid any vendor lock-in. Not all the components have smooth transitions since some systems use their own data models to store enterprise data, and in such cases, we might need to get help from the new vendor to transform and migrate the existing data set to it.

Observability

Failure is inevitable in enterprise software systems. Recovering from failure is the utmost important aspect of such systems. Observability is the mechanism that allows developers to identify the root causes of failures by looking at external outputs that are produced within the system. As an example, enterprise applications produce outputs through multiple channels such as log entries into a file, events published to a topic, or even an email sent to a system admin when something abnormal happens. Then these admins can go over these events and identify the sequence of events that caused this erroneous behavior in the system and make necessary measures to fix the issue.

Large enterprise software systems with hundreds of applications running in parallel with complex integrations within these applications can make it harder to troubleshoot if no proper observability is implemented. Hence, it is a best practice to implement observability from the initial stages of the system design and implementation so that the system's observability, which is a property of the overall system, keeps on improving with time. Monitoring is a function within the enterprise that uses various observability outputs to keep an eye on the stability of the system. It helps developers to keep the system in a good state and recover from failures as soon as possible.

Adaptability

Executive leaders always look to improve the performance of the enterprise due to the steep competition coming from the alternate enterprises. This sheer competition impacts all the different functions within the enterprise, and hence, enterprise software systems need to adapt to the continuous change requests coming from the executive leadership. As an example, as part of a global expansion within the enterprise, executives ask enterprise architects to bring in more and more systems to manage global operations. In such a scenario, the enterprise systems should have the capability to integrate with those systems without impacting the existing applications. It also means that the system is agile and flexible to adopt the changes fast and move forward.

Sometimes, enterprise software vendors come with drastic changes across versions to their applications and suddenly stop supporting existing product versions. In such scenarios, the enterprise architects must be able to evaluate alternative vendors that would provide better functionality with better pricing and support. Enterprise technology evolves with time, and enterprise architects should do a technology refresh periodically to make sure that enterprises are reaping the benefits of advancements in enterprise technology. Having an enterprise system that can adapt based on these requirements is critical for enterprises to be on the cutting-edge technology rather than stuck in year-old technology platforms and products.

Now you have an idea of what enterprises are, how enterprises use software, and the characteristics of enterprise software systems. Let us discuss a few example enterprise software systems in brief to expand our understanding further.

Practical Examples of Enterprise Software Systems

Enterprise software systems have common characteristics that we discussed in the previous section. At the same time, there are many differences that are specific to the enterprise domain that a particular software system is implemented for. Let us take a few enterprise domains that make a significant impact on our day-to-day lives and go through software architecture diagrams in brief to understand the similarities and differences better. The enterprise domains we will be discussing are as follows:

- Healthcare

- Transportation

There are many other enterprise domains that we will be discussing in the upcoming chapters of this book. But we have taken the two domains mentioned previously to explain the concepts of enterprise software systems here.

Enterprise Software System Architecture for Healthcare

Let us imagine that we need to build a software system to be used in the healthcare domain that consists of hospitals owned by the government and private organizations. The first thing we need to do is identify the people and processes that we can consider as stakeholders of the system. Figure 1-2 depicts some of the main stakeholders of a software system built for healthcare.

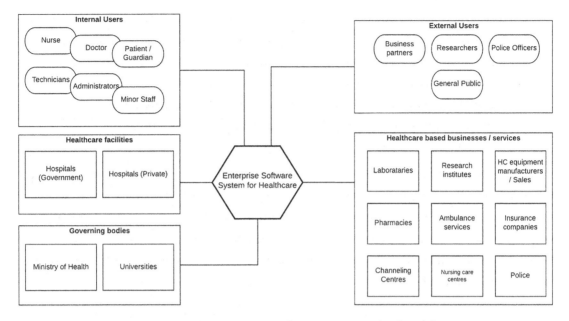

Figure 1-2. *Stakeholders of enterprise software system for healthcare*

As depicted in the figure, the mentioned stakeholders make use of the enterprise software system that is designed for healthcare:

- Internal users – These are the users who interact with the software system from within the hospital itself. These users have more privileges to access information since they play a critical role in the healthcare process within the hospital.

- External users – Certain information in the hospital software system can be exposed to external users for business, administration, and research purposes. These users have less privileges than the internal users.

- Healthcare facilities – This is the core of the system where all the healthcare facilities reside. It can be a government hospital or a private hospital.

- Governing bodies – In certain countries, healthcare systems are governed by government departments. In addition to that, there are universities that produce healthcare professionals that interact with the system.

- Healthcare business and services – There are other external stakeholders who partner with hospitals to provide supportive services such as pharmacies, care centers, ambulance services, and insurance services that need to interact with the healthcare system to provide better services and gain more customers to their businesses. The FHIR standard along with healthcare regulations such as the CMS rule that was introduced in the United States encourages and pushes healthcare organizations to share health information with external parties over a standard format.

The next step in designing an enterprise software system for healthcare is to identify various units within hospitals and identify the data that each unit needs to store, access, and manipulate and come up with an entity relationship (ER) diagram. Once that is done, enterprise architects can start putting together a solution architecture diagram to lay out the technical components of the system. Figure 1-3 depicts a sample solution architecture diagram for a healthcare software system.

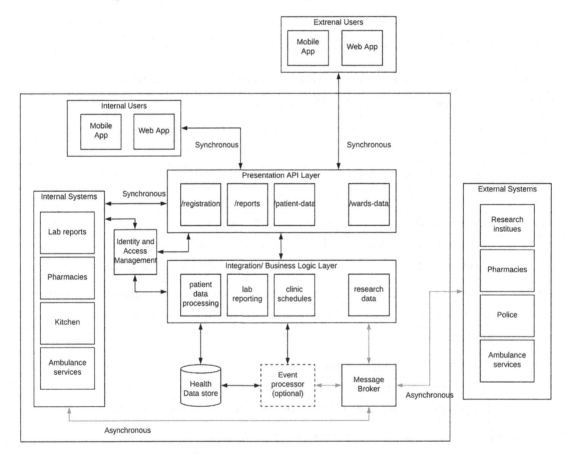

Figure 1-3. *Solution architecture for healthcare software system*

Figure 1-3 depicts a possible solution architecture diagram that explains how different units within a hospital and outside a hospital interact with the healthcare system with technical details. If you feel this is a steep move from the previous diagram to this diagram, don't worry about it since we will be discussing these solutions in detail in an upcoming chapter. In the interest of this chapter, let us discuss in brief what the figure depicts.

Let's start from the top layer where users (internal and external) interact with the system through client applications. These applications can be mobile or web applications installed on a laptop/desktop/tablet or even mobile phones. These applications access information within the healthcare system through the presentation API layer, which controls the access to the healthcare data with security, monitoring, and rate limiting. A few example APIs can be

- Patient registration

- Patient report card

- Lab reports of a patient

- Ward statistics

There can be many such APIs according to the requirements of the consumers. If a doctor wants to register a new patient to the system, they will do so via the mobile or web application by providing the credentials related to the doctor. There is an additional component called the Identity and Access Management (IAM), which takes care of the sensitive nature of data and how people access that data. It provides the required security capabilities to the platform such as authentication and authorization along with consent management. Authentication identifies who the user and validates the user's identity, while authorization validates the permissions that the validated user has in relation to the system and the resources that they can access. Consent management is used to get the user's confirmation (consent) to collect the user's data such as personally identifiable information (PII) by the system. This information will be used to provide better experiences to the user.

Underneath this presentation API layer, there is a layer that does the actual heavy lifting and the processing of the data and orchestrates between multiple raw data systems to produce results that are consumable through presentation APIs. This layer collects data from real-time sources, historical event sources, and static data sources and produces valuable results for end-user consumption.

There is another major component within this architecture that is the "message broker," which will be used as the reliable messaging layer for asynchronous information exchanges. Some examples are

- Releasing lab results

- Police reports

- Birth/death reports

- Research data

- Drug reports

In addition to that, there can be a real-time event processing component that analyzes various events and produces results that are then communicated to relevant medical personnel and systems so that they can act immediately. As an example, if a certain report results in a severe health condition of a patient, the system can send notifications to relevant people to take immediate action rather than waiting till they get the report and analyze the report.

There is a lot more to be discussed on this solution, but we will do that in a future chapter within the book.

Enterprise Software System Architecture for Transportation

Transportation is as important as anything we could imagine to make the world moving forward and connected. At the same time, it is one of the domains that technology is used in a largely uneven manner. The reason for me saying that is technology is heavily used in innovating different vehicles and building infrastructure such as roads, but at the same time, it is not used much in controlling the transportation systems. If you've been to any major city in the world such as London, New York, Paris, Tokyo, or any other, you would wonder why we cannot solve the traffic problem that is common in these cities. In fact, there are countries and cities who improved traffic behaviors within cities significantly using technology.

Let us first understand the different stakeholders that are involved in a ground transportation ecosystem. Figure 1-4 depicts some of the main stakeholders that we need to consider when designing a software system for transportation.

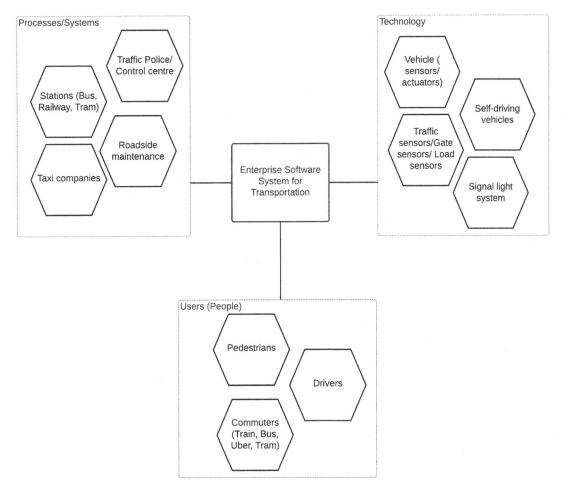

Figure 1-4. *Some main stakeholders of transportation ecosystem*

As depicted in the figure, we can identify the following main stakeholders related to ground transportation:

- Commuters – People who travel as passengers of vehicles. They need information about traffic conditions, vehicle locations, capacities, and vehicle conditions.

- Drivers – People who drive the vehicle and use the infrastructure in reality. Their responsibility is to move commuters from the starting point to the destination in a safe, timely manner. They are interested in traffic conditions, traffic light systems, commuters who are waiting for their travel, roadside maintenance activities, events happening in that area, etc.

- Pedestrians – People travelling on foot and walking around the city. They want to know about air pollution, crowded areas, and traffic light systems.

- Vehicles (including self-driving) – This is the actual tool drivers are using to carry commuters around. These vehicles have sensors to capture data and actuators to act upon receiving data. Self-driving vehicles are solely driven by these two types of data, while other vehicles use those data points to improve drivers' efficiency and eventually contribute to the overall improvement of the system.

- Sensors – Sensors can be used to improve the overall system efficiency. There can be different types of sensors depending on the positions they are located in.

  - Traffic sensors – These sensors can be installed in the road near junctions. They will capture raw events about how many vehicles passed through the sensors. That can be used to derive the traffic flow of a particular direction within a junction and eventually communicated to the traffic control system so that the overall traffic lighting system can be improved.

  - Platform gate sensors – These sensors can be used to measure the capacity at a given platform of a station, and based on that, users can be distributed to different sections of the platform to have a uniform distribution of load to the compartments.

  - Air pollution sensors – By measuring the air quality of an area, pedestrians can select healthy areas to take a walk, and vehicles can be moved away from roads that are heavily used by pedestrians

- Traffic control system – The main component of the control system is the signal light system. Adaptive signal light systems can take feedback from roadside sensors and change the durations of green light and control the traffic flows as a whole, and based on the day of the week and the time, it can decide the timing of lights across the entire system. Traffic police can also receive this information through the control center.

- Roadside maintenance – In a developing city, there can be many maintenance activities going on within the road network, and this information needs to be properly fed into the system so that users can receive and act based on that. Prior notifications allow people to plan their routes in advance.

- Stations (bus, railway, tram) – These are places that show a lot of information about the transportation system status. They show details about schedule, current running vehicles, and locations. With the usage of sensors on vehicles, more detailed information like capacity of each compartment, locations of buses, and predicted time can be communicated to the users through public communication mechanisms available in these stations.

- Taxi companies – These companies have a huge impact on the traffic condition by reducing the number of personal vehicles entering the city, ride sharing, and professional drivers with advanced devices. These drivers can make smart decisions and be more effective on the roads with quality information and experience.

- Transportation authorities – Most of the public transportation is controlled by these authorities. They can impose rules for a better transportation system and run buses, trains, and trams within cities. There can be more than the aforementioned stakeholders within a specific transportation ecosystem. But the aforementioned can be considered as the most common denominator.

Once we identify the main stakeholders, we need to come up with a solution architecture that can help us build an effective ground transportation software system. Figure 1-5 shows an example of such a solution architecture.

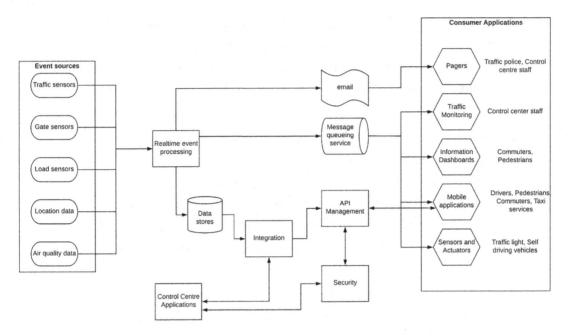

Figure 1-5. *Solution architecture for transportation software system*

Figure 1-5 depicts the technical components of an enterprise software system that is designed for the transportation domain. It contains the following mentioned components:

- Event sources – These are the various devices and systems that generate data. This data is then processed and used to enhance the transportation system.

- Real-time event processing – This component processes the events in real time and makes measures to filter, cleanse, and calculate various statistical information that are useful for making better decisions to reduce traffic.

- Data stores – This is the data store that stores different types of data such as raw data, processed data, and intermediate data that will be used by other components of the solution.

- Message queueing service – This component is critical to decouple the source systems from the target system. It will receive events from the real-time event processor and publish them to targets using a queue or a topic.

- Integration and API Management – The integration component integrates other systems that keep less dynamic information such as population data, maintenance data, government policies, and similar type of data with the real-time events as and when necessary. API Management component exposes these integrated services to clients through a secured interface using APIs.

- Security – This component provides the required authentication and authorization capabilities to the system so that consumers access data in a secured manner.

- Control center applications – These are the applications used by traffic controlling authorities to monitor the real-time traffic status and apply necessary measures to efficiently route vehicles and people within the area.

- Consumer applications – These are various applications used by the general public and control center staff to access publicly visible data. This data would guide these consumers to follow better routes to save their time and health.

We will stop explaining the solution here since we will be discussing this in more detail in an upcoming chapter.

Summary

In this first chapter of the book, we discussed what enterprises are and how those enterprises use software systems to offer great customer experiences to their users. We went through a few examples of real-world enterprise software systems at a high level and discussed the functions of these systems. Then we discussed some of the common characteristics of enterprise software systems that are critical for the success of those systems. Finally, we took two examples of healthcare and transportation domains and discussed how a real-world enterprise software system would look like in those domains. We discussed those examples at a high level in this chapter, and we will be discussing them in greater detail in a future chapter.

In the next chapter, we will be discussing the concepts of solution architecture in detail and lay out the foundation for the solution architecture patterns that we are going to discuss throughout this book.

CHAPTER 2

Introduction to Solution Architecture

Enterprise software systems solve complex business problems in an efficient manner using a technology-driven approach. These systems are designed as a solution to an existing challenge or a problem within the enterprise. Solution architecture is the high-level blueprint of the enterprise software system that is going to be built to offer a technical solution to the enterprise requirement. Each and every enterprise is unique in many ways while sharing commonalities at the same time. Coming up with a good solution architecture requires

- A good understanding of the business requirements

- Experienced solution architects with domain knowledge

- Technical architects with technical knowledge on tools to be used

A good solution architecture covers the business use cases, the technical solution, and the underlying infrastructure services as separate components. It also can be used to come up with total cost of ownership (TCO) of the system so that business people can understand the financial impact of the solution. In addition to that, it also serves as the technical reference document (such as a plan of a house) for developers who actually build the solution (similar to the builders of the house). Hence, it is really important to come up with a good solution architecture before starting any enterprise project by taking enough time to analyze the business requirements and technical requirements properly.

In this chapter, we are going to discuss what is solution architecture and how it captures different levels of information so that the entire project can rely on it throughout the project life cycle. We will be discussing the following topics in this chapter:

© Chanaka Fernando 2023

C. Fernando, *Solution Architecture Patterns for Enterprise*, https://doi.org/10.1007/978-1-4842-8948-8_2

- What is enterprise architecture?

- What is solution architecture?

  - Business architecture (Level 0)

  - Technical architecture (Level 1)

  - Deployment architecture (Level 2)

- Moving from solution architecture to implementation

- Advantages of solution architecture patterns

Let us first take a look at what enterprise architecture is and how it correlates to the solution architecture.

What Is Enterprise Architecture?

Enterprises can be different in size and different in the operational models. Some enterprises may have a centralized operational model where everything is controlled from one location such as a head office or a global headquarter. There can be other enterprises that operate in a totally decentralized manner where individual units within the enterprise take their own decision to run their part of the enterprise. Technology can also be a part of this operational model, and hence, different units of an enterprise can have their own solutions and tools in a decentralized operational model. The term "enterprise architecture" discusses an enterprise-wide technology approach to optimize the operations while adapting to changes requested by the business needs. It provides a technology framework to the entire enterprise so that it can focus on delivering value to their customers in a uniform manner regardless of which business unit these requirements are coming from. Some benefits of the enterprise architecture include the following:

- Improved business operations:

  - Reduced business costs through shared capabilities

  - Flexible and agile working models

  - Streamlined decision-making

- Improved IT operations through shared services and interoperability:
  - Reduced time to market with shared services
  - Less friction between teams due to better alignment of requirements and expectations
  - Improved resource efficiency via reusability
  - Extending effective reach of the enterprise through digital capability
  - Better decision-making on enterprise-wide requirements such as security and infrastructure
- Improved ROI and reduced TCO:
  - Reduce the complexity of overall IT ecosystem and management overhead
  - Improved usage of existing IT resources
  - Ability to consider different vendors and make better financial agreements such as enterprise license agreements (ELA) that could significantly reduce the TCO
- Improved procurement process:
  - Making a buying decision is much simpler since all the information is readily available.
  - Fast procurement process due to the availability of technical and nontechnical requirements.
  - The ability to procure heterogeneous, multivendor open systems.
  - The ability to secure better economic capabilities.

To get a better understanding of enterprise architecture, let's take a look at a couple of enterprise architecture examples from the real world. The following are two enterprise architecture diagrams that depict the high-level, enterprise-wide technology approach for two practical scenarios.

Layered Enterprise Architecture Pattern

We can design an enterprise software system using a layered architecture pattern as depicted in Figure 2-1. This is a sample enterprise architecture pattern that describes the overall approach to solve technical problems within an enterprise.

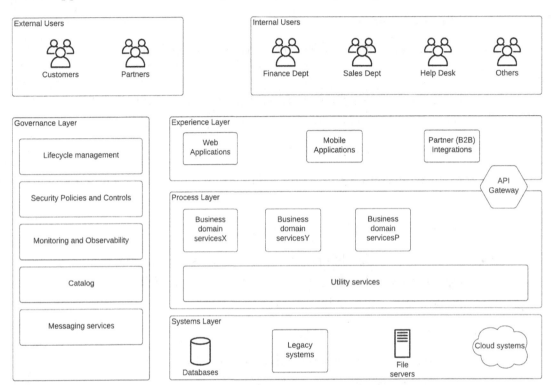

Figure 2-1. *Layered enterprise architecture pattern*

Figure 2-1 depicts the users of the system, the high-level technology components, and the interactions between systems and users. There are a few main components you can identify in this enterprise architecture:

- External users – These are the customers and business partners who interact with the enterprise platform to consume services offered by the enterprise.

- Internal users – These are the internal users such as employees working on other departments such as finance, sales, and help desk to name a few.

- Experience layer – This is the layer that exposes enterprise services to the internal and external users using different client applications such as mobile, web, or partner applications.

- Process layer – This layer is designed to implement function (domain)-specific services that will be consumed by the experience layer through an API gateway. In addition to domain services, there can be shared services that expose common functions to the experience layer as well as domain services.

- Systems layer – The core data sources and system of record systems are included in this layer. These core systems will be exposed to the customers carefully through the two upper layers.

- Governance layer – This component is a shared services component that provides functions that are shared across all three layers. Examples are security, messaging, and observability. In addition to that, there are specific services such as Catalog that will be used to expose the experience layer, and process layer services to external developers are included here.

This is a perfectly valid enterprise architecture that can be used in many different industries including banking, healthcare, and manufacturing domains to implement enterprise software systems.

Microservices-Based Enterprise Architecture Pattern

We can design an enterprise architecture using a microservices-based approach where new services that are developed in the platform need to follow microservices design principles. Even though most of the concepts around microservice architecture assume a greenfield platform where every service needs to be implemented as microservice and the entire platform needs to follow the microservice architecture, the real-world enterprise software systems do not work like that. Instead, there are heterogenous applications and systems developed by in-house developers, third parties that are deployed in on-premise, and cloud and hybrid infrastructure that we need to coexist with when implementing microservice architecture. This kind of enterprise platform is called a brown-field enterprise. This type of enterprise architecture is depicted in Figure 2-2.

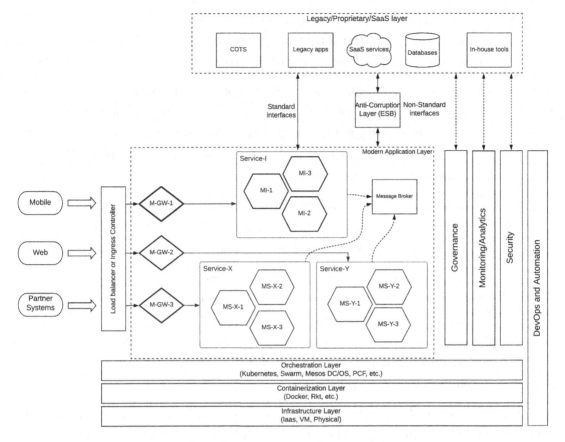

Figure 2-2. *Microservices-based enterprise architecture pattern*

Figure 2-2 depicts an enterprise architecture for a brown-field enterprise using a microservices-based approach. It depicts an enterprise platform that contains existing legacy systems as well as modern applications that are developed using microservice architecture. We can identify several key components in the figure:

- Client applications – These are the user applications that internal and external users utilize to access the enterprise software system.

- Load balancer or ingress controller – This is the network-level entry point to the platform from external client systems.

- Micro Gateways (MGW) – These are the domain-specific gateways that control access to each domain service implemented as a set of microservices.

- Microservices – These are the domain-specific business services implemented using microservice architecture where each service is deployed as a set of containers or pods.

- Infrastructure services – These are the underlying containerization, container orchestration, and infrastructure layers of the platform

- Shared services – The functionality that is common across all the microservices will be implemented as shared services. This includes security, governance, observability, and automation.

- Existing services – There can be already implemented systems and services in the enterprise that needs to integrate with the newly designed enterprise architecture. That can happen through standard interfaces such as HTTP and AMQP or via an anticorruption layer such as an ESB in the case of proprietary interfaces.

This enterprise architecture pattern defines how new services are to be developed as microservices and the integration points of existing systems and applications. This architecture can be utilized by different enterprises including retail, education, and financial services industry.

Enterprise architecture itself is worth a separate book of its own, and we will not go into much detail of it within this section of the book. Instead, we will use this brief introduction as a way into our main topic, which is solution architecture. If you need to learn more about enterprise architecture, you can refer to this link: `https://pubs.opengroup.org/architecture/togaf92-doc/arch/`.

What Is Solution Architecture?

The term "solution architecture" itself provides you with a hint of what it entails. In layman's terms, a solution architecture is a technical blueprint of a solution that caters to a certain enterprise requirement. It is like the "plan" of a "house," which is referred to by the builders and engineers from time to time when building the house. Similarly, the software engineers and software architects use the solution architecture as a reference when building the enterprise software system.

If we compare enterprise architecture with solution architecture, enterprise architecture mostly talks about the overall technology vision for the enterprise while solution architecture focuses on real-world problems at hand and coming up with a workable model as a solution to those problems. You can derive multiple solution architectures for different problems using the same enterprise architecture. In a small enterprise, both enterprise architecture and solution architecture can overlap so we cannot figure out a difference. In a nutshell, enterprise architecture is more of a conceptual model, while solution architecture is a model that is ready to be realized using the technical components.

Coming up with a solution architecture for a complex enterprise requirement can take a considerable amount of time, and different enterprises go about it in different ways. I have seen many large organizations having a dedicated enterprise architecture team that discusses the business needs and coming up with an overall enterprise architecture strategy. In such a scenario, solution architecture comes at a secondary phase and will take time to realize a project. There are other organizations that follow a more flexible and agile mode of execution who work on the solution architecture first and start building projects immediately. These are small and medium enterprises that do not have an enterprise architecture team, but they will find the need for such a team once they start implementing several projects.

In the preceding section, we discussed what an enterprise architecture is and how it allows an enterprise to come up with an overall technology framework for an organization to develop software systems. In this section, we will discuss more on the specific business problems within an enterprise and how those problems are solved with specific "solution architecture" patterns.

We took the analogy of "house" vs. "plan" when talking about "enterprise software system" vs. "solution architecture." If you ask an engineer or a builder about the most important piece of information for building a house, they would most probably say it is the plan. It is the same for building enterprise software systems as well. The most important piece of information for developers and architects when building an enterprise software system is the solution architecture. Not only that, it also acts as the bridge between the financial influencers such as business executives and architects and the developers. Due to these reasons, we need to make sure that the solution architecture captures all the information for different stakeholders to make their decisions.

There are several approaches people follow when coming up with solution architecture. Throughout this book, we will use a methodology that I used in my own work as a solution architect, which provides a clear separation of business, technology, and deployment aspects so that relevant people can utilize the respective components most effectively. In this model, we are going to define three main components of solution architecture. We call these components as different levels of the solution architecture from Level 0, Level 1, to Level 2:

- Business architecture (Level 0)

- Technical architecture (Level 1)

- Deployment architecture (Level 2)

Let us discuss each of these aspects in detail in the following section with a few practical examples.

Business Architecture (Level 0 Architecture)

The first step in solving any problem is understanding the problem as it appears in the real world. Once we do that, we can come up with a solution using the technical knowledge and the domain knowledge. The idea of the business architecture is to come up with a possible solution to the real-world problem or problems and depict that in the form of a diagram or a document using the systems, applications, and users that are considered in the scenario with minimum technical details. This component is mainly useful for business executives and other nontechnical stakeholders so that they can understand what the technical solution is going to be built using this architecture.

Let us take an example of a bank that is planning to implement a mobile application to its customers. The technical team and the business analyst team at the IT department have done the research on the customers, their needs, and competitive products and have come up with a proposal to the business leadership with the business architecture document that showcases how different stakeholders interact with the solution. Figure 2-3 is such a sample business architecture diagram.

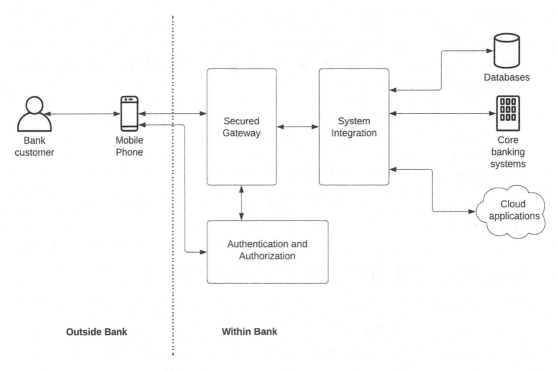

Figure 2-3. *Business architecture for a mobile banking application*

The figure showcases how a banking customer uses their mobile phone to access their banking data and services through a secured gateway. It also depicts a certain level of technical details about the existing systems within the bank such as databases, core banking systems, and some cloud applications that are used in the system. The functionality of each component can be described as follows:

- Secured gateway – This component exposes the banking services in a secured manner so that it can be accessed through a mobile phone.

- System integration – Since there are multiple systems and data sources that keep customer data and financial details, an intermediary integration component is required to orchestrate and transform the data across systems.

- Authentication and authorization – Users need to be authenticated and authorized to use the banking services via the mobile application.

Once the business architecture is designed, the next phase is to use this to build the technical architecture by identifying the nitty-gritty details of technical requirements that need to be covered from each component.

Technical Architecture (Level 1 Architecture)

The business architecture or the Level 0 architecture does not go into the detailed features and functions of each component. That is the task of the technical architecture or the Level 1 architecture. Coming up with the technical architecture requires a thorough understanding of the existing requirements of the business problem as well as any future demands. As an example, in the mobile banking application, the BA suggests using a secured gateway to expose the banking services to the mobile client. It is the solution architect's duty to identify which functionality is required from a secured gateway.

Based on the previous experiences that I have, I will come up with a list of functionalities that need to be available for each component:

- Secured gateway functions required:

    - API gateway

    - API Security (OAuth2 and Basic Auth)

    - Caching

    - Throttling

    - Developer portal

    - Monitoring

- System integration functions required:

    - Data transformation

    - Service orchestration

    - Data services

    - Enterprise connectors

    - Monitoring

- Authentication and authorization functions required:

    - Authentication

    - Authorization

    - Single Sign-On

    - Multifactor authentication (MFA)

    - Adaptive authentication

The list of functions mentioned previously is based on the experiences that I have working on similar projects in the past. This can be different for a different use case and for a different solution architect. But the process is the same. With these major requirements at hand, now we can decide what concrete software components we are going to use in this solution and how they are going to interact with each other. That is what we are going to include in the technical architecture component. This can be a diagram along with a supportive document in most cases. Figure 2-4 depicts a sample technical architecture designed for the mobile banking application that we discussed before.

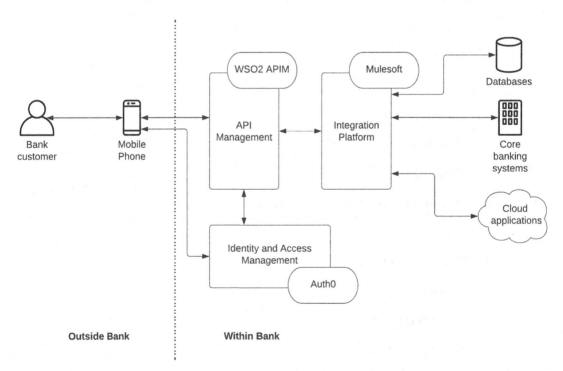

Figure 2-4. *Technical solution architecture for a mobile banking application*

As depicted in the figure, we have clearly mentioned what technical products we are going to use in the solution along with some example names for those products. As per our understanding of the feature set, we have decided to go with the following mentioned technical products:

- API Management product for secured gateway – Given the required functionality for the current use case and the future use cases, we have decided to use an API management vendor here. WSO2 is an APIM vendor who offers support for the required features.

- Integration platform for system integration – Based on the required features, we have decided to use an integration platform for this component. MuleSoft is a vendor that offers integration software.

- Identity and Access Management for authentication and authorization – An IAM vendor is selected based on the security functions that are identified by the team. Auth0 is a vendor that offers the required feature set.

The technical solution architecture diagram gives us a clear understanding of what technology products and tools are used in the solution and how they are laid out in the overall solution. Mentioning exact vendor names is not a must, but it is good to have so that the technical teams can do the deployment architecture easily.

Selecting the vendors for the technical component can be a long, tedious task with multiple product evaluations, proof of concepts, request for proposals (RFPs), and many other mechanisms. Having the technical architecture helps a lot in these evaluation phases since we have a better idea on what we are looking at rather than purchasing something that is out there but does not fit into our use case.

The next phase in the solution architecture design is the capacity planning where we capture the capacity requirements from the different stakeholders of the problem at hand and decide on how to actually deploy the solution in a real computing infrastructure. That is what we are going to cover under the deployment architecture section.

Deployment Architecture (Level 2 Architecture)

Once the problem is identified, a solution is defined, and the technical products have been recognized, then it is time to deploy it in a real computing infrastructure and start implementing the use cases. The deployment architecture or the Level 2 architecture within the solution architecture provides the details of how the actual deployment looks like in a data center or a cloud infrastructure. It is designed based on the current and projected capacity requirements of the system.

Let us extend our mobile banking application to define the deployment architecture for the solution. Here, we got to know that the typical capacity requirement for mobile applications is around 200 requests per second in a peak time such as payroll dates and tax paying dates. We take a look at the performance benchmarks of API Management vendor (WSO2), integration platform vendor (MuleSoft), and IAM vendor (Auth0) and decide to have the deployment similar to the one mentioned in Figure 2-5.

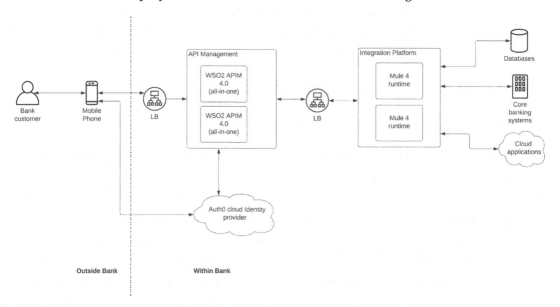

Figure 2-5. *Deployment architecture for a mobile banking application*

In the figure, you can find the details of the components that are going to be used in the system. These are the following:

- LB (load balancer) – This component is used to share the load between multiple instances of the WSO2 API Manager as well as Mule 4 runtime.

- WSO2 APIM (all in one) – This is the APIM component that is deployed as a two-node cluster for minimum high availability. At the same time, it can support more than two times of the capacity requirement, which is 400 rps.

- Mule 4 runtime – This is the integration component that is deployed as a two-node cluster for minimum high availability. Here, the capacity requirement is estimated as four times of the original estimate, which is 800 rps (200×2×2), assuming that each API call can result in two integration calls on average.

- Auth0 cloud Identity Provider – For the authentication and authorization requirement, we have used a cloud-based IAM solution Auth0, which is priced based on the number of active users. This is a SaaS product that is managed and maintained by the vendor itself. We only need to integrate with that using standard interfaces. It has a scalable deployment model that automatically scales as per the number of users active in the system.

With the deployment architecture component at hand, the development teams can start setting up the deployment in a computing infrastructure such as on-premise data center or a cloud infrastructure-as-a-service (IaaS) platform and get into the implementation phase of the project. Instead of designing the solution architecture for the entire project, it is also possible to do that for a proof-of-concept (POC) scale and then improve the design based on the outcome and the experience of the POC as well.

There are different approaches that we can follow to come up with the solution architecture for an enterprise software system. At the end of the day, what is important is the solution that we come up with and how well that solution adapts to the requirements of the business. In the next section, we will take a look at a generic process that can be used to guide the solution architects when designing solution architecture for enterprises.

Solution Architecture Defining Process

Enterprises have varying sizes and structures within enterprise software teams. Depending on the size and the structure, these teams may follow different processes to come up with a technical solution to a business requirement. We call this technical solution as the solution architecture, which will be the blueprint for the actual implementation. So far, we have discussed different components of solution architecture and how these components such as business architecture, technical architecture, and deployment architecture help different teams to get clarity on what is going to be built. Figure 2-6 shows a simple process flow that can be adopted by many different enterprise teams regardless of their size and structure to get a good solution architecture designed for a business requirement.

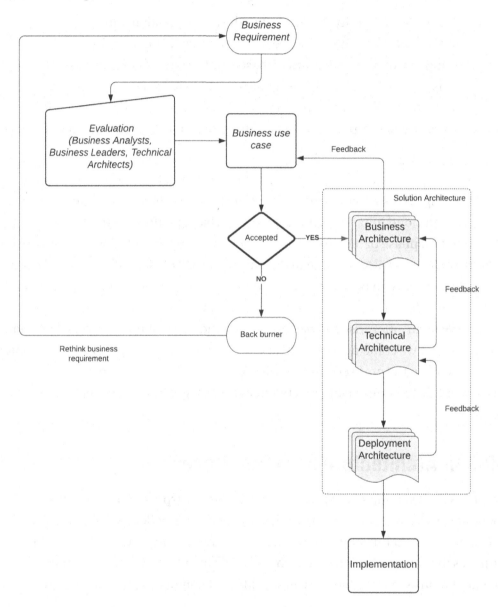

Figure 2-6. *Sample process flow to define a solution architecture for a business requirement*

The figure depicts a generic workflow to design a solution architecture from a business requirement. The flow as appeared in the figure can be explained as follows:

- An individual or a team comes up with a business requirement that they think will improve the overall efficiency of the enterprise or bring more glory.

- There is a team of evaluators (can be the enterprise architecture team) who interviews the people who came up with the idea and decides on the technical and financial feasibility of the proposal.

- If the proposal is accepted, then it will move to the next phase where the solution architects along with the domain experts and the idea presenters come together and design the business architecture. During this process, if they identify any improvements or suggestions to the use case, that would be updated in the project proposal.

- If the proposal is rejected, the team will go back and rethink their proposal and may come back in a later time.

- Once the business architecture is finalized, solution architects along with technical architects will get together and figure out the best matching technology for the solution and come up with the technology architecture. During this time, the team would do their own technical evaluations for choosing the vendors and talk with the enterprise architecture team (if there is any) to get their opinion on technology choices.

- Then the process moves to the next phase where the solution architects and technical architects design the deployment architecture by going through the capacity requirements of the current and future needs.

- Once the solution architecture is done, the project implementation team will use the created solution architecture to build the real enterprise software system.

Even though the process is depicted as a waterfall approach, if required, you can use that in an agile manner where you don't need to wait until one step is completely done before moving to the next step. As an example, you can take a portion of the business use case and start building the solution architecture and the implementation rather than waiting till the solution architecture is built for the entire use case. This can also happen in a situation where you need to build a proof of concept before making the final decision on technology vendors.

Now we have a good understanding of what solution architecture is and how to build a solution architecture for an enterprise business requirement. To improve this understanding further, let's take a more example where we start from an enterprise architecture and then derive the solution architecture for a particular business use case.

Complex Solution Architecture Example

Let us think of a large organization that has a dedicated enterprise architecture team that designs the overall technology vision for the enterprise. They have already come up with a solid enterprise architecture that needs to be adopted for any future solutions that are built within the enterprise. Let us start with the microservices-based enterprise architecture (Figure 2-2) that we discussed in a previous section of this chapter. Let us assume that we are building a modern omni-channel banking solution for the enterprise using this enterprise architecture. The first thing we need to do is come up with the business architecture based on the requirements that are presented by the business teams. The following is the initial set of requirements for the proposed solution:

- Provide customers with access to banking services via multiple channels:

    - Mobile application

    - Internet banking

    - Agents

    - SMS banking

    - ATMs

    - Call centers

- Integrate with third-party applications and services.

- Provide insights into customers and their behaviors.

- Manage business processes and workflows.

- Integrate with internal customer and business management systems.

Once the requirements are presented to the technical committee who evaluates the feasibility of the project, they would give their feedback and the green light (or red light) to start the project. Assuming that they have already given the green light, let us try to come up with a business architecture for this complex requirement.

Business Architecture for a Banking Solution

In business architecture, we need to capture the main business stakeholders and the systems that are already available in the system along with the proposed components that solve the business problem. Figure 2-7 is a sample business architecture for the requirements that were mentioned in the previous section.

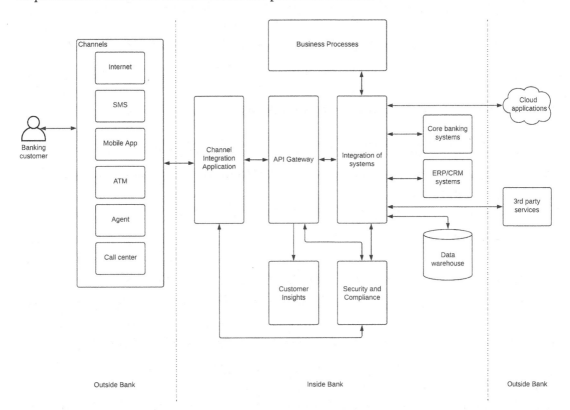

Figure 2-7. *Business architecture for omni-channel banking solution*

The figure depicts the main components of the banking solution. It captures the high-level view of these components and their interactions. As depicted in the figure, the following is a list of components used in this solution.

Banking Customer

This is the user who consumes this solution via different channels such as mobile application, SMS banking, web application, and so on. This customer should be able to use the services such as balance inquiry, fund transfer, bill payments, money withdrawal and deposit, and many other services offered by modern banking platforms.

Channels

These are the different mediums used by the customer to interact with the banking services. All of these channels act as a client to the banking solution, and these clients are sitting outside the banking system.

Channel Integration Application

Handling different consumer channels requires a dedicated infrastructure to manage these connections and service requests. As an example, to handle SMS and voice calls, there should be a different telecommunication infrastructure. Similarly, to handle mobile and web application requests, there need to be separate application components. We are going to use an integrated omni-channel platform to handle all of these different channel communications with the banking data.

API Gateway

Banking systems are highly sensitive applications, and we need to have a secure gateway to protect all the access coming into the system. That is the task of the API gateway, and it will control access to the banking systems by applying various quality-of-service measures on top of the requests coming into the platform.

Integration of Systems

In a banking ecosystem, there are different types of applications and systems used to store data related to customers, transactions, banking products, card systems, other bank transactions, currency conversions, and many other different types of information. When a customer wants to use a banking service via a mobile application, several of these systems need to be integrated to offer that service. As an example, if a customer wants to make a payment via Internet banking to a retail vendor using a different currency, that request needs to verify the customer profile, account balance, and currency conversions while fulfilling the customer request. Similarly, there can be many situations that involve orchestration of multiple systems to support a particular customer service request. That is the task of the integration component, which is capable of integrating with on-premise banking systems, cloud applications, and third-party systems and applications connected over the Internet.

Business Processes

Banks provide services such as leasing, personal loans, and housing loans that would require long-running business processes to execute in the enterprise software system. These types of processes can be implemented using a workflow product that supports designing and implementing long-running business processes in a programming model such as BPMN or BPEL. This component will communicate with the other systems as and when required to move the business process forward until it comes to a conclusion.

Security and Compliance

Financial activities need to be regulated and secured with the best possible mechanisms available while providing a good experience to the user. That is the task of the security component, which secures access to the financial information and lets customers control their consent. Compliance is another key aspect of financial transactions where certain systems need to be compliant with standards such as GDPR, PCI DSS, and PSD2. The security component takes care of this functionality.

Customer Insights

In the modern competitive banking market, every other bank tries to acquire customers from competing banks by analyzing customer behaviors, financial usage patterns, and buying patterns. This is the function of the customer insights component, which provides details of how the customers are using different banking services via different channels so that business teams can offer attractive services to the customers in a personalized manner.

Other Banking Systems

There are common applications and systems used by banks to store the customer information (CRM), transactions processing (core banking), and banking products (data warehouse) to operate the daily functions of a bank. These systems will interact with the solution that we are proposing here.

Once we identify the business architecture and the components required to build a solution for the banking system modernization project, we need to select the best technology vendors and their interactions with the technical architecture. The following section describes this process.

Technical Architecture for a Banking Solution

Identifying the correct technology components to build the solution based on the business architecture requires a fair amount of technical knowledge as well as domain knowledge. There are certain vendors who provide turnkey solutions for the kind of requirements that we identified in the previous section. It is important to understand the difference of "build" vs. "buy" approach when selecting a vendor for this type of business architecture.

Build vs. Buy

The world of enterprise software has evolved so much that most of the industries have turnkey solutions that are built by software companies based on their past experiences and domain knowledge. Most of these companies are started by some technical or business leaders who worked in the industry for some time. With the experience and the exposure they get during their tenure at the organization, they will come up with the idea of building a turnkey solution that would solve most of the common problems related to that industry. If you are looking to build a solution for a particular domain, let's say banking, you would find such turnkey solutions that you can "buy" from the market and use it directly. This has advantages such as better time to market, lesser management overhead, and lesser consumption of human capital. There are a few disadvantages as well. Less flexibility when it comes to implementing custom solutions, too much dependency on the vendor, and pricing and support complications over time are some disadvantages.

The other option is to build the solution using the best components that we can select from the market. This gives the advantage of flexibility, control, and independence from a single vendor. Technical architecture is mostly valuable in this sort of "build" scenario rather than the "buy" scenarios.

Figure 2-8 is a technical architecture that we can use to map with the business architecture we designed in the preceding section.

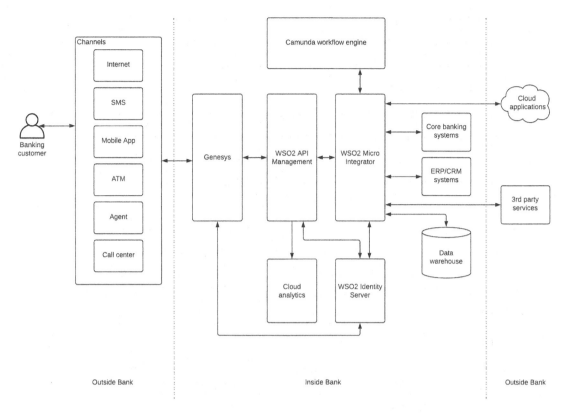

Figure 2-8. *Technical architecture for an omni-channel banking solution*

The figure depicts the technical components that we are going to use to build the banking software system. Depending on the functional requirements of the business use case and the overall enterprise strategy of using microservices-based components for middleware, we have chosen the following mentioned components within the technical architecture:

- Genesys – This is a multichannel platform that allows providing support for customers over channels such as phone (voice and SMS), mobile applications, and web applications and aggregates these channels to provide a unified experience.

- WSO2 API Management – This is an open source full API life cycle management vendor that allows protecting banking services via a set of managed APIs. This tool also allows exposing these APIs to not only Genesys but also other third-party applications that would develop in the future. It supports container-based deployments natively.

- WSO2 Micro Integrator – This is the integration product that supports all the different application integration requirements as well as data integration use cases. It can be deployed in a container-based environment.

- Camunda workflow engine – This is the component that will be used to implement long-running business processes within the solution. It uses a BPMN-based workflow design model to implement the processes such as loan approvals and leasing approvals. This can be run within the container environment.

- WSO2 Identity Server – This component provides the authentication and authorization capabilities for business applications and APIs. It also provides tools to comply with financial regulations such as PSD2 and GDPR. It is an open source product that can be run in any infrastructure such as VMs or containers.

- Cloud analytics – For business insights, we use a cloud-based analytics solution since managing analytics in an on-premise environment sometimes causes unnecessary overhead to the operations teams.

In addition to these components, there are already-existing applications and systems in the enterprise that have been used for a long time, and the new solution integrates with these components either directly or via the integration component.

Given that this solution needs to be developed according to the enterprise architecture that is designed by the architecture team, we need to follow the container-based deployment model for the new solution since all the new solutions developed in the enterprise are using that infrastructure. In the next section, we will look at how our technical architecture can be deployed in a real computing infrastructure.

Deployment Architecture for a Banking Solution

Enterprise architecture teams are always looking to improve the efficiency of overall IT infrastructure and save costs wherever possible. Most of the enterprises are moving toward container-based deployments due to the many advantages they provide over a traditional VM-based or a physical server–based model. For our banking solution also, we will be utilizing a container-based deployment model. This was considered as a major factor when selecting vendors for our solution. Figure 2-9 depicts how we can deploy the proposed banking solution in a container environment.

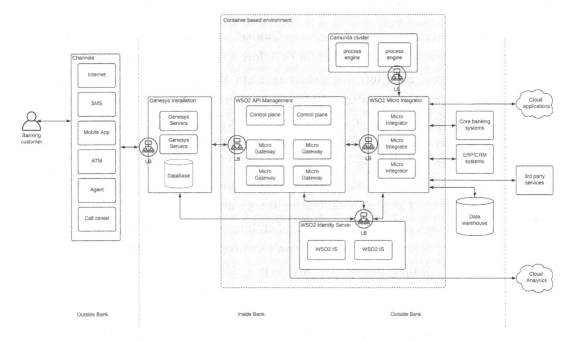

Figure 2-9. *Deployment architecture for an omni-channel banking solution*

As depicted in the figure, the deployment architecture captures the details of the actual deployment within the computing infrastructure. Each product has its own way of deployment according to the capacity and scalability requirements of the solution. There are certain components that cannot be deployed within containerized environments because of certain technical requirements and limitations. In our banking solution, the Genesys application is deployed outside of the container environment due to the nature of that system. All the other components including WSO2 API Manager, WSO2 Micro Integrator, WSO2 Identity Server, and Camunda workflow engine are deployed within the containerized environment. The analytics is provided as a cloud-based solution that comes with the WSO2 API Management solution.

Now we have gone through two examples of designing solution architecture for real-world enterprise use cases. The next phase of the project is to move to the development phase from the architecture designing phase. Even though solution architects won't actively work on writing code, they need to be involved in the implementation phase as well. In the next section, we will talk about the involvement of the solution architecture and the solution architect in the project implementation phase.

Moving from Solution Architecture to Implementation

We talked about the analogy of the "plan" of a "house" to the "solution architecture" of an "enterprise software system" a couple of times before when explaining the importance of solution architecture to an enterprise software system. We can start the implementation conversation using the same analogy. By the time solution architecture is designed and discussed among the architects and business stakeholders and approved, the funding will follow right after. The technical leads of the project need to put together a plan on how to implement this proposed solution. In most cases, planning of the project implementation also starts once the business and technology architecture components are finalized. The project implementation timelines would have a direct impact on the vendors that we select during the technical architecture design phase. Hence, it is essential to have a rough idea on the overall project timelines so that these vendors can be notified about the project delivery as early as possible. The actual project timelines must include tasks such as solution architecture design, proof-of-concept (POC) developments, and vendor evaluation processes as well even though these are not directly producing any tangible outcome to the actual production implementation. Different teams use different mechanisms to communicate the project timelines to the stakeholders. Some people use spreadsheets, some use timetables, and some use Gantt charts.

Sample Project Timeline

Let us take an example and discuss how to come up with a project timeline based on a solution architecture that we design. Let us consider the first example we discussed in the previous section where we designed a solution architecture for a mobile banking application. For a project of that nature, we can follow a timeline similar to the one mentioned in Figure 2-10.

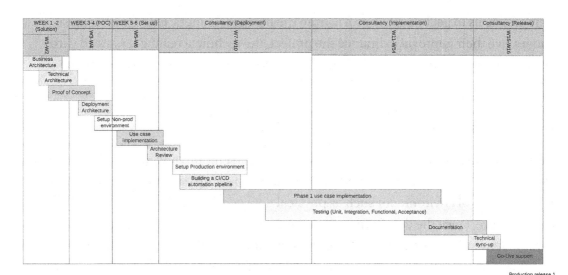

Figure 2-10. *Gantt chart for mobile banking application project timelines*

The figure depicts a project that spans approximately 4 months (16 weeks) from the start of the solution design to the first major production release. Let us discuss the tasks included in the Gantt chart in detail.

Weeks 1–2

At the beginning of the project, we spend time on designing the business architecture by going through the business use case and the requirements. This process involves technical architects, business analysts, business leaders, and solution architects. Once everyone provides their input and the business architecture is designed and agreed upon, the technical architects and solution architects move to the next phase where they design the technical architecture by evaluating the products that are required to the solution. They do various POCs and evaluate vendors as per the experiences and preferences. This could span two to three weeks for a simple project and could take months for a complex project with multiple vendors.

Weeks 3–4

Once the evaluations are done, the technical team finishes the technical architecture and comes up with a possible deployment architecture based on the capacity requirements of the business use case. Sometimes, they plan the deployment ahead of time and make sure the solution can withstand future growth as well. Then they present

55

their proposals to get budget approval from the business leaders. Once the business leaders give their approval to finance the project, the technical team goes ahead with the next phase of setting up computing infrastructure according to the deployment architecture.

Weeks 5–6

After designing the solution architecture within the first month and getting the financial approvals, the team starts working with the vendors to set up development environments in their choice of environment such as physical data centers, virtual machines, or cloud infrastructure. Once the development environments are set up, the development teams start implementing the use cases and testing the different services, integrations, and workflows. At the end of the development environment setup, the technical teams will review the architecture along with the environment details to make sure it aligns with what is discussed in the solution architecture.

Weeks 7–10

The next phase of the project is the setting up of the production environment and automating the development and deployment process so that it can release projects in a timely manner in the future. This is an important aspect of the production deployment since it will allow developers to independently release their new products and services without bothering the operations teams. Though it will consume some resources during the setting-up process, it will result in valuable benefits in the future. Use case implementation continues to happen, and the development team will start utilizing the production environment and the build pipelines to test their implementation.

Weeks 11–14

Once the production environment is ready and the deployment process is automated, the development teams start on-boarding their developer-tested implementations to the production environments so that quality assurance (QA) teams can perform the required testing in the production environment in a rigorous manner before releasing them to the customers. Development teams will start documenting the implementations, user guides, and other critical information for the test teams and the end users.

Weeks 15–16

In the final two weeks of the project, the development teams stop implementing new features, and the QA teams will sign off their testing and hand it over to the go-live support team so that they can be prepared for any post-release questions or queries coming from the users. The production deployments will be rolled out in a blue-green approach where all the services become available for the users at once or in a canary approach where services are rolled out to the customers step by step. In either case, the technical teams will stay alert, and the vendor support teams are also informed about the production release ahead of time so that they can allocate dedicated resources during the rollout hours. The system will be monitored for a few hours, and if all goes well, the release is successful and will be handed over to the standard support teams who provide customer support on the system.

What we have discussed in the preceding section is a typical enterprise software project that involves different teams within an enterprise. The teams will utilize the solution architecture that is designed in the early phases of the project throughout the entire project timeline. Even after the production release, the architects will keep the solution architecture document as the blueprint of the system so that whenever they need to troubleshoot a problem or need to expand the system, they will refer to it as the single most important document.

Advantages of Solution Architecture Patterns

Now we have a better understanding of what is solution architecture and how it helps enterprise teams to build solutions to enterprise problems using technology. We talked about the importance of the solution architecture throughout the life cycle of an enterprise project. Let's take a step back and think about what we have designed as solution architecture for some of the use cases we discussed in this chapter and the previous chapter. We designed solutions for mobile banking applications, omni-channel banking systems, hospital systems for the healthcare domain, and a solution for transportation. If you take a closer look at these solutions, you could identify some similarities in all of those solutions. Some notable similarities are as follows:

- API gateways are used to expose services to consumer channels.

- Integration component is used to connect different systems within different use cases.

- Security component is used to provide authentication and authorization services.

There can be more similarities that you could recognize. What that means is that there are certain components within the solution architecture that we can reuse across industries and use cases. What we design in solution architecture is the way data flows through an enterprise system and the intercepting points of that data in the manner of different software components. There are distinct aspects of the way these systems communicate with one another in terms of the protocols (e.g., HTTP, TCP), message formats (e.g., JSON, XML), communication style (synchronous, asynchronous), and encryption (e.g., TLS, SSL).

After working in the enterprise software domain for more than a decade, what I observed was that there are many common patterns appearing in the enterprise software systems that we can reuse. We can categorize these patterns into different categories based on technical aspects or based on industries. This book is written with the intention of sharing such common patterns with you and helping you understand the value of these common patterns so that you can use them for your enterprise software projects in the future. These patterns are similar to the design patterns you use in the software development world. It will reduce the time you need to spend on reinventing the solutions that are already there and well tested across many enterprises. Some of the advantages of using solution architecture patterns for your enterprise software projects are as follows:

- Patterns include a ton of knowledge from experienced solution architects who worked on similar projects before. It is hard to earn this knowledge otherwise.

- Domain-specific patterns provide solutions that are well tested within those domains across organizations of different sizes.

- Don't need to fail twice for the same reason. These systems are designed with the learnings from previous failures, and you don't need to fail again for the same reason.

- Patterns provide a blueprint that you can change according to your needs. You don't need to do exactly as it says. But you can use the best from these past experiences that are converted to patterns.

You will learn more about the patterns and the advantages in the upcoming chapters.

Summary

In this second chapter of the book, we discussed what enterprise architecture is with a few examples. Then we discussed what solution architecture is in detail. We discussed the relationship of these two concepts and how solution architecture becomes the blueprint of enterprise software systems. We went into detail about solution architecture and discussed the business, technical, and deployment components of solution architecture with a few examples. Then we talked about moving from solution architecture to the implementation with a sample project using a Gantt chart. Finally, we discussed the importance of using solution architecture patterns when building enterprise software systems. Figure 2-11 depicts the concepts that we discussed in this chapter in a nutshell.

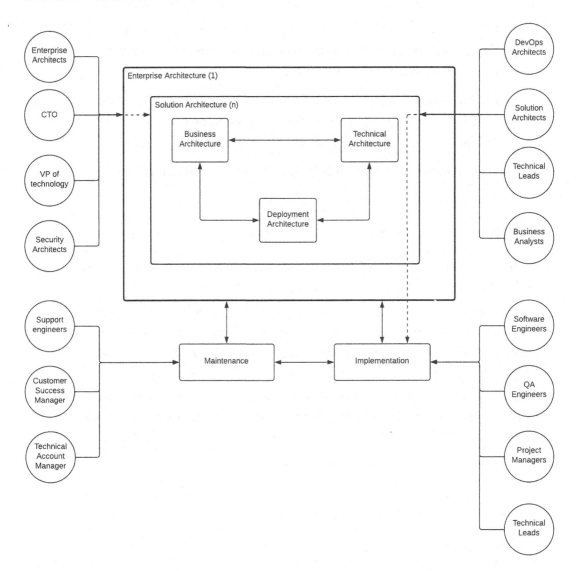

Figure 2-11. *Enterprise architecture, solution architecture, and stakeholders*

The figure depicts the correlation between enterprise architecture, solution architecture, and its components, implementation, and maintenance with the relevant stakeholders. The diagram depicts the idea of having one enterprise architecture that can fork many different solution architectures (n) for different use cases in the enterprise. It also depicts (in dotted lines) the idea of stakeholders spilling over their responsibilities to the next layer as and when required. As an example, the enterprise architecture team members can sit on the solution architecture discussions as well as solution architects can sit on the implementation discussions.

This chapter concludes the first section of the book where we covered the concepts of enterprise, enterprise architecture, and solution architecture. The next chapter marks the beginning of the second section of the book where we discuss different reusable solution architecture patterns based on technological categorization.

CHAPTER 3

Building Enterprise Software Systems with Microservice Architecture

Enterprise software systems have evolved rapidly over the last few years due to the increasing demand of consumers purchasing products through digital mediums. The global economy has shifted from a vendor-driven economy to a consumer-driven economy with the advancements in the technology. Organizations such as Uber, Airbnb, and Netflix have become global phenomena with the usage of technology in a short period of time. These Internet-based companies were able to achieve this much of a success due to the flexibility they had on their enterprise software systems that ran the show behind the curtain. Serving billions of customers a day globally required solid enterprise software systems that we have not seen before. The microservice architecture played a pivotal role in these organizations to become successful business corporations with the use of technology.

In this chapter, we are going to discuss what is microservice architecture and how it can be used to design global-scale enterprise software systems. We will be discussing the following topics in this chapter:

- Introduction to microservice architecture (MSA)

- A reference architecture for an enterprise software system with MSA

- What is a service mesh and how to use that with MSA

- Designing MSA with a message broker

© Chanaka Fernando 2023
C. Fernando, *Solution Architecture Patterns for Enterprise*, https://doi.org/10.1007/978-1-4842-8948-8_3

- Implementing security for MSA with policy agents

- Implementing governance for MSA

Microservice architecture itself is worth a few books of its own, and we will be giving a brief introduction to the concept and cover a few major aspects of it with possible architecture patterns that can be used in building enterprise software systems. Let us first take a look at what microservice architecture is and how it correlates to enterprise software systems.

Introduction to Microservice Architecture (MSA)

Microservice architecture is an architecture pattern that helps developers and architects to build distributed systems by dividing the functions of the system into domain-driven, small (micro), independently manageable components (services). This definition highlights two important aspects of microservice architecture:

1. Size and the scope of the service

2. Nature of the service

Let us discuss in detail how these two aspects are important in building enterprise software systems with microservice architecture.

Size and the Scope of the Service

The term "microservice architecture" itself has the word "micro" in it to highlight the fact that the components that are designed and developed in a microservice architecture–based distributed system need to be small. A given service has various attributes such as

- Functionality (domain)

- Lines of code (size)

- Number of functions (scope)

Let us take a detailed look at each of these attributes and the size associated with them in a microservice architecture context.

Functionality (Domain)

In a system that follows the microservice architecture pattern, the services need to have a clearly defined functionality or a domain. This is sometimes referred to as domain-driven design (DDD). Sometimes, this is the most difficult task, and if you wait until you do it right for the entire system, you will never be able to get your system implemented. Hence, it is advisable to start with a manageable design and then keep on improving the boundaries or scopes of the services as the time goes on. You may start assuming that one word (noun) is a one function and start developing microservices for that. But later on, you may identify that this one word can be divided further into subfunctions and separate microservices down the line. That is perfectly fine. As an example, for a banking system, you may think that you can divide the functions based on various account types such as

- Fixed deposits
- Current accounts
- Savings accounts
- Remittances
- Loans
- Leasing

You can start your implementation based on the aforementioned domains or boundaries. But when you start utilizing the system, you will realize that there are certain subdivisions that you need to make such as fixed deposits need to be divided into different categories such as foreign currency deposits, senior citizen deposits, and local currency deposits that require different functionality. This is a perfectly valid approach, and the boundary of the service domain can change accordingly. But it needs to be clearly defined and relatively small at any given time.

Lines of Code (Size)

Another aspect of the size of a service is the lines of code required to implement a service. This is a highly debatable topic since different technologies require different number of code lines. As an example, if you write a service using a low-level language such as C or C++, you may require more code lines than a service implemented in a language such as Python or Java. If you use a domain-specific language (DSL) such as

Apache Synapse (XML) or Ballerina, you may require even fewer code lines. Hence, defining the size of the service with the usage of the number of code lines needs to be done carefully, and it should be done with proper understanding of the technology that is used.

Number of Functions (Scope)

An ideal microservice should have a single method (or function) that serves a single task. But that is highly unlikely in a real-world microservice. The developers will decide the number of methods (or functions) based on the requirements of the service. As a developer, you can write a one large method with hundreds or thousands of lines or divide that into utility methods of few lines of code per method. This again needs to be considered with the technology that is used for the development. There can be high-level languages and frameworks with a lot of built-in functions and libraries that can be utilized with a few lines of code with a minimum number of methods. But during the runtime, it will require all those additional libraries and frameworks to be packaged into the deployable artifact, making it heavy in the runtime. Such an application would perform not so well and may consume more resources than a service developed with a low-level language with higher number of methods and code lines.

As a summary, the size of the service is a relative thing, and it needs to be decided based on the needs and the technology. But it needs to be comparatively small in a given context.

Nature of the Service

The other important aspect of microservice architecture is the nature of the service. This includes the following properties:

- Development
- Deployment
- Governance

Let us discuss in detail what each of these properties entails in a microservice architecture.

Development

Once the service scope is defined based on the requirements by following an approach such as DDD, the next step is to develop it with a suitable technology. Microservice architecture allows teams to select their own technology stack instead of using the same technology for all the services. This can add a bit of complexity to the overall maintenance of the solution. But it is a viable option in case a particular service needs a specific technology to be used. We call this approach polyglot programming where different microservices developed with different technologies. The other important aspect is that the teams can be agile and they don't need to be dedicated center-of-excellence (CoE) teams with rigid boundaries. Instead, enterprise architects who overlook the projects can formulate teams as and when necessary to develop microservices with the relevant roles such as

- Business analyst

- Programmer

- UX developer

- QA engineer

- Project manager

These team members can be picked from existing teams, and the new team can work in an agile manner to release the service within a given time duration. Companies like Amazon follow the two-pizza rule for team sizes where each team consists of less than ten team members. These teams can work on the end-to-end development of the service.

Deployment

Once the development is done, the services need to be deployed into various environments such as development, testing, and production. Different organizations follow different approaches to deploy the services, and microservice architecture encourages teams to automate the deployments as much as possible using technologies such as DevOps or DevSecOps. In both approaches, the deployment of a service into different environments is automated so that human interaction is minimal. This type of an approach will minimize human errors such as developers saying "it worked on my machine" when the service is failing in production environments. The usage of container technologies such as Docker allows developers to package their services into highly portable deployable artifacts so that they no longer need to defend themselves with statements such as "it worked on my machine." Once the developer tests the service with a container on their own computer, that should behave identically in other environments as long as runtime configurations are properly done by the DevOps and DevSecOps teams. Hence, in a microservice architecture, the following two aspects are important related to deployment.

1. Deployment automation

2. Container-based deployments

Let us take a detailed look at each of these two aspects.

Deployment Automation

Enterprise software teams used to take a long time to do a product release due to the complexity of the system and the critical nature of the services. This is no longer the case with highly competitive business requirements and consumer demand. Companies such as Google and Facebook do several releases within a given day. If you are in the enterprise software domain and think that you have three or six months to do a feature release, you are not in a good position. How these large Internet-based companies do frequent releases is through the automation of their deployment. As an example, once the developer makes a commit to the source code repository such as GitHub, that would automatically trigger a build and that will package the code into a runtime container and that will be deployed automatically to a lower environment such as development and the tests are getting triggered to validate the functionality and to make sure there are no regressions. Once the testing is completed in the lower environment, it will trigger a build on the next environment until it goes to the production environment.

This may sound magical in the first pass. But implementing such a comprehensive build pipeline requires a good amount of time, and most of the companies push this task to the back burner assuming that it is not an important task. But companies such as Google and Facebook have shown the world that building these sorts of build pipelines provides many benefits in the long run. In a microservice architecture–based platform, it is really important that each service can be deployed independently without impacting the other services.

Container-Based Deployments

Microservices are designed in such a way that they can run on their own. But when we develop these microservices, we use different technologies and frameworks. These frameworks will add dependencies to the microservice, and running the microservice requires a certain runtime environment. Containers allow the developers to package all these required components to be packaged into a single artifact and share that with the operations teams or in case of an automated deployment, to be added to the pipeline. There are many technologies available to run containers, and Docker is one of the most popular technologies out there.

In addition to running the service in containers, managing the container deployments in a given infrastructure is also important when it comes to scalability and availability. As an example, what happens if a container goes down. In such a scenario, there are container orchestration systems such as Kubernetes that help the service to be available by automatically monitoring the status of the container and restarting. In addition to that, these technologies can also scale the deployments based on the incoming load into the system and control the way containers are distributed across the computing infrastructure. Given the fact that microservices are independently deployed and scaled, having a container-based deployment with an orchestration technology such as Kubernetes helps a lot to provide better availability and scalability.

Governance

Even though the microservice architecture allows individual services to be developed, deployed, and managed independently, at the end of the day, these services need to work cohesively to offer a complete solution to the end users. That is why it is important to have a proper governance at overall solution level while providing the freedom to individual microservices teams to run with their own technologies and methodologies. As an example, if one team uses Open API Specification (OAS) to define the rest interfaces and another team uses a proprietary standard like RAML, it will make the overall solution a bit ugly when you need to expose different services through a common development portal. Hence, it is important to have a proper governance model and a structure to define the common standards across microservices teams so that they can use the freedom offered by the microservice architecture while adhering to common standards, which makes the overall solution manageable.

With that brief introduction, let's jump straight into using microservice architecture for designing an enterprise software system by defining a reference architecture in the next section.

A Reference Architecture for Enterprise Software System with MSA

We discussed the characteristics of enterprise software systems in Chapter 1, "Introduction to Enterprise Software Systems," and possible solution architecture of such a system in Chapter 2, "Introduction to Solution Architecture." In this section, we are going to design an enterprise software system using the microservice architecture concepts that we discussed in the preceding section. A typical enterprise software system consists of different types of systems and applications based on the industry that system is built for. As an example, a healthcare enterprise software system may contain systems to hold electronic medical records and hence use systems such as electronic health record (EHR) systems or electronic medical record (EMR) systems, while a banking enterprise software system may consist of systems that hold financial data such as ISO 8583 formatted data.

Components of Enterprise Software Systems

While there are different systems to hold different types of data based on the industry, there are many common applications and systems utilized across most of the enterprise software systems. In this section, we are going to identify those common systems and design a solution based on microservice architecture. The following is a list of common software components that are used in most of the enterprise software systems:

- Databases
- Core business applications
  - Cloud-based software
  - Commercial off-the-shelf (COTS) software
  - In-house built applications
- Integration software

- Application Programming Interface (API) software

- Accessibility software

- Security software

- Monitoring software

- Infrastructure management software

Let's discuss each of these different components of an enterprise software system in detail. Figure 3-1 depicts how these components are positioned in a typical enterprise system.

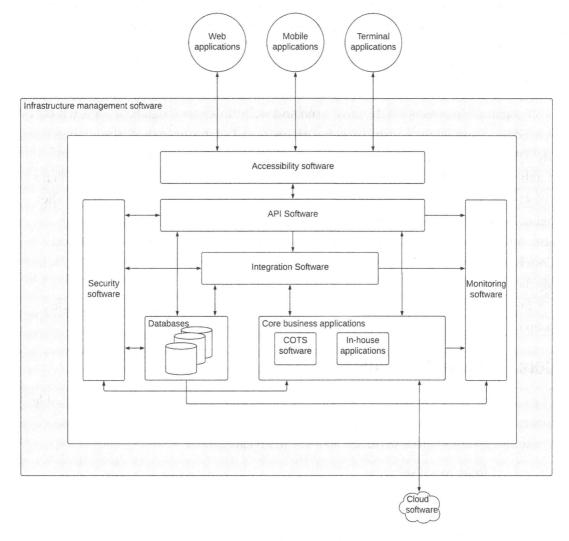

Figure 3-1. *Key software components of an enterprise software system*

As depicted in the figure, different software components work together to provide digital services to different types of client applications such as mobile, web, and terminal applications that consumers use. Let us discuss in detail the unique functionality of these components and how they interact with one another.

Databases

The world of business is dominated by data in the modern world. Holding valuable information about customers, products, and buying patterns allows businesses to offer great experiences to the customers and expand their businesses regardless of the industry. Hence, databases play a major role in any enterprise software system. There are two main types of databases that we can identify in mainstream software systems:

- Relational databases

- Nonrelational (NoSQL) databases

Relational databases are the most used and well-understood database type, which is used by almost all the enterprise software systems. Database technologies such as MySQL, Oracle, PostgreSQL, and MS SQL Server are popular examples of relational databases. These databases are used to store transactional and structured data, which needs to be stored in a tabular format for easy retrieval and consumption. On the other hand, NoSQL databases are used to keep large amounts of data that are consumed after further processing. A few examples are MongoDB, Cassandra, Cosmos DB, and Couchbase. These databases are used to store semistructured and unstructured data in big data, analytics, and machine learning–based use cases.

From the perspective of an enterprise software system, databases hold the single source of truth when it comes to data.

Core Business Applications

The data that resides in databases needs to be accessed in a manner that is consumable for end user applications. This happens through a set of core business applications. These applications can be divided into three main categories:

1. Cloud-based software

2. Commercial off-the-shelf (COTS) software

3. In-house built applications

Cloud is no longer a strange space for enterprise software. More and more enterprises are utilizing cloud-based business applications for their common needs such as customer relationship management (CRM), enterprise resource planning (ERP), and human resource management (HRM). In addition to these common requirements, there are many industry-specific applications available as cloud solutions in the market.

COTS applications are still in use even in the cloud era to provide business applications that require high performance, strict security requirements, and on-premise installation options. These applications are typically installed within enterprise premises and managed by internal teams with the help from the vendor through product support.

In-house built applications are also common in the business applications space where enterprises need to "build" their solutions rather than "buy" from another vendor. The advantage of building an application within the enterprise itself is that it can be designed to match the exact requirements of the business and control over the applications is fully within the enterprise itself. In most cases, microservice architecture is utilized in this type of application development.

Integration Software

Once the databases and core business applications are in place, most of the mandatory requirements of the business are covered. Each of these applications serves a specific business purpose, and having these systems installed and configured within a computing infrastructure provides the required tools to serve the customers. But these systems individually cannot fulfill the full experience that is expected by different stakeholders of the business such as customers, business leadership, and investors. That is why integration software is required to connect these different systems and build a cohesive enterprise software system that utilizes and compliments the capabilities of each system. Integration software allows software systems developed and designed by completely different vendors using different technologies to share data with one another without changing any of the applications. Instead, integration software translates the communication such as a language translator who helps an English speaker talk to a Japanese speaker.

Integration software is capable of integrating cloud-based systems as well as on-premise systems. The software itself can be deployed in any of the selected environments including on-premise, cloud, and hybrid models. In a microservice architecture–based enterprise software platform, integration software can also be deployed as microservices. We will discuss how to do that in the reference architecture section.

Integration software includes the message broker software that acts as a messaging framework for different applications to communicate with one another in an asynchronous manner. These message brokers may include as separate components along with traditional integration software components such as enterprise service bus (ESB) or integration platform as a service (iPaaS) in an enterprise software system. Some examples are Kafka, RabbitMQ, ActiveMQ, and NATS.

API Software

Once the databases and core business applications are integrated with the integration software, these aggregated services need to be exposed to internal and external consumers. These consumers may use web applications, mobile applications, and sometimes terminal applications to access core business data over these integrated services. API software is used to standardize access to these services by exposing the services over standard interfaces such as REST over HTTP or GraphQL over HTTP. These APIs also hide the complexity of the underlying systems and provide a well-defined interface to the client applications so that they can build their own experiences without worrying about the details of underlying implementations of the platform. On top of these standard interfaces, enterprises can apply various quality-of-service measures such as

- Security to protect data from unauthorized access
- Access controls with rate limiting
- Caching to improve performance
- Monitoring to understand usage

Instead of implementing these features at services level for each and every service, using an API software such as an API gateway allows enterprises to rapidly deliver services and standardize the services and the interactions. API gateways are equipped with the required functionality such as security, rate limiting, caching, and monitoring so that these capabilities can be added to the services without changing anything from the services side. Most of these API gateways create a "virtual" or "proxy" service by connecting to the actual business service and implement the required QoS functions at the virtual service level.

In addition, to allow services to be exposed with QoS applied, API gateways also provide the capability to publish all the services in a common portal so that API consumers can come and find out the available services. This feature is quite useful in cases where your enterprise is having hundreds or thousands of services that need to be exposed to the consumers such as application developers and third-party business partners. It helps your business to grow and reach a much wider audience through these automated interactions through the portal. Otherwise, each partner or application developer has to contact with your enterprise team to get details of available services and request access. Having a centralized developer portal avoids that manual interaction and saves a lot of time from both enterprise and partners.

Accessibility Software

Once the APIs are designed in such a way that various consumer applications such as mobile, web, and terminal applications access them to provide great experiences to the users, the next challenge is to allow these applications to access our enterprise network through the Internet with better performance. This is the task of accessibility software, which resides at the edge of the network. In most cases, it is the first point of contact for client applications before actually connecting to the enterprise services. There are different types of components used in different scenarios to provide better accessibility from external networks and from the Internet. Some common tools used as accessibility software are

- Proxy servers
- Load balancers
- Ingress controllers
- Content delivery networks (CDNs)
- Firewalls

Let us discuss each of these tools in detail to get a better understanding.

Proxy Servers

These servers hide the actual details of the backend services and provide a fake URL to the client applications to access the system. There are different types of routing rules that can be applied to this component to route traffic to certain services based on the need.

Load Balancers

This component is used to distribute the load across different instances of the same backend service, and it also acts as a proxy by hiding the details of the backend services. This is a must-have component in case you have more than instances of the same service.

Ingress Controllers

In a scenario where you use a container orchestration technology such as Kubernetes, you can use this to allow traffic from external networks such as the Internet so that client applications can access the services.

Content Delivery Network (CDN)

This component is used to improve the performance of the users by caching the content at this component and providing static content without going back to the services or databases layer. It lives along with proxy/load balancer or ingress controller.

Firewalls

This component is used to prevent malicious users accessing the enterprise software system from external networks and the Internet. This is configured at the very first level of the network interactions and filters out unwanted users before they hit the services layer.

Security Software

Security is no longer an afterthought of enterprise software systems. It is a primary requirement for any enterprise software system. While there is a physical security required to protect the infrastructure and buildings, we are mainly focusing on the virtual security or the data security of the enterprise systems here. There are two main aspects of securing enterprise software:

- User management
- Access management

Let us take a closer look at each of these aspects of the software security.

User Management

There can be different types of users who will be accessing the services offered through APIs. It can be internal users (employees) or external users such as customers or partners. Depending on their category, the access levels can be different. But these users need to be stored and managed by a user management component. Active Directory (AD) and openLDAP, which are both Directory software, are examples of user management software. In addition to these directory services software, some applications use databases to store and manage users. A typical user management software defines users according to a particular model or schema with user attributes such as username, password, email, and organization. There can be hundreds of these attributes associated with a particular user based on the application requirement. In addition to this, user management software also provides the capability to group the users into common user groups according to the requirements of the applications. As an example, if there is a need to provide access to salary details of employees only to a particular group of users (say, HR team), then these users will be added into a common group, and the access controls will allow only the users under that group to access salary details.

Access Management

Once the user information is stored in a user management component, the next step is to implement access control policies to protect APIs and services from malicious users and to provide easy access to authorized users. This entire process of storing user information and controlling access to services is referred to as "Identity and Access Management" or IAM in the enterprise software world. There are two main aspects related to access management:

1. Authentication – Verifies the identity of the user (who am I)

2. Authorization – Verifies the things that user can do (what can I do)

Let's discuss these two aspects in a bit of detail.

Authentication

Each and every user has a unique identity in the user management system that can be used to identify the user separately from others. This can be the "username" or "email address" or any other attribute associated with the user. If a user needs to access a certain service or API that is protected with authentication, the user must provide a valid "credential" to certify that the user has the right to access that service. This credential can be a username along with a password or an access token received via a login flow using a mechanism such as OAuth2. In either case, the security enforcer, which is the component that acts as the gateway to the services, needs to validate that this credential is valid and this user is someone who is in the system with required permissions to access the service. Once that is validated, the user can access the service or API.

This authentication is a complicated process, and depending on the application in use, the users may need to provide a username-password pair or an additional information such as an OTP (one-time password) that is received into your phone. This sort of additional security measures is required for sensitive data exchanges such as medical data or financial data. Such an authentication mechanism is called two-factor authentication (2FA) or multifactor authentication (MFA). There are additional capabilities such as login with social media accounts such as Facebook, Google, or GitHub; in such cases, users do not need to create new username and password in the system but rather give consent to the social media site so that the particular application can access the required information about the user from that site. With all these different options, what actually happens at the end of the day is to verify the identity of the user.

Authorization

Once the user is identified as a particular user in the system, the next step is to verify the "permissions" of the user to make sure that this "authenticated user" has the authority to access the requested data. Authorization is an advanced security feature that may not be required always. But it is becoming a common requirement in enterprise applications due to the different types of users accessing sensitive business data. Like we discussed in a previous section where an HR team is the only team who can view the salary details of employees, there can be many situations where we need to control access to certain sensitive information to only a selected set of users.

There are two main types of access control mechanisms used to implement authorization in enterprise software:

- Role-Based Access Control (RBAC)

- Attribute-Based Access Control (ABAC)

RBAC uses user groups called roles to implement access control policies. With this option, a particular user group or multiple groups are linked to a particular service or API/resource so that only the users within that group can access it. This is very common in the enterprise software systems and easier to implement when compared with ABAC.

In the ABAC model, user attributes are used to implement access controls, and specific policies are written to implement this capability using specific models such as XACML or Rego. This is a bit complicated model but provides fine-grained access control for applications.

Monitoring Software

Once the enterprise data, applications, and services are integrated and exposed with security, the next step is to monitor them to get insights into what is happening and provide feedback to business operations so that enterprise can continuously improve. With the complexity of modern enterprise software systems, monitoring has become ever so important. There are two different aspects of systems monitoring:

- Monitoring for insights

- Observability

Let's take a closer look at each of these aspects.

Monitoring for Insights

This type of monitoring is used to collect different types of statistical information related to the enterprise software system. It can be related to things such as

- Infrastructure monitoring (CPU, memory, disk usage)

- Application performance monitoring (latency, transaction rates)

- Business insights (usage per month, popular services, usage patterns)

This type of monitoring is important to keep the system stable and make the necessary changes according to the business requirements and usage patterns of the consumers.

Observability

The other important side of the monitoring is the observability, which is an attribute of the system that provides the ability to recreate a certain scenario with the help of the external outputs of the system such as logs and traces. This is helpful in troubleshooting issues when things go wrong. Having a proper observability implemented on the system is critical to maintain the system with minimum outage when things start to fail. Given that complex enterprise systems are distributed in nature and use unreliable networks to communicate data, failure is inevitable in these systems. Observability tools help the system to keep track of the various states of the application by the means of logs and traces so that a failure scenario can be identified quickly and resolutions can be provided without further delay.

Infrastructure Management Software

All the software components that we described so far run on top of computing infrastructure. Most of the enterprise software systems used to run on physical computing infrastructure managed by the enterprises themselves within their own data centers. This provided them with the control of their resources and the physical security and availability. But managing such data centers comes at a cost. Hence, some of these enterprises have started moving into cloud computing infrastructure, which is offered by cloud vendors such as Amazon, Google, Microsoft, and IBM. In either of these scenarios, these computing infrastructures were managed by some software components running on top of the hardware. There are different types of infrastructure management software used in enterprise software systems.

- Virtualization software

- Containerization software

- Container orchestration software

- Application management software

Virtualization software is pretty common in enterprise software systems and used to create virtual machines on top of the physical computing infrastructure so that multiple users can access the underlying infrastructure as per the requirements of applications. As an example, a same physical computer can run multiple virtual machines so that different users can use them for development or run different applications without interfering with one another.

With the popularity of container-based applications, containerization software becomes prominent, and Docker has become the most popular containerization software. This allowed users running separate applications similar to virtual machines without the overhead of an additional guest operating system.

Once the containers started getting traction, there came the need for managing container deployments across multiple computers so that failure of one computer does not cause the application to be unavailable. That is where the container orchestration software such as Kubernetes became popular. These systems allow running applications with minimum failures by monitoring the state of the containers and restarting them and distributing them in an optimal manner.

Even though the aforementioned infrastructure management software provides a lot of flexibility to enterprise application developers, it comes with the need for learning those technologies. Due to this, certain cloud providers have built some software components called application management software so that the users do not need to worry about any of the underlying infrastructure management such as VMs, containers, or Kubernetes and just focus on application development. These software components are easy to use but come with their own restrictions.

Now we have a better understanding of an enterprise software system architecture and the fundamentals of the microservice architecture (MSA). In the next section, let us discuss how to build a reference architecture for enterprise software system with MSA.

A Reference Architecture with MSA

Microservice architecture suggests having independently manageable, small services to build a software application. This approach is suitable for organizations that have fresh requirements and start from scratch. These sorts of organizations are called green-field enterprises. A startup organization or a small to medium size enterprise may have similar environments at the beginning of their journey. Implementing microservice architecture is much easier for such green-field enterprises.

With time, even these green-field organizations have to purchase some third-party software applications and solutions to cater to their various business needs as part of their growth. On the other hand, most of the existing enterprises that have established IT systems already have different types of components in their enterprise software system. We discussed about such an architecture in the previous section. This kind of enterprises is called brown-field enterprises. If we go with the 80/20 rule, 80% of the time we find enterprises with similar environments. The challenge we have at our hands is to design a microservice architecture–based platform for a brown-field enterprise. We will be discussing a possible approach for doing that in this section.

The first thing in solving any problem is understanding the problem and identifying the areas of improvements. Let's go ahead and identify which components can be moved into a microservice architecture from our enterprise software architecture diagram.

Figure 3-2 depicts the software components that we can move to a microservice architecture with a hexagon symbol. As per the figure, the following components can be designed according to an MSA.

- In-house applications

- Integration software

- API software

- Security software

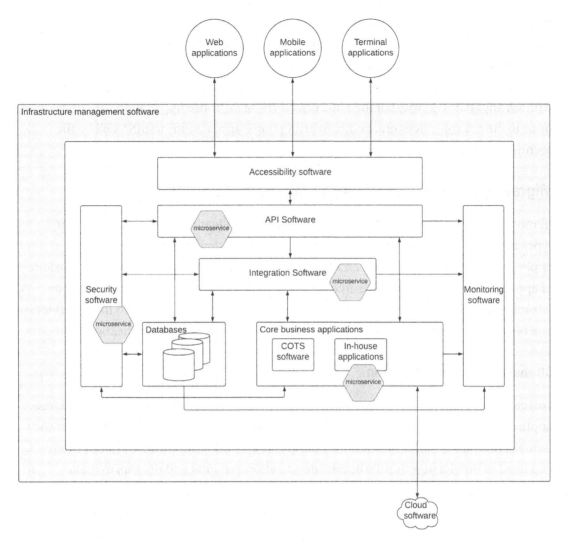

Figure 3-2. *Microservice architecture–compatible components of an enterprise software system*

Let's take a look at how these components can be deployed in a microservice architecture.

In-House Applications

Let's start with the software component that is developed and designed in-house within enterprise platforms. These applications are architected by the internal development teams, and they have the luxury of selecting the best possible technology and architecture when building these applications. Given the benefits provided by the microservice architecture, most teams start adopting MSA at this layer. If you are implementing a new application from scratch, you can follow the standard practices around MSA and deploy these applications in a microservice-friendly infrastructure without any issues. In most of the enterprises, these in-house applications are developed prior to the microservices era, and converting these applications to MSA will be the second phase of the MSA adoption.

Migrating Existing Applications to Microservice Architecture

In most of the enterprises, there are in-house built applications to execute different types of functions, and most of these applications have developed as monolithic applications or service-oriented architecture–based applications. Converting these kinds of applications to a microservice architecture can be done with technologies such as "strangler pattern" where the application's functionality is converted into microservices in a phased approach without impacting the clients or users of the application.

Strangler Pattern for Migration

You can start with one particular application or a specific function or domain of a larger application and convert that to a set of microservices based on an approach similar to domain-driven design. Let us take an example of a healthcare software system where you need to build a new mobile application to allow patients and doctors to make doctor's appointments. You can start this project as a new initiative and evaluate the best possible architecture to implement this application. If you decide that microservices-based approach is the way to go, then you have to review the existing in-house applications and services to decide on which functionality needs to be converted to the microservice architecture first. If you don't have an API gateway in front of your existing services, you can introduce an API gateway and hide the implementation details from the clients as the first step. Then you can start converting the functionality step by step into the microservice architecture. Since there is an API gateway that hides the internal details, the different types of clients such as web applications and the newly built mobile applications will not experience any difference during the migration from existing monolithic applications to microservices. Once the migration is completed, you can either remove the API gateway or keep it as it is since it will help in future changes as well.

Figure 3-3 depicts this approach.

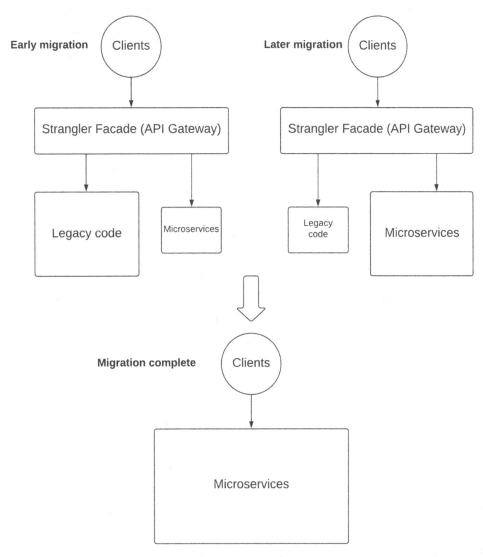

Figure 3-3. *Migrating to microservice architecture with strangler pattern*

As depicted in the figure, existing applications can be converted into microservice architecture in a step-by-step manner without disturbing the experience of the clients by using the API gateway. This process may take some time since you need to change the mindset of your organization to move from developing applications in a traditional waterfall type of methodology to agile methodology where you keep adding new features to the system continuously without waiting for big-bang releases. Adopting microservice architecture in an enterprise requires the support from your top-level executives in addition to the technical leads since it will create resistance within internal development teams such as center-of-excellence (CoE) teams who used to dominate the development activities. Hence, it is important to bring in the technical evolution along with the people evolution when starting a microservice architecture–based development journey.

Integration Software

The next component that we can consider moving into microservice architecture is the integration software. In some cases, this component is also developed by the internal development teams using some open source technologies such as Apache Camel, Spring Integration, or Apache Synapse. If you are following a similar approach, you can easily migrate your integration software into microservice architecture based on the same domain-driven design sort of an approach given that the open source tools you use support such an architecture. As of the writing of this book, both Apache Camel and Spring Integration support container-based deployments and hence can be used to build integration software component with a microservice architecture.

One difference between building in-house business applications and integration software with microservice architecture is that integration software layer works with different microservices and other services at a given time. Specially in cases where you need to orchestrate multiple services and systems to produce results for consumer applications, integration services have to interact with different microservices domains. Hence, defining domains or scopes for integration services may not be as straightforward as core business applications in most cases. But still it is a doable thing, and high-level segregation of duties or functions can be done to make the integration runtime to carry one or a few integrations at once.

If you are an organization utilizing an external vendor for integration software, you need to check the feasibility of those runtimes to run in a microservice architecture. Similar to the open source technologies, most of these vendors are also supporting container-based deployments as of this writing. Hence, you can follow a similar approach with vendor-based integration software as well. Figure 3-4 depicts how these different integration services can be deployed as separate integration runtimes to adopt a microservice architecture with coarse-grained domains at the integration layer.

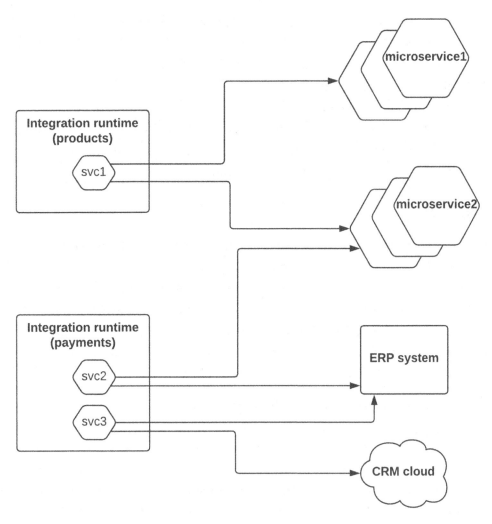

Figure 3-4. *Creating integration microservices*

The figure depicts two integration runtimes with different characteristics. The first one contains a single integration microservice (svc1), which integrates with two different microservices. These two microservices may contain a particular high-level domain such as product information where each microservice may contain details of a single product. This integration runtime instance can be run in a container or a similar deployment mode so that it is independently manageable.

The second integration runtime instance contains two integration microservices (svc2 and svc3), and these are integrated with the ERP and CRM software for payments and order related operations. Given that it is a separate high-level business domain, we can consider it as another domain for integration microservices. This integration runtime can also be run in a container or a similar deployment model so that it is managed independently from the first integration runtime. Similarly, you can convert your entire integration software layer into a microservice architecture.

In addition to the standard integration runtimes, message brokers are also becoming an essential component of the integration layer in recent years. Most of the time, these message brokers run as monolithic applications in high-performing computing infrastructure and act as the messaging hub for asynchronous communications. Hence, it is advisable to keep the message broker as a centralized component.

API software

The next component that is possible to migrate to microservice architecture is the API software. Before we discuss about migrating your existing API software into a microservice architecture, let us discuss the typical architecture of an API software product. There are many types of open source and commercial software available for API management, and different tools have different features and functionalities. But in general, most of the tools have a common architecture when it comes to the main components of the tool. Those main components contain

- API gateway or microgateway (data plane)
- API manager (control plane)
- API developer portal

Let us take a closer look at each of these components so that we can identify which components can be migrated into microservice architecture. Figure 3-5 depicts how these components work together in a typical API manager deployment.

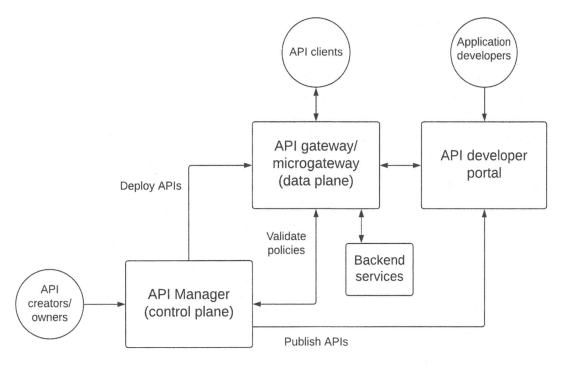

Figure 3-5. *API management components*

The figure depicts how the main components of a typical API management software interact with one another in a deployment. Let us discuss each of these components and their functionality in detail.

API Gateway or Microgateway (Data Plane)

This component is the main runtime unit of API software that receives all the requests (traffic) from consumer applications. It verifies the security and various other policies with the help of the control plane before allowing the request to pass through it and connect to the backend services components that contain the business data. It also connects with the control plane to receive the latest APIs that need to be deployed into the runtime. Some API management vendors provide support for container-based deployments with a separate gateway component called "microgateway," which is optimized for such deployments. But some vendors provide a single gateway runtime for both standard VM-based deployments and container-based deployments.

API Manager (Control Plane)

API management goes beyond just creating proxy APIs wrapping business services with security, rate limiting, and monitoring. That is where the control plane component is becoming a commodity in the API management software world. This component is responsible for configuring the API data plane with the required APIs using API definitions such as schemas and applying security, rate-limiting, and mediation policies and enabling analytics data publishing. Once everything is configured at the control plane, API is deployed into the data plane by a person who has the authority to do so (e.g., API product owner). In addition to that, API will also be deployed into a developer portal so that the application developers can discover the API and create innovative applications to expand the business beyond the traditional consumers. Hence, this component provides API life cycle management (LCM) in addition to acting as the configuration component of the API data plane.

API Developer Portal

Most of the API programs start with the basic need of exposing business services wrapped as APIs for security, control, and monitoring along with standardization. For such requirements, you can live with the data plane and the control plane explained in the preceding sections. But when you have more and more APIs and more and more consumers, you need a place where you can publish information about APIs and how to use those APIs. That is the primary functionality of a developer portal. It allows people who want to use these APIs to discover APIs and try them out and understand them before designing their client applications. Regardless of whether you are developing APIs for internal usage or external usage, having a developer portal makes life easier for API owners as well as API consumers since that will reduce a significant amount of manual integrations between these two parties. Some vendors offer this as a standard feature, while other vendors offer this as a plug-in or an optional feature.

Now we have a good understanding of the API software that we typically use in an enterprise software system. Let us discuss how we can migrate such a component to microservice architecture. As we discussed so far, APIs are wrappers of actual business services. These services can be core business services or integration services. One important aspect of APIs is that those are designed with the intention of interfacing directly with client applications. Hence, we need to consider that when coming up with a domain-driven design for API segmentation for microservice architecture. What this means is that our segregation of API runtimes into separate components needs to consider more on the consumer usage in contrast to the business objectives that we typically use for backend business services segregation. Figure 3-6 depicts how we can do this with an API management software that we discussed in the preceding section.

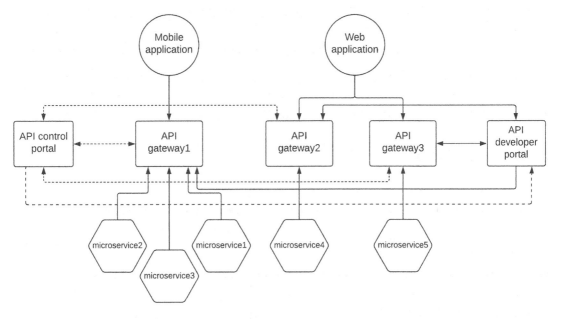

Figure 3-6. *Migrating API management software to microservice architecture*

The figure depicts how your APIs can be moved into a microservice architecture according to the needs of the consumer applications. It depicts that the API gateway is the component that needs to be deployed as separate components and scale based on the number of APIs that needs to be deployed in the system while the control plane and the developer portal components can remain the same. In some cases, control plane components also need to be scaled when there are a large number of API gateways deployed. But it is not a 1:1 ratio rather a much higher ratio such as 10:1 where one control plane component is required to support ten gateways.

The most important aspect is how you partition your APIs into independently deployable API gateways or microgateways based on the need. In Figure 3-6, there is a dedicated API gateway (gateway1) that is deployed to cater the APIs required for the mobile application. It is just an indication that you can have a single gateway per client type when you have a lot of different clients. As an example, if you are a video streaming service such as Netflix and your client devices ranged across a larger set of different screen sizes and resolutions, you may have to expose APIs per particular screen size and resolution range so that each device gets the best video quality. That needs to be backed by separate microservices in the backend side as well.

The other two gateways are deployed as dedicated gateways per each microservice. This provides the maximum-level isolation when it comes to managing the gateways along with the APIs. It is a good approach if you are implementing an API gateway in a sidecar pattern where each microservice runs with its own gateway in the same container or VM to reduce the latency between calls from/to gateway and microservice. It is up to you to decide how many gateways are required and how you partition the APIs across these gateways. You can use accessibility software such as proxy servers and load balancers to hide the details of the gateway deployment model.

Security Software

Security software is instrumental in enterprise software systems since it provides the required access control to different components within the platform. Sometimes, different software components use different mechanisms to implement security. As an example, core business applications may use their own security implementation with their own user store and authentication mechanism, while API software and integration software utilize a third-party security software vendor with standard authentication mechanisms such as SAML2 or OIDC-based protocols. Consolidating multiple applications to use the same security software is a challenging task due to the nonstandard implementation used by some applications. But this is becoming better as of the writing of this book where most of the modern applications have started supporting standards-based authentication mechanisms. In case there are nonstandard applications, the security software needs to be extended and customized to bring those applications into the common security solution.

The more popular method of implementing security software is to deploy it as a monolithic application that connects with all sorts of different software components within the enterprise software system. But there are new technologies coming with ways to implement security in a microservice architecture–friendly manner. One such example is the usage of a policy-based security agent that runs along with the microservice to provide security. This approach is depicted in Figure 3-7.

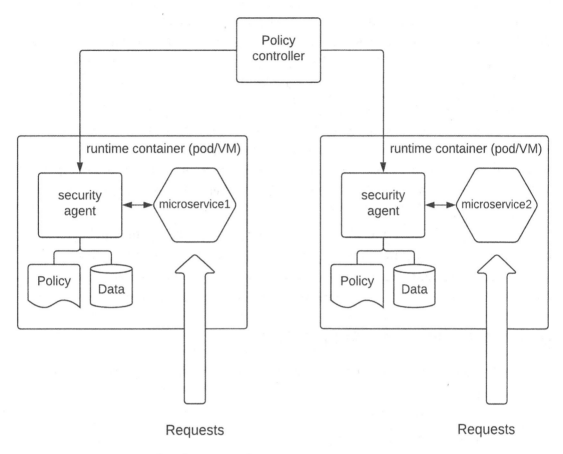

Figure 3-7. *Decentralized security for microservices*

The figure depicts how the security can be implemented in a decentralized manner with the usage of a policy-based security agent. As per the figure, each service that needs to be secured accompanies a dedicated security agent that uses a policy and a data source to determine the required access controls for that service. These policies and data sources can be configured through a policy controller per each service. This approach avoids the need to have a centralized security software for authentication and authorization purposes. But there are many additional functionalities offered by these security components that will not be provided through these kinds of decentralized models as of the writing of this book. With time, these features will also get incorporated into these tools so that the entire security capabilities can be implemented in a decentralized architecture that suits a microservices-based approach.

In addition to these main components, the infrastructure layer needs to support the decentralized deployment architecture that is required for microservice architecture.

The best possible option is to use a container-based environment if you are moving this kind of architecture. There are many organizations that are moving their enterprise architectures to cloud-based infrastructure models, and most of these vendors offer container-based deployments as managed services so that the overhead of managing containers and container orchestration technologies is offloaded from the enterprise teams. If you are considering a cloud migration along with moving to a microservice architecture, considering such a managed container service would be a better option. With such a deployment infrastructure, you can focus more on application development and business innovation rather than spending time on learning infrastructure management technologies and dealing with them.

Now we have a better understanding of how individual components can be moved into a distributed architecture, which is the basis of microservice architecture. Let us put these learnings and transform the enterprise architecture that we discussed at the beginning of this section to be compatible with microservice architecture.

Defining the Reference Architecture

Let us put together a reference architecture for an enterprise software system following a microservice architecture.

As depicted in Figure 3-8, we can design an enterprise software system adhering to the principles of MSA by implementing certain components of the brown-field enterprise as microservices while other components implemented as centralized components. It is important to have the underlying infrastructure layer that supports deploying these components as microservices. The figure depicts that the infrastructure management layer needs to have a container platform such as Docker as well as a container orchestration platform such as Kubernetes. Additionally, source code management software such as GitHub as well as continuous build and integration software such as Jenkins is also provided through the infrastructure management layer.

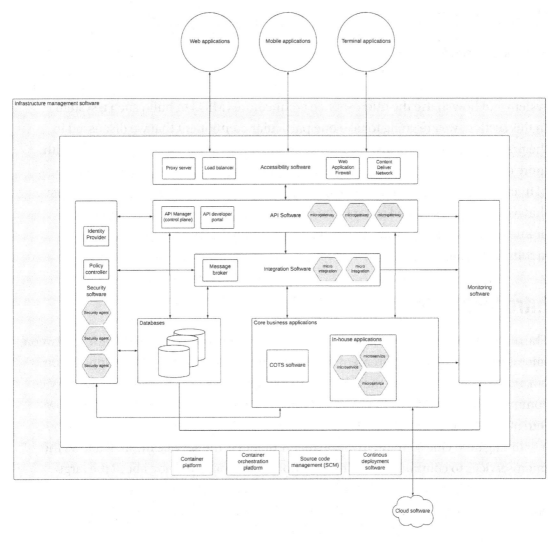

Figure 3-8. *Enterprise software system reference architecture with MSA*

The components depicted with the hexagon sign in the figure can be deployed as containers or pods depending on the technology that is available. Development of these components can follow an agile approach to reap the full benefits of the architecture.

The reference architecture discussed here can be realized with open source software as well as commercial software that is available in the market. It is up to the enterprise architecture team to decide on which software is used for each component. This architecture is designed in such a way that it is independent from any specific vendor or industry vertical. In the next few sections of this chapter, we will discuss the details of implementing microservices with certain technology patterns such as service mesh, distributed security, and microservice governance.

What Is a Service Mesh and How to Use It with MSA?

So far, we have been discussing about the architectural aspects of an enterprise software system and how to use the microservice architecture (MSA) to build such a system. In this section, we are going to take one particular component that we discussed in the previous sections and discuss how to implement that component with MSA with more details. We already discussed the designing of microservices and deployment of microservices so that they can be managed independently. One important aspect that we have not discussed so far is the communication between microservices or inter-service communication. It is one of the critical aspects of microservice architecture design.

Introduction to Service Mesh

The distributed nature of the microservice architecture makes communicating between microservices a major requirement. If you are coming from a monolithic application era, most of the in-memory function calls will happen over the network as interservice communications in MSA. On the other hand, since the number of services can grow into hundreds or even thousands, making one-to-one links between services can be a daunting task. One solution to tackle that problem is the service mesh. It allows the microservices to communicate with one another without worrying about the large network of microservices. It uses a "proxy" that runs along with the microservice to control incoming and outgoing traffic to and from the microservice. In addition to the "proxy" component, there is a control plane component that is used to configure the network of proxies and apply various policies related to routing, load balancing, and security. Figure 3-9 depicts the high-level architecture of a service mesh.

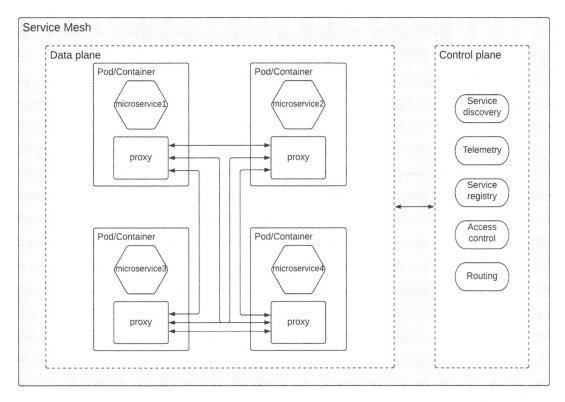

Figure 3-9. *Service mesh architecture*

As depicted in the figure, the data plane consists of the individual pods or containers that contain the microservice along with the proxy that is injected by the service mesh. These individual microservices communicate with other microservices over the proxy that is running in the same host. The control plane is connected with the data plane to configure the different routes between microservices and acts as the service registry so that microservices can be discovered dynamically. Also it provides access controls and captures telemetry data from individual pods to implement monitoring and observability.

Using Service Mesh for MSA

Let us take a closer look at how a service mesh operates in a real use case. Figure 3-10 depicts a scenario where we have two microservices running inside an enterprise network that is receiving traffic from external clients. Once the traffic is received at the first service, it will call the second service and produce the response to the client.

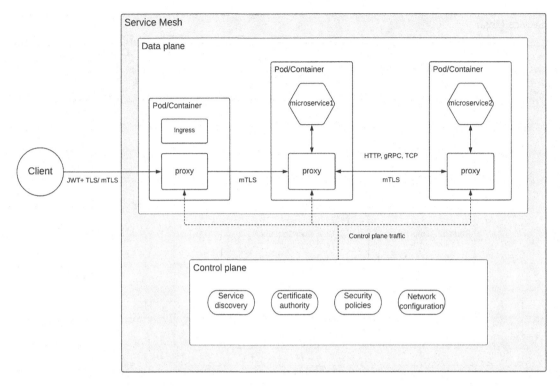

Figure 3-10. *Service mesh traffic routing*

The figure depicts a simple request flow of a message that is coming into a service mesh in a Kubernetes kind of an environment. Here, we are using Kubernetes pods as the containers for microservices and ingress controller, which is the access software in this case. The request flow is mentioned as a sequence of steps:

1. The client sends a request to access an API exposed by microservice1. This request contains a valid JWT to validate the authenticity and the authority of the client.

2. The request is received at the ingress controller, which has a proxy that is deployed as part of the service mesh, and it will validate the required security and access policies at the access layer and pass it to the next phase.

3. Microservice1 receives the request and uses mutual TLS (mTLS) to validate the authenticity and the authority of the ingress controller client and any other policies associated with the service. This validation is done at the proxy level, and the microservice does not need to worry about it.

4. Next, the request goes to the microservice, and it finds out that it needs to communicate with microservice2 to fulfill the client request. It sends a request to microservice2 via the proxy that is running inside the microservice1 pod.

5. Then the request received at the proxy of microservice2 pod and the proxy will do the security validations. Once the validations are done, the request is forwarded to microservice2 and receives the response from that. Then this response is forwarded back to microservice1 via the proxy.

6. Finally, microservice1 will receive the response via the proxy and forward it back to the client via the proxy of microservice1 and then through the ingress proxy.

While the requests are passing through the proxies, observability-related data such as logs and tracing information are captured and pushed toward the control plane. In addition to that, the control plane is used to configure security policies and networking policies in the proxy layer.

This pattern can be used to implement different software components that we discussed in the preceding sections. The most common use case is the in-house application development where core business services are developed with MSA. Additionally, service mesh pattern can also be used to implement API software as well as integration software.

Designing MSA with a Message Broker

Another approach that you can use to implement interservice communication for microservice architecture is using a message broker. This approach removes the need for having a proxy deployed along with each service, and hence, it will reduce the overall complexity of the solution. On the other hand, each microservice communicates with other services in an asynchronous manner. As an example, if microservice1 needs to send a message to microservice2, microservice1 will publish a message to a topic that is created in the message broker to continue its execution without waiting for a response. In the meantime, microservice2 will receive this message via a subscription to a topic that it has created on the message broker and process the message. If there is a response to the message, this response will be published to another topic (reply topic), and microservice1 will receive that via a subscription to that topic. This approach completely decouples the individual microservices from each other, and the message broker takes care of the different levels of message guarantees such as exactly once, at least once, or at most once depending on the use case. You can use a message broker such as Kafka, NATS, or RabbitMQ to implement this pattern. With advanced features such as durable subscriptions and persistent message storage, applications can receive messages that were distributed while those applications were offline. This kind of message processing is hard to implement with the synchronous messaging models without introducing complexity. Hence, the usage of a message broker for interservice communication can simplify the overall architecture while providing better message delivery guarantees. Figure 3-11 depicts this architecture in a typical microservice implementation.

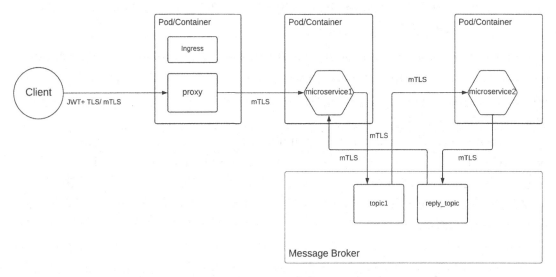

Figure 3-11. *Interservice communication in MSA with the message broker*

The figure depicts how individual microservices communicate with one another using the message broker over the topics that are predefined. In this case, topic1 is used to communicate the "request" messages, and the "reply" messages are shared using the reply topic. With this approach, microservice acts as a smart client where it needs to implement code to communicate with the message broker and handle the required communication protocol. That is the only thing it has to worry about, and there is nothing to worry about the existence of any other microservices. As long as the communication from microservice to message broker is successful, that particular message broker can consider that as a successful communication.

Different message broker solutions use different keywords to define the communication "channel" that is used to send messages between services. Some use the term "channel," and others use the term "subject" to name this message carrier. But in either case, there is a topic or a queue associated with the communication that will hold the messages and distribute among the associated subscribers. The major advantage of this pattern over service mesh is the simplicity it brings to the overall architecture. This message broker component is usually considered as an integration software component, and it is deployed in a monolithic or centralized deployment model.

Implementing Security for MSA with Policy Agents

Microservice architecture increases the risk surface of the overall application since it divides the application into multiple components and makes each component accessible over the network. Comparing this approach with a monolithic application, a monolithic application does not expose that level of functionality to access over the network, and instead it makes most of these calls in-memory. But we have to live with the complexity that microservice architecture brings, if we are to reap the benefits of the microservice architecture. There are different approaches to implement security for microservices. At a high level, there are two main approaches that we can use to implement security for microservices:

- Security for external communications (north-south traffic)

- Security for internal communications (east-west traffic)

Figure 3-12 depicts these two approaches for implementing security for microservice architecture.

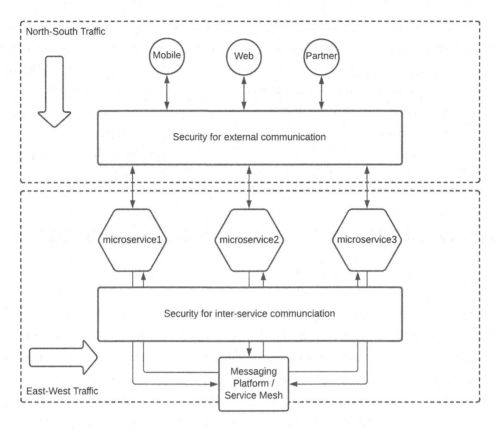

Figure 3-12. *Implementing security for microservice architecture*

As depicted in the figure, security for external communications can be implemented with a security gateway solution such as an API gateway. We need to implement strict security measures and use standards-based security approaches such as OAuth2 to implement security in this layer. Security for internal communications happens within a controlled networking infrastructure, while security for external communications happens over the Internet. We can use a microservices-friendly, distributed security solution to secure east-west traffic. We discussed in a previous section how to use API gateways to implement security for external communications. Let us discuss how we can use a policy agent–based approach to implement security for interservice communication in a microservice architecture in this section.

Microservice architecture recommends having independently manageable, self-contained components as services. These services can have their own databases, technology stacks (polyglot programming), and own security implementation. At the same time, these choices need to align with some sort of a standardization for certain aspects such as security. Policy-based security solutions allow microservices to run the security as part of the microservices container in the same host so that it does not need to depend on an external service. A common solution that provides this sort of a capability is open policy agent or OPA. Let us discuss how this distributed security concept for east-west traffic can be implemented with OPA. Figure 3-13 illustrates this idea.

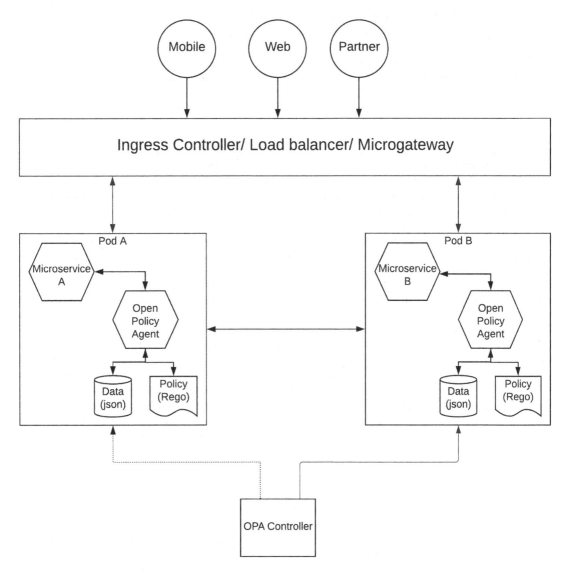

Figure 3-13. *Microservice security with open policy agent*

The figure depicts a scenario where two microservices communicate with each other using the policy agent as the security component. This policy agent uses a data store and a policy to define the security controls for the respective microservice. This agent runs in the same host along with the microservice and communicates over localhost for security validations. The figure depicts a deployment pattern based on Kubernetes where both microservice and the policy agent run on the same "pod." The policy controller is an external tool such as a command-line interface (CLI) that can be used to update the policies and data within the pods. What this means is that the microservice does not need to change its implementation to apply new security policies since that is handled in the policy agent through the controller. For north-south traffic or ingress traffic, you can use an API gateway to implement security.

Implementing Governance for MSA

The microservice style of development allows teams to operate with a lot of freedom where they can select the technology, methodology, team members, and even the timelines. It is a good approach to take the innovation out from each team member. At the same time, microservice architecture also suggests the cohesiveness of the overall solution, which is the need for teams to work together to achieve a wider organizational goal. This is where the governance comes in handy. Governance in the IT domain means an interaction of people, policy, and technology to achieve a common goal. It allows IT teams to align their technical innovations with the business goals of an enterprise.

Let us first try to identify what are the governance capabilities that are required in an enterprise that uses a microservice architecture with a polyglot programming model and an agile development approach. Figure 3-14 depicts these core governance capabilities that are required to align business needs with technology innovations.

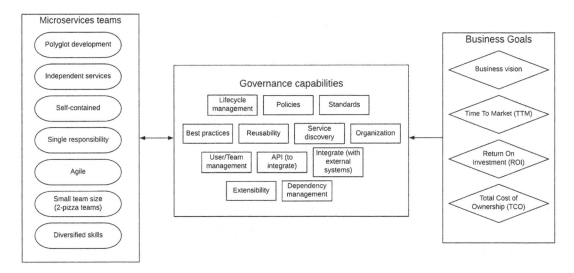

Figure 3-14. *Governance capabilities of enterprise IT systems*

As per the figure, individual microservices teams and the services they develop need to work cohesively to achieve the business goals such as business vision, time to market, return on investment, and total cost of ownership. To do that, we need to have a proper governance model within the organization with capabilities such as

- Reusability

- People management

- Standards

- Policies

- Extensibility

- Interfaces for integration

- Life cycle management

Let us take an example and understand how this governance capabilities are useful in building a microservices-based application. Let us assume that we are developing an application that has two microservices and two different teams are working on developing these microservices. For obvious reasons, let us assume that the first microservice needs to communicate with the other microservice. Then the first team should be able to reuse the functionality that is already built by the second team. Then the interaction needs to happen through a standard interface such as REST. If the entire

team has only a UX developer, then there should be someone who can manage the
allocations of that person across two microservices teams. This shows the usage of these
governance capabilities within an enterprise.

The enterprise reference architecture that we designed earlier on this chapter
contains core business microservices, API microservices, integration microservices, and
security microservices. We need to consider all these components as well as the non-
microservices-based components when implementing governance for the IT system.
We can utilize API management as a mechanism to implement governance for API
microservices, integration microservices, and core business microservices since all of
these components are connected to the API management platform. Figure 3-15 depicts
how a governance framework can be used to manage different types of microservices
within an enterprise software system.

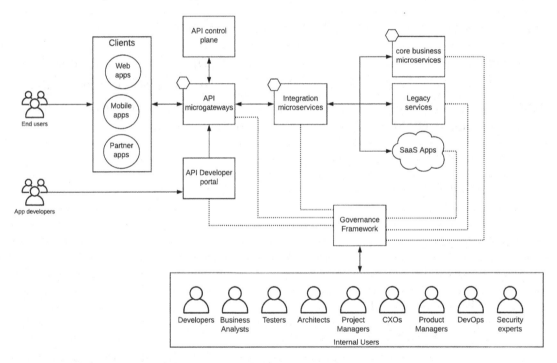

Figure 3-15. *Implementing microservice governance*

The figure depicts how to use an external governance framework along with an
API management platform to implement governance within an enterprise software
system that uses microservice architecture for software development. In this solution,
there are certain capabilities such as API reusability, API life cycle management, and
API standardization, and integration across different components is handled by the

API management and integration components. In addition to that, there is a dedicated governance framework that takes care of functionalities such as life cycle management, policy definitions, and standardizations for integration microservices and core business microservices. This governance framework connects with the API management component to provide a seamless governance experience for microservices teams who develop different types of microservices for a given use case. These teams can start with the service definitions that are defined at the governance framework and build the core microservices and then convert them to relevant integration and API microservices and track the overall progress of the application through this tool. It also can provide dependency graphs where you can identify which core microservices are related to which integration and API services. This will help you to modify your services properly without breaking the functionality of other related services. Figure 3-16 depicts how the life cycle of services can be managed at the governance framework and then moved to the API management layer in a continuous manner.

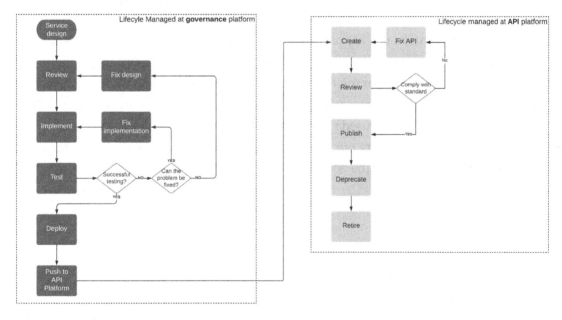

Figure 3-16. *Integrating life cycle management of microservices with APIs*

As depicted in the figure, the core microservice's life cycle is managed at the governance framework, and once it is ready to be published as an API, it will be pushed toward the API management platform where the newly created API's life cycle is managed through the API management component. When you are selecting tools for governance and API management, make sure those tools can work together and integrate with others so that you can build an integrated experience to the development and architecture teams.

That concludes the chapter on using microservice architecture–based patterns to build enterprise software systems.

Summary

We started this chapter by defining the microservice architecture and then moved into discussing software components that you commonly find in an enterprise software system. Then we discussed which components can be moved into a microservices-based model and a few methodologies to do so. Then we designed a reference architecture for an enterprise software system that utilizes microservice architecture. We discussed that most of the enterprise software systems are brown-field instead of green-field and how that impacts the design of our reference architecture. Then we discussed how a service mesh can be utilized to implement interservice communication within a microservice architecture. We also discussed an alternative approach to implement interservice communication for microservices with a message broker. We then moved to implementing security for microservice architecture and discussed in detail how a policy agent–based approach can be used to do so. Finally, we discussed about putting all things together and making sure our technical solution is compatible with the enterprise vision and goals by discussing the governance aspects of microservice architecture.

CHAPTER 4

Building Enterprise Software Systems with Hybrid Integration platforms

In today's highly competitive world of business, technology is a key differentiator that can make or break an organization. Some technology experts express this idea by saying "every company becomes a software company in the near future." It is evident that today's consumer-driven market urges enterprises to bring technology to their ecosystems to attract young generation as well as older generation due to the popularity of smartphones, tablet computers, and intuitive applications. The digital experience offered by these applications teases consumers to purchase products and services from the comfort of their homes. All these aspects converge to building enterprise software systems that are capable of serving these demands. The need for having systems to cater to different requirements becomes so important that enterprise architects tend to onboard various third-party systems into the enterprise ecosystem in quick succession. As an example, an enterprise who used to sell clothes through their brick-and-mortar showrooms has to build an online retail shopping website so that customers can easily make their purchases without physically coming into the store. This requires enterprise teams to bring in CRM software, billing software, shipping and handling software, and many other on-premise and cloud-based systems. These systems cannot work in isolation and need to integrate with one another to build a complete solution to the customers. On top of the integration, we need to expose the enterprise's products and services through multiple channels such as web applications, mobile applications, and

© Chanaka Fernando 2023
C. Fernando, *Solution Architecture Patterns for Enterprise*, https://doi.org/10.1007/978-1-4842-8948-8_4

terminal applications. That is where the need for hybrid integration platforms comes into the picture, which allows us to integrate systems and expose these integrated services via common interfaces such as APIs. Finally, all these consumer-facing applications that offer products and services need to be secured with modern Identity and Access Management (IAM) capabilities to make sure that the user gets the best possible experience.

In this chapter, we are going to discuss why hybrid integration platforms are needed for enterprise software systems and how to use these solutions to build great customer experiences. We will be discussing the following topics in this chapter:

- Introduction to enterprise integration

- Introduction to enterprise API management

- API-led connectivity pattern for enterprise

- SOA governance to API Management pattern

- Legacy platform modernization with hybrid integration platform

Let us first take a look at what enterprise integration is and how it correlates to enterprise software systems.

Introduction to Enterprise Integration (EI)

A typical enterprise software system contains different kinds of applications to cater consumer, technical, and business needs. These applications come with different vendors, different technologies, and different deployment models. It is the task of enterprise architects and developers to build an integrated platform that serves the consumer demand and achieves business goals using these disparate applications. Let us divide this broader task of integration into a subset of tasks so that we can come up with suitable solutions for each task. At a higher level, we can divide the integration requirements of an enterprise into the following tasks:

- Data integration

- Application integration

- Business integration

- Consumer integration

Let us take a somewhat detailed look at each of these integration concepts.

Data Integration

The core of any enterprise software system is the data that the system works with. This can be related to customers, products, prices, discounts, processes, and many other types of data that are required by the business. In most cases, applications operate on these different data types and models that are stored in a data source such as a database or a data lake. The storage of data is an important aspect of the entire enterprise system, and without a proper data storage and data handling mechanism, the entire system can become obsolete. Let us first identify the two main kinds of data that are generated within enterprise software systems:

- Structured data (e.g., XML, JSON, CSV)

- Unstructured (semistructured) data (e.g., emails, images, videos)

Different use cases require different mechanisms to deal with data. Some use cases require collecting data at very high rates and storing them for later processing. There can be other use cases that require processing data in real time and generating results in real time. Another use case would be to take data, process it, and produce a result in a synchronous and an asynchronous manner.

Structured Data

If we think about a use case where we need to showcase the available models of a particular product (e.g., washing machine) in a website, we need to retrieve this data from some kind of a data source and show that to the user. In this case, a given product has a specification, and all different models follow a common specification of a washing machine. We can store this information in a tabular format. This sort of standard, well-defined data points that can be stored in a tabular format is called structured data. This sort of data is typically stored in relational databases or relational database management systems (RDBMS). The advantage of structured data is it is easier to process using computer programs or applications. One disadvantage of structured data is the limitations with usage due to the strict schema that is enforced on data. This is sometimes called quantitative data since it can be quantified. Applications such as CRM, online banking, and online booking use structured data heavily.

Unstructured (Semistructured) Data

There can be other use cases where we collect data from sources that does not have a defined structure or schema. Most of this type of data is generated from human interactions instead of machine-to-machine interactions. As an example, if we are to process or store a set of emails and word documents, each and every email and the document contain a different number of characters and combinations. If we are to process this information and derive some valuable insights, we need to use advanced technologies such as machine learning and artificial intelligence due to the complex nature of data. Due to this nature, this type of data cannot be stored in a tabular format in an RDBMS system. Instead, we need to use special types of databases such as NoSQL databases like MongoDB, Hadoop, or DynamoDB. The advantage of unstructure data is the flexibility it provides to store data in native formats rather than restricting users into rigid schemas. A possible disadvantage is the need for specialized tools to process this type of data.

There is no silver bullet when it comes to data modelling, and hence, a typical enterprise may need to work with both structured and unstructured data types. The task of an integration software component is to bridge the gap between these two data types and apply the necessary transformations when moving data from one system to the other system. As an example, the unstructured data that is stored in NoSQL databases or data lakes can be consumed by ML applications, and the generated results may be stored in relational databases. In that sort of a scenario, we can use an integration software component to make data accessible from both databases through data services instead of allowing direct database access from ML applications. This use case is depicted in Figure 4-1.

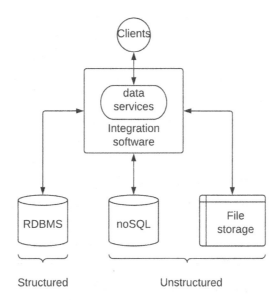

Figure 4-1. *Integrating different data sources and exposing as data services*

The figure depicts how different types of data sources can be integrated with the usage of integration software and exposes these data sources as standards-based data services. This will allow us to control access to these data sources and apply various quality-of-service (QoS) capabilities such as security, rate limiting, monitoring, and caching to manage the overall data access requirements in a fair manner by avoiding scnearios such as one malicious application blocking all the other applications from accessing data. It also hides the internal details of data sources, which would otherwise cause data leaks and various malicious activities.

Another common data integration requirement is moving data from one system (source) to another system (destination) in a periodical manner. This is referred to as either extract, transform, and load (ETL) or extract, load, and transform (ELT). Depending on which task execution order follows after extracting data, the functionality becomes ETL or ELT. Figure 4-2 depicts how an integration software can help with achieving these data integration tasks.

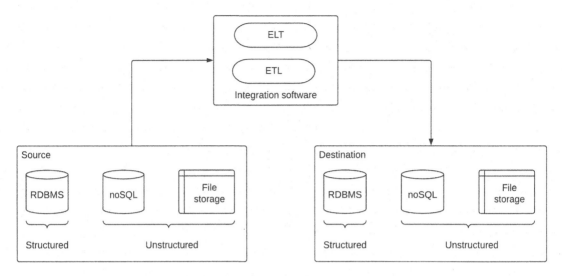

Figure 4-2. *Data integration with ETL and ELT tasks*

As per the figure, the source system can be structured or unstructured data store. The integration software component extracts (reads) this data and either does transform and load into the destination system or does load and transform into the destination system using the functionalities available in the integration component and the requirements of the connecting systems. Usually, these ETL jobs run from a dynamic data storage (source), which updates data very frequently, into a static (destination) data storage, which is rarely updated. These tasks were used to execute during off-peak hours such as midnight or late in the night when there are not much changes happening on the source system side.

A more modern flavor of ETL and ELT is called the "streaming" ETL or ELT where the data moves from source to destination in a near real-time manner using a technology called streaming integration. This approach is suitable in case if you need to reflect the changes on the source system more frequently than on the destination system. In this scenario, whenever there is a change happening on the source side, it will generate an event that will be triggered in the integration component, and it will move the changed data into the destination system in near real time. Capturing such changes on a database is called change data capture (CDC), and modern integration tools offer this functionality for streaming ETL and ELT tasks.

Application Integration

Another key aspect of enterprise integration is the application integration. Enterprise applications come in various forms. We can categorize these applications into three main types:

1. On-premise applications

2. Cloud applications

3. Hybrid applications

Let us discuss these application types in detail.

On-Premise Applications

Enterprises require specific applications to perform specific tasks. These applications can be available in different flavors depending on the vendor you select and the requirements you have. As an example, certain high-performing applications might be only available as on-premise installers since those applications require special computing resources and networking infrastructure as well as security constraints due to the type of data that application operates on. There can be other cases where you have the option of choosing an on-premise version or cloud version that is available through the selected vendor. In such a scenario also, you can select an on-premise version of the application due to reasons such as flexibility, the ability to keep it under your control, and performance. Additionally, there can be many scenarios that you develop in-house applications and deploy those in on-premise infrastructure, which is already available within your IT ecosystem. These are some of the reasons that you would go with on-premise applications instead of the other two variants mentioned here. These on-premise applications require a dedicated resource to manage and maintain the infrastructure, which can be a challenge if you do not have enough IT resources. But it is a trade-off that you have to deal with when using on-premise applications.

Cloud Applications

Cloud applications solve the challenge of infrastructure management by providing a managed service for users. Fully managed applications are called software-as-a-service or SaaS applications, which offer the application as an easily consumable service. Users do not need to worry about the infrastructure, scalability, and availability of the

115

application since these are offered with well-defined SLAs by the cloud vendor. Some examples of SaaS applications are Salesforce, GitHub, Gmail, and People HR.

Another flavor of cloud applications is platform as a service or PaaS in which the vendor provides the infrastructure layer such as computing, memory, networking, and the required runtimes. The user has to configure these platforms to run their applications or workloads by configuring the infrastructure layer. In these platforms, the user needs to be aware of the scalability, availability, and aspects and design the infrastructure accordingly. These platforms provide pre-built templates and packaging models to make life easier for developers to implement automated builds and deployments so that they do not need to spend time on setting up these tools. Vendors such as Heroku, Google app engine, and AWS Fargate are examples of PaaS.

One challenge of these cloud applications is the lack of flexibility when it comes to implementing business use cases. This heavily depends on the application and the vendor you select.

Hybrid Applications

When you need to gain the benefits that are offered by cloud applications and yet there are mandatory requirements to run your applications within your on-premise data centers, you can go with hybrid applications. These applications allow the user to run certain components on the cloud while keeping the other more restrictive components in on-premise infrastructure. These applications are designed to offer the best of both cloud and on-premise worlds. Some examples are API management solutions that allow running gateways that interact with business data to run within on-premise infrastructure while running control plane components such as developer portal, security components, and API designers on cloud. In general, these applications are complex in design, but given the fact that only the part of the overall solution needs to be managed by the user, it is a viable option.

The task of the integration platform is to integrate these different types of applications and allow these applications to share data as and when required through their application-specific interfaces without needing to change it. Hence, the integration platform has the important responsibility of acting as the translator between systems that speaks in different languages as in the form of wire-level protocols, messaging formats and standards. Figure 4-3 depicts how an integration platform acts as the hub for communicating among different types of applications.

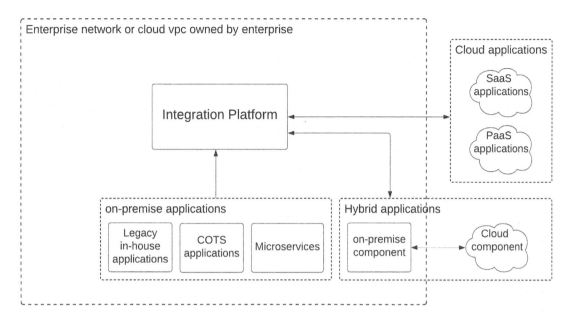

Figure 4-3. *Application integration with an integration platform*

The figure depicts an integration platform that is deployed within an enterprise network or an enterprise-owned cloud virtual private cloud (VPC). This integration platform connects with applications that are running on-premise in the same network, cloud applications that run on the Internet, and hybrid applications that run on both on-premise and cloud networks. This platform is capable of connecting to cloud applications over the Internet or virtual private network (VPN) depending on the requirements of the enterprise.

Business Integration

As an enterprise, we need to work with other enterprises in the form of dealers, distributors, suppliers, and partners. It is a common requirement that the enterprise platform integrates with the systems that are running on these external partners' IT system. As an example, assume you are an enterprise that manufactures shoes and you work closely with dealers who sell the shoes that you manufacture. These dealers need to place orders for shoes by connecting with your enterprise system. This is where the dealer's IT system integrates with your IT system. This sort of integration is called business integration or more commonly B2B integration. One major challenge with B2B integration is that the partner system resides outside of our enterprise ecosystem and it is not easy to change the behavior of the partner system as per our need. Hence, we need to be flexible and capable of integrating with the partner system without changing anything on the partner side. Partners may have some proprietary protocols, different message formats, and specific standards that we need to adhere to. Integration platform provides this interoperability between partner systems and our own enterprise systems.

Figure 4-4 is an extension of Figure 4-3 where partner-owned systems are integrated with enterprise-owned applications using the integration platform. The important point to note here is that partner-owned applications won't be as flexible as internal applications and having a good integration platform that supports B2B protocols such as AS2/3/4, HL7, and EDI is critical for business integration. Additionally, there can be situations where you need to integrate with nonstandard and proprietary protocols when doing business integration, and your integration platform should be extended with custom components to cater to these requirements.

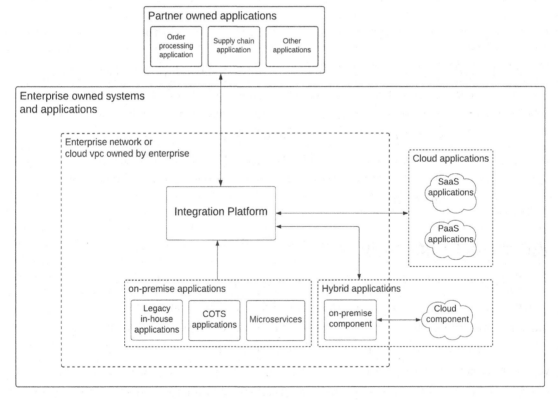

Figure 4-4. *Business integration with integration platform*

Consumer Integration

The ultimate goal of a modern enterprise software system is to offer great consumer experience since the consumer is the source of revenue for any business. It is essential to integrate consumers with the enterprise software system. The approach to integrate consumers with the enterprise software system is to offer the services through multiple channels. This is sometimes called omni-channel experience. As an example, you should be able to offer your services through web applications, mobile applications, and terminal applications such as kiosks, counters, and point-of-sale (POS) machines. This allows you to engage with a wider range of consumers based on their preference. The approach to integrate with consumers via an omni-channel experience requires a standard interface that can sit on top of the integration middleware layer and hide the internal implementation details and is easily consumable via a standard interface. API management is the functionality that offers this capability. Through an API management capability of an integration platform, we can control how we integrate with consumers. Figure 4-5 depicts the usage of API management capabilities in an integration platform to integrate consumers with the enterprise software system.

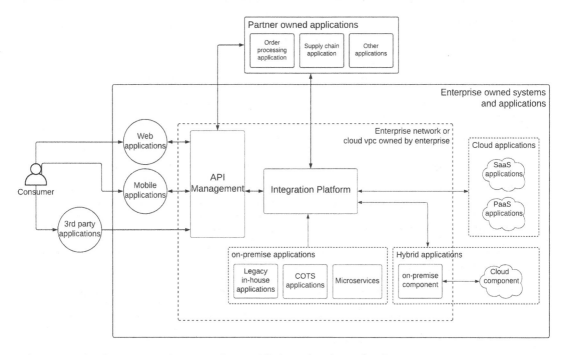

Figure 4-5. *Consumer integration with integration platform*

The figure is an extension to Figure 4-4 where an API management component is introduced to integrate consumers with the enterprise software system. In most cases, API management component is considered as part of the integration platform. This component exposes the business services as standard interfaces so that different types of client channels such as mobile, web, and third-party applications can access them.

Now we have a better understanding of the different types of integration requirements within an enterprise software system. In the preceding section, from time to time, we discussed various functional requirements demanded by these different types of integrations. The following is a list of integration functionalities required by the enterprise software system:

- Data transformation

- Protocol translation

- Application connectors

- Routing and orchestration

- File processing

- Partner engagement

- API management

Data transformation is a common requirement for almost all the types of integrations that we discussed in the preceding section. The data that is generated from one system may not be the same as the expectation of the other system. As an example, a legacy in-house application may produce a result in an XML format, while the client application, which is a mobile application, expects a JSON response in a simple format with only a few fields. This type of data transformation is pretty common in enterprise use cases.

Protocol translation is another requirement in enterprise integrations where one system communicates with a particular protocol that is not the same as the other system. In a healthcare enterprise software system, your health data may reside in an electronic health record (EHR) system that exposes data in HL7 protocol while the end client application requires that data in HTTP protocol. In such a situation, the integration platform translates the protocol from HL7 to HTTP during the communication from client to backend EHR system.

Application connectors are easy-to-use components that allow the enterprise software system to connect with different types of applications that are onboarded into the ecosystem. These applications may use standard interfaces such as REST or proprietary interfaces such as ISO 8583 and may use their own data models and formats. These application connectors hide the complexity of these differences in protocols, formats, and data models and offer a simple interface as a "connector," which you can easily use in your integration flow implementation.

Routing is another common functionality needed by the enterprise integration use cases where a certain message (data) needs to be routed to one of the multiple systems based on a condition. As an example, let us assume that a government information system stores citizen data in separate tables according to the province or state mentioned in their address. If the client application is searching for some information about a citizen given that the address is known, a routing logic will redirect the request to the relevant data service that exposes data from the database relevant to that specific province or state. Orchestration is a bit different use case where you need to connect with multiple services to get a response for a particular client request. It is also a common use case in enterprise integration.

Files are a simple mechanism to store structural data, and there are many practical use cases in enterprise software systems that require data to be stored in files. Hence, working with files is a common requirement of an integration platform. This includes use cases such as reading from files, writing to files, creating and deleting files, and moving files across systems. In more advanced use cases, you may read a file and update the information to another system such as a database or do vice versa.

Partner engagement is where B2B integration use cases come into the picture. Enterprises need to connect with software systems run by partners, and integration platforms bridge the communication gap between the system in your enterprise and the partner software system. A common use case in B2B world is electronic data interchange or EDI-based integrations. There are different formats of EDI such as AS2, AS3, AS4, EDIFACT, X12, and HL7 that need to be supported by the enterprise software system. The integration platform helps the enterprise software system to interface with these message formats.

API management is a topic of its own, and we will be discussing it in detail in the next section of this chapter. But at a high level, it allows enterprise software systems to expose business data through standard interfaces so that different clients can consume the services without worrying about internal details.

Introduction to API Management

Consumer integration or allowing consumers to get access to products and services through digital means is critical in today's business landscape. We talked a bit about the need for API management in the preceding section. Let us discuss that in detail in this section. In the world of enterprise software, it is important to understand the fact that any new technology you introduce to the platform comes at a cost. It will be the cost of the software, infrastructure, and human resources for development and maintenance. Because of this, executives who make decisions on technology have to consider the long-term and short-term benefits of the technology before making investment decisions. Let us try to understand the value of API management in the context of enterprise or business so that we can be confident in front of those decision makers when talking about it. Some common questions that business leaders may ask include the following:

- What will this project bring to the company?

- How will this project make us gain more business?

- What are the initial cost and recurring cost? (OpEx vs. CapEx)

- How long will it take to reap the benefits of the program and return the investment?

- How the business is going to be profitable with this?

As technical leaders or developers who design enterprise software systems, we should know the answers to these questions so that we can convince business owners to approve the technology choices that we make. The best way to find answers to these questions is to define some key performance indicators (KPIs) for the technology so that everyone can measure the success of the decision and come up with answers to the aforementioned questions. These KPIs need to be quantifiable and make sense in the context of the organization. As an example, these KPIs need to align with the business goals of the enterprise. Let us assume that there is a hypothetical organization named "ZZZ company" that is planning to introduce API management to their existing enterprise platform. This company is a financial services organization that offers financial services for a healthcare domain. Their business is trying to capture a niche market instead of covering a broad range of customers. The business leadership team has defined their business goals as follows:

- Revenue growth

- Cost reduction

- Data security

- Business expansion

- Citizen engagement

It is important to support these business goals with the technology choices that you make within the enterprise platform. We can use these as goals when setting the KPIs for APIs. The following is a list of KPIs that you can define to cater the ZZZ company's vision.

- Total sales executed through APIs

- New customer sign-ups via API channel

- Cost reduction through automation via APIs

- Average time to build a new functionality

- Count of API-related security incidents

- Number of partners integrated through APIs

- New revenue generated through APIs

This list covers the main business goals that are identified by the leaders of the ZZZ company. By measuring these KPIs, anyone in the organization can measure the benefits of the API platform that is utilized. Most of these numbers would be mere estimates at the beginning. But with time, these numbers will become more sensible and valuable for the enterprise to make decisions on technology direction.

The next phase of the project is to identify the key technical requirements of the API platform based on the identified KPIs. The following is a list of capabilities that need to be available in the API platform:

- API gateway

- API developer portal

- API security

- API monetization

- API governance

- Business insights

API gateway is the gatekeeper that receives all the requests from various client applications and applies required policy controls. These policies can be related to security, throttling, mediation, and monitoring. The traffic gets filtered through the gateway and forwarded to the backend services that offer data from the core components or integration components. API gateways should be capable of handling large volumes of traffic and need to be scaled horizontally accordingly. Performance is another key aspect of a gateway where it should be able to do the policy validation without adding unnecessary latency to the response time.

API developer portal is the marketplace for APIs where API consumers can find the related APIs from the list of available ones. It provides the ability to search APIs by using different attributes such as name, version, category, and tags. Additionally, it also allows consumers to try out the APIs, register client applications, and provide feedback on the APIs as comments or ratings.

API security is one of the most important functions of an API platform, and it will make the platform secure without compromising the user experience. Different client applications interact with APIs using their own mechanisms. Hence, security component needs to be flexible enough to support such clients without compromising the security. As an example, there can be clients who use OAuth2-based security with different grant types such as client credentials, password, and authorization code. It is important to have these capabilities in the API platform.

API monetization is critical when you are planning to sell your data through APIs. If your financial services company offers financial insights, predictions, and other analytical data that are not available through competitors and add value to the consumers, you can sell access to these APIs via monetization features. A common approach to implement monetization is to use a tier-based subscription model where a user can select the consumption rate and the way forward when limits are reached.

API governance is useful to build a sustainable API platform with best practices and standardization. It allows managing API development, deployment, and maintenance activities with proper controls and auditing capabilities. Sometimes, different teams in the enterprise require managing their own set of APIs without interfering with other teams. In such a scenario also, API governance helps isolate APIs across teams.

APIs provide a way to monitor the business trends using business insights. Information such as popular APIs, latency, usage, and consumers allows business leaders to identify areas where they can invest more based on the demand. It also can be used for real-time notification sending by identifying certain anomalies such as fraudulent token usage, unexpected latencies, and backend failures.

Figure 4-6 depicts the main components of an API platform and how those components interact with one another. It also depicts how different user profiles interact with the platform using different components. API gateway receives the requests that are coming from end users of the platform such as customers. It will enforce the security, rate limiting, monetization, and monitoring with the use of other components. API developer portal is consumed by the application developers who build different types of applications such as web, mobile, or terminal applications. They can be internal or external developers. API governance component is used by the API creators and API owners who build these APIs and manage them. It allows these API owners to manage the life cycle and configuration of the APIs based on the business requirements. Business insights are useful for analyzing different usage patterns and performance of the APIs and subsequently take decisions on the overall platform direction and investments. API security component provides security keys, tokens, and required security credentials to the users and validates them during the API consumption. Depending on the token type, API gateway will contact the API security component to validate the tokens before allowing the requests to go through the gateway toward the back end. API monetization is one of the many optional components available in the API platform. It allows the API platform owners to monetize the APIs directly by selling API subscriptions to the users such as third-party organizations who utilize these APIs to grow their businesses. A typical example is Google Maps API where Google provides a paid subscription for business applications to consume advanced maps APIs.

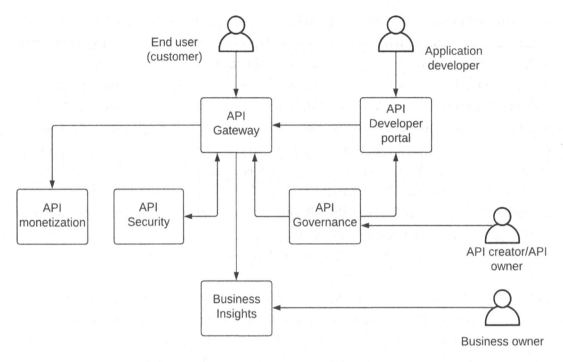

Figure 4-6. *API platform components*

Now we have a proper understanding of enterprise integration and API management in the context of enterprise software systems. Let's try to use these concepts to build real-world enterprise software systems with a few well-known architecture patterns in the following sections.

API-Led Connectivity Pattern for Enterprise

Enterprise software systems require heterogeneous components to fulfill the needs of the customers as well as business leaders. The ability to innovate is a critical factor that decides how an enterprise can compete in a highly competitive business environment. Innovating within a highly complex enterprise ecosystem requires a well-organized architecture to define the boundaries of each component. The API-led connectivity architecture is one such approach that we can use to build an enterprise software system that can innovate faster.

Let us first identify different types of applications that are developed in an enterprise software system:

- Consumer-facing applications – These are the applications that are used by customers to access the services offered by the enterprise. Omni-channel experience is a key aspect of digital consumers. That includes web applications, mobile applications, and various terminal applications running on kiosks.

- Experience-creating applications – Consumer-facing applications require a separate set of applications or services to retrieve data in a secured and dynamic manner. That is the task of experience-making applications to connect with other systems and applications and produce the results in a consumable manner to the consumer applications.

- Business processing applications – Experience-creating applications require to execute certain logical operations to aggregate, transform, and translate data that are retrieved from core business applications. That is the task of business processing applications.

- System applications – There needs to be a set of applications that directly connect with databases and various legacy data sources and expose the business critical data in a highly performant manner. That is the task of system applications.

- System-of-records applications – These are the core data sources that store and retrieve business information. These include databases, file systems, SaaS applications, and mainframe systems.

In a more traditional enterprise ecosystem, there are well-defined IT teams to manage these different types of applications. But in a more modern IT environment, there won't be separate teams based on the application type. Instead, teams can be formed based on the tasks to be performed and based on the style of development (e.g., agile, waterfall). According to the aforementioned definition of application types, we can formulate a layered architecture for an enterprise software system as depicted in Figure 4-7.

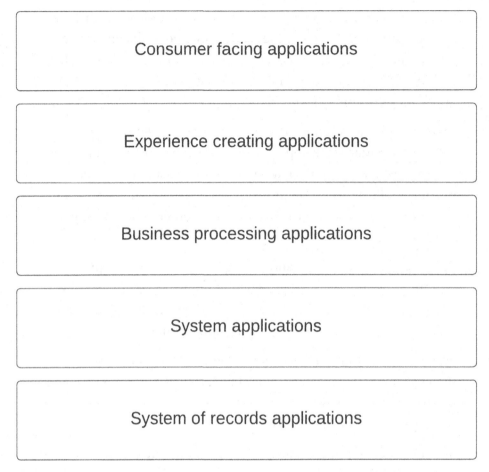

Figure 4-7. Layered architecture for enterprise software applications

As depicted in the figure, we can stack these different applications in a layered architecture so that one application is connected to the other application. This is similar to the OSI model that we discuss in computer networking where each layer is connected to the upper layer through a defined interface. The real challenge of an enterprise software system is the interoperability of these different types of applications. That is where the standards have evolved and the complex nature of enterprise software systems has made even standards-based interoperability a challenge due to the number of different standards available based on the industry. As an example, if you are building an enterprise system for healthcare, you need to work with standards such as HL7, FHIR, EDIFACT, and X12. If the system is developed for financial domain, you need to work with standards such as FIX and ISO 8583. Likewise, there are many different standards and protocols that we need to understand if we are building an enterprise software system. This layered architecture allows us to use the required software components to hide the complexity of these industry-specific standards and allows applications to work with more standard protocols such as HTTP for sharing data.

Let us improve the layered architecture to deal with the complex protocols and standards while allowing teams to do innovation without friction. We can use an API-led approach to convert this architecture into a more manageable and standard architecture that can be utilized across different industries. The first step in designing such an architecture is to identify the ownership of different applications and the control we have over them so that any change that we introduce to the architecture is feasible. If we start from the top, consumer-facing applications are in most cases controlled and owned by the enterprise. These applications can be designed according to the requirements and architecture defined by the enterprise teams. Experience-creating applications include higher-level APIs that are defined based on the needs of consumer applications, and these are also controlled and owned by the enterprise teams. Business processing applications do the heavylifting of complex integrations and transformations that are required for the experience and consumer applications. This layer can utilize third-party software products such as integration platforms and message brokers. Still, the control and ownership are within the enterprise teams. System applications are in-house built components that extract data from core systems according to the specific needs of a particular organization. These are also controlled and owned by the enterprise teams. System-of-records applications are the ones that store the critical business data in their own formats based on the needs of the application domain. Examples are databases, COTS systems, mainframe systems, legacy applications, and SaaS applications. These systems are controlled by system-specific development teams, and enterprise development teams need to interact with them using the available interfaces, which can be proprietary and industry specific in some cases. What this means is that there are certain components that we can control and define while there are other components that we cannot control and define the interoperability. We can improve the layered architecture by introducing APIs for enterprise-controlled components while working with proprietary protocols for third-party components as depicted in Figure 4-8.

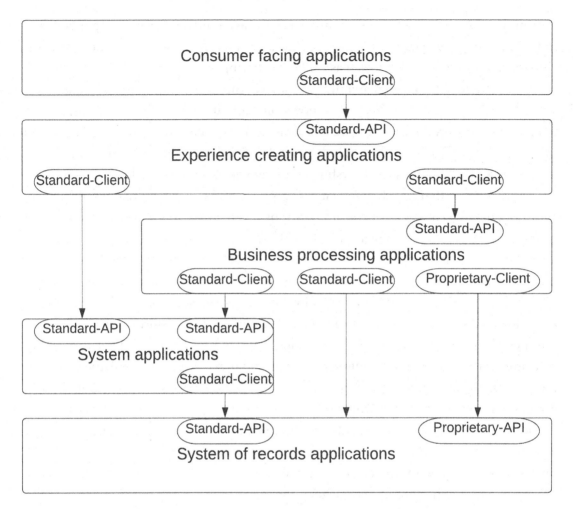

Figure 4-8. *Layered architecture with API-led interoperability*

The figure illustrates how different application layers interact with one another using an API-based architecture. Here, we have used the term "standard" to denote the idea of a common protocol such as REST, SOAP, and GraphQL over HTTP and the term "proprietary" to denote the idea of a proprietary or an industry-specific protocol such as HL7, ISO 8583, and AS2. As per the figure, we can utilize "standard" client and API in most cases to interact between layers except for the interaction between system-of-records applications and business processing applications. We can use an application such as an ESB to create this interoperability at the business processing applications layer. Let us convert this into a real-world enterprise architecture with software components that are used in enterprise software systems.

Figure 4-9 depicts an improved version of the layered architecture where each layer is updated with sample software components. It depicts the interoperability between layers with the usage of these software components. The consumer-facing applications such as mobile, web, and terminal applications connect with the enterprise platform using an API gateway component. This component allows enterprise teams to innovate faster and create digital products and experiences using the underlying layers. The business processing layer utilizes an integration platform to connect with system applications and system-of-records applications using standard and proprietary APIs. It exposes these integrated applications over standard APIs to the API gateway. The system applications layer can be implemented as microservices or Service-Oriented Architecture (SOA) applications, and it can expose standard APIs so that the upper layer components such as experience layer and business layer can interact with it. The system-of-records applications may expose standard or proprietary interfaces to interact with the upper layers. In the case of proprietary interface, the integration platform can act as the intermediary to translate from standard interface to proprietary interface. One additional component that is included in the figure is the API developer portal, which can be used to organize all types of APIs into a common repository and expose them as managed APIs to application developers.

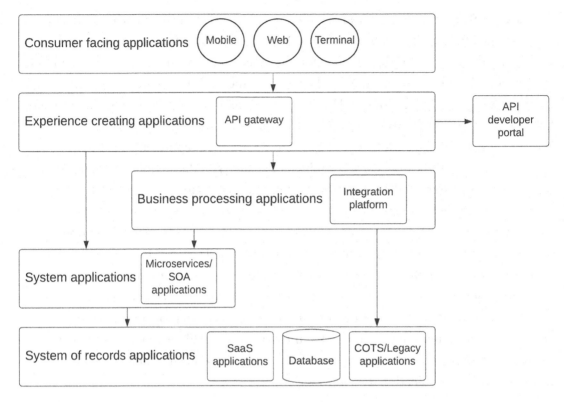

Figure 4-9. *Layered architecture with real-world software components*

This API-led architecture can be implemented with different technical approaches such as monolithic or microservices based. It is also independent of any specific enterprise domain or industry, and hence, it can be used to build enterprise platforms for many different use cases.

SOA Governance to API Management Pattern

Service-Oriented Architecture (SOA) is still a heavily used concept in the enterprise software systems. Many aspects of SOA are still utilized to design enterprise software systems. Given that most people consider microservice architecture (MSA) a successor of SOA or an approach to do SOA right, it is still a key in any enterprise. If there was anything that people struggled in the SOA world, it was governance. One reason for that is people did not consider it as a "must-have" capability in an SOA-based architecture. But with the introduction of brown-field enterprise platforms with microservices, APIs, and integrations along with cloud/on-premise software applications, governance has once again become a key requirement in enterprise software systems. In a typical brown-field enterprise software system, each system offers capabilities through a service or API. Let us consider both of these types as services for easy reference given that both provide some sort of a service to the other systems or end users. A typical service goes through a set of life cycle stages that we need to govern from the enterprise ecosystem. A sample set of life cycle stages is as follows:

- Requirement identification

- Design and review

- Implementation

- Test

- Deploy

- Consume

- Support

- Deprecate

- Retire

These different stages involve different stakeholders in the enterprise. Some examples are

- Business analysts

- Product managers

- Software architects

- Developers

- QA team

- DevOps team

- Project managers

- Support engineers

- Consumers

- Business leaders

Governance is the process that integrates these stakeholders with different life cycle stages of the service and produces better experiences to the customers. It uses various tools and techniques to make sure respective stakeholders interact with the related life cycle stages during the service life span. A governance tool makes sure that services are delivered in a timely manner with a predefined quality standard. Such a tool requires to have capabilities such as

- Policy management

- Dependency management

- Life cycle management

- Source code management (through integration)

- Deployment management (through integration)

Policy management is crucial for a governance tool since there can be different types of policies needed to develop and maintain services. Some examples are service definitions (WSDL, Swagger, OAS) and security policies and security questionaires. These policies need to be properly managed with access controls so that only the authorized stakeholders can apply and change these policies.

Dependency management is useful when changing the services since it allows you to see the impact your change is going to have on other services. As an example, if you are going to change the WSDL of a service, you should be able to see what other services are impacted with this change and take the necessary actions to update those services accordingly.

Life cycle management is a key aspect of service governance since it makes the service available to the consumers in a proper manner and makes it unavailable in a graceful manner when there is a new service available to replace the existing one. It also assures the quality and the compliance of the service by verifying these aspects at different stages by different stakeholders.

Each service will hold its source code in a source code management system that resides outside of the governance tool. But it is essential that the governance tool integrates with this SCM system and pulls and pushes the changes to the source code whenever required. As an example, whenever a change is committed to the SCM by the developers, that needs to be reflected in the governance tool so that whoever manages the life cycle stage can view these change and gets notified on the changes.

Once the service is ready to be deployed into a given runtime environment, the governance tool should be able to integrate with the required tools and deploy the service into the respective runtime environment. Figure 4-10 depicts how different stakeholders interact with the governance tool and how it integrates with the other components of the enterprise ecosystem.

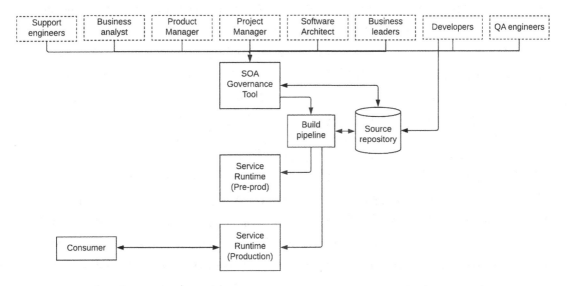

Figure 4-10. *Service governance in an enterprise software system*

The figure depicts how an SOA governance tool interacts with the infrastructure layer of an enterprise software system to provide the service governance. It also shows the different stakeholders that interact with the tool. Business analysts and product managers use the tool to capture the requirements and do the reviews on them and formulate a specific product or project that can be implemented by the developers and architects. Project managers will use the tool to keep track of the progress of the implementation and delivery and escalate any challenges during the implementation process. Developers will implement the services and commit the source code to the repository and make the necessary changes to keep the project and the life cycle moving forward. Once the implementation is done, the deployment process is kicked off, and the services are getting deployed into the relevant runtime environments with the automated build pipelines that are triggered by the governance tool. Once the services are deployed and serving the consumer traffic, support engineers provide updates on service failures, feature improvements, and feedback from the customers on the governance tool. Once the service has come to an end of life, the service will be marked deprecated and subsequently gets undeployed from the runtimes with the retirement of the service.

So far, we discussed the governance from the perspective of services, and we considered both APIs and services as a single entity. But in modern enterprise software systems, there are different types of services called APIs that really are just "proxy services" that wrap real services that implement business logic. As we discussed in a previous section, API management platforms provide the capability to govern the life cycle of these APIs within an enterprise ecosystem. Let us see how our SOA governance tool can be integrated with an API management tool in a real-world enterprise system.

As depicted in Figure 4-11, API management capabilities overlap with the SOA governance tool specifically on the life cycle management, policy management, and deployment management fronts. Hence, we can consider both the SOA governance tool and the API management control plane as common governance solutions for enterprise services and APIs. An API management control plane may provide different options for deployment such as directly deploying APIs from the control plane to the data plane (gateways) without using a source repository or build pipeline. In that case, there will be direct connections from governance solution to the API gateways without going through the build pipelines. But these API management tools provide command-line interface tools to automate the deployments through build pipelines that can be used to deploy the APIs to the gateways. Using such a mechanism will make the overall governance process easier to manage. The SOA governance tool can be used to govern system applications (e.g., microservices) and business applications (e.g., integration services), while the API management tool can be used to govern experience applications (e.g., APIs). If you can integrate these two components together, you can govern macro-level services that contain multiple services and APIs related to a particular business function or domain.

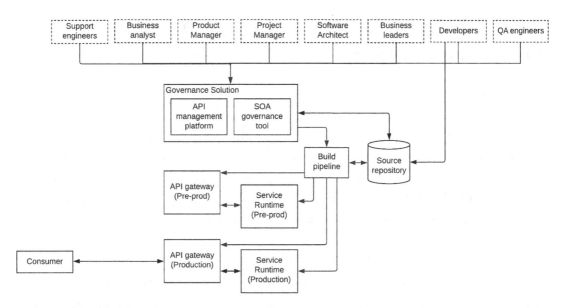

Figure 4-11. *Service and API governance in an enterprise software system*

Another key usage of a governance solution is to manage the runtime service discovery for dynamic environments. This is called the "runtime governance" of services. As an example, a service can be deployed across multiple environments. There can be references to other services from this particular service (e.g., service1). Let's say that service1 is calling an endpoint that changes its URL based on the environment. In this scenario, service1 may refer to the endpoint with an identifier rather than the actual URL. During the runtime, it will query the identifier from the governance solution and find out the correct URL for the environment. A proper governance solution is capable of handling runtime governance as well as the design time governance that we discussed earlier. This runtime governance aspect is becoming a requirement of its own, and there are tools available to just implement the runtime governance or service discovery.

One common misconception about the SOA governance and API management is that people think that API management can replace the SOA governance tools in an enterprise. It is not true since API management tools are only capable of managing or governing the API proxies that are created on top of the system and business services that need to be governed by a separate governance tool. API management solutions are not capable of managing the life cycles of these services.

Legacy Platform Modernization with Hybrid Integration Platform

Enterprise software systems have been there for decades, and introducing modern architectures and tools to such systems needs to be done carefully. Enterprise software is a unique domain where it is not possible to introduce cutting-edge technologies as we wish. These systems execute the most important business processes of an enterprise. Hence, it is not wise to change these systems unless there is a necessity. At the same time, as an architect or developer, you need to make sure that your system is up to date and reaps the benefits of technological advancements in the world of enterprise software. This is where the need for "platform modernization" arises, and people refer to this with different terms such as "digital transformation," "cloud migration," and "decentralization" to name a few. No matter which name you use, the fundamental goal of platform modernization is to improve user experience while reducing operation overhead and costs in the long run.

Before we discuss the architectural approach of platform modernization, let us first understand the challenges of a so-called legacy enterprise software system. The following is a list of challenges that you may encounter with such a system:

- Difficult to update and upgrade

- Takes a long time to develop new services

- Resource underutilization

- Lack of shared knowledge

There can be many other challenges that exist based on the specific industry or domain you are in. But the aforementioned are a common set of challenges that are more or less applicable to any legacy enterprise software system. Let us understand these challenges in a bit more detail.

This sort of legacy enterprise systems is not easy to update since they have become stable after many iterations of configurations and changes that were done based on a trial-and-error method. Hence, changing any configration can cause unexpected behaviors and results that can cause greater damage to the business operations. On the other hand, doing an upgrade is a much more complicated process where you need to get approvals from highest levels before even starting the process. In most cases, these updates and upgrades can only be done by the vendor, and sometimes, you need to pay a good fortune of money to do such an upgrade. These systems are mostly developed and deployed in a monolithic fashion so that any change can impact the entire system. Hence, it is a challenge to do updates and upgrades to such a system.

Most of these legacy systems rely on the excellence of few individuals and teams who dominate the operations of the respective components. If you are to develop new services that interact with different systems within the legacy platform, you need to align with their timelines and get approvals before even thinking about the service. This would take a long time to get the logistical aspects organized and eventually impact the timelines of service delivery.

In a centralized IT environment, provisioning computing resources is a tedious task, and hence, most of the enterprise software teams ask for more resources than necessary at the beginning of a project to make sure that they don't need to waste time on asking for resources again and again. What this does is that there can be enterprise applications running on computing resources that are highly underutilized. Since most of these legacy systems are running on physical computers or virtual machines, it is not easy to scale the resources dynamically than allocating the resources at once.

One of the major challenges of legacy enterprise software systems is the lack of shared knowledge. This may be due to the fact that vendors do all the installation, configuration, and maintenance activities. But it can cause a lot of trouble when you need to make changes or migrate from one system to another system. In most cases, there are few individuals who keep the knowledge within themselves without sharing with wider teams, and whenever that team member leaves the organization, it becomes a black box for the entire team.

So any approach that we take to modernize the platform should tackle these challenges and provide an improved version of the platform at the end. Additionally, it should also provide the benefits offered by the new technologies and architectures. Let us take a sample enterprise software system with commonly used applications and components and migrate that into a modern enterprise platform by applying architectural and technological changes to that in the following section.

A Sample Legacy Enterprise Software System

In a typical enterprise software system, there are business applications such as ERP, CRM, HRM, and other in-house applications that are integrated with an integration component such as an ESB along with databases to store business data as well as user data. Figure 4-12 depicts a sample enterprise software system.

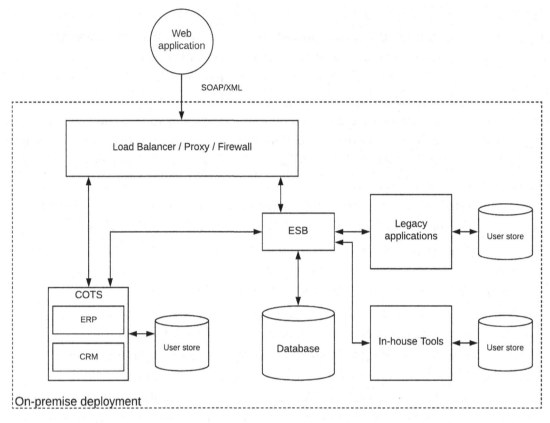

Figure 4-12. *A sample legacy enterprise software system*

The figure illustrates an enterprise software system that exposes a web-based access to enterprise data. It uses SOAP/XML-based services to interact with the internal systems. It has a set of COTS applications for business operations, a few core business applications (legacy) that have not been updated for a long time, a database, and a few in-house software tools developed by the internal IT teams connected with an ESB. This system is installed in an on-premise infrastructure and exposed through a standard LB/ Proxy and Firewall layer for security.

If we are to migrate this system to a modern architecture, we need to first identify which components need to be migrated and in which order. That decision is crucial, and it will have a larger impact on the outcome of the migration effort. There are enough examples out there in the industry where people stop such modernization efforts in the middle, which makes the systems highly unstable and unmanageable. It is not a good position to be in if you are an architect or a developer.

Using a Strangler Facade to Begin the Modernization

When you publish the idea of platform modernization, different teams will come up with their own plans and requirements to include in the project. You need to listen to their ideas and prioritize the order based on the business needs and the vision without disrupting the user experience. For the legacy enterprise system that we discussed in the preceding section, teams might come up with following ideas:

- Change the web application to use modern technologies such as REST/JSON instead of SOAP/XML.

- Convert in-house tools to more distributed microservice architecture.

- Utilize more cloud-based (SaaS) products instead of COTS applications.

- Move infrastructure from on-premise to cloud or cloud-native infrastructure.

- Consolidate users into a centralized identity management solution.

These are great ideas, and implementing all of them at once would be too much or a risk. Instead, we can start with tasks that would not disrupt the user experience largely yet provide enough benefits to move forward with modernization. Let us take the first three requirements and understand what changes can be made to accommodate them.

If we are to change the client side to work with REST/JSON instead of SOAP/XML, we need a mechanism in the server side that can cater to this requirement. But we cannot do this by changing the core business applications or the COTS applications since those are not developed by the enterprise IT team. Those are third-party vendor products that we cannot change as we wish. But we can refactor the existing in-house tools into a microservice architecture since it is within our control. But we need to do this without impacting the client-side services. Utilizing more cloud services for COTS services is a decision that needs to be made based on the features, budget, and overall ROI. It can take more time than the other two aspects. To do all these things, we need to change the existing legacy platform architecture by introducing a "strangler facade" where we put an intermediary component between the client and the old system and eventually transform the old system to a new architecture by hiding the details from the client. Figure 4-13 depicts this idea with the usage of an API gateway, which is introduced into our legacy enterprise architecture.

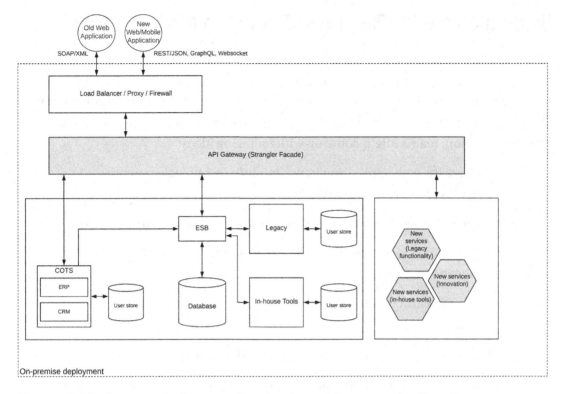

Figure 4-13. *Legacy platform modernization with a strangler facade*

As depicted in the figure, API gateway acts as the intermediary between the client and the enterprise systems. It is used to hide the changes that are happening in the enterprise system while supporting the existing clients. As an example, the existing web application can still access the backend services through the API gateway using SOAP/XML protocol without any disruptions. At the same time, there will be new services exposed through REST/JSON that will connect to the old systems as well as newly developed applications. These services can be used to build modern web applications as well as mobile applications. At the same time, this allows the refactoring of in-house tools and legacy applications wherever possible and exposes their functionality to new clients. In case that the business leaders agree to purchase SaaS products instead of on-premise COTS applications, these applications can also be onboarded to the platform without disrupting the clients since API gateway can do the transformations that are required for the clients. This is where the need for a modern integration component that can work together with API gateway arises, and if your ESB is not capable of supporting modern architecture, it is time to replace that with a suitable integration product.

Figure 4-14 depicts a scenario where a modern integration component is introduced instead of the legacy ESB, which was there in the older system.

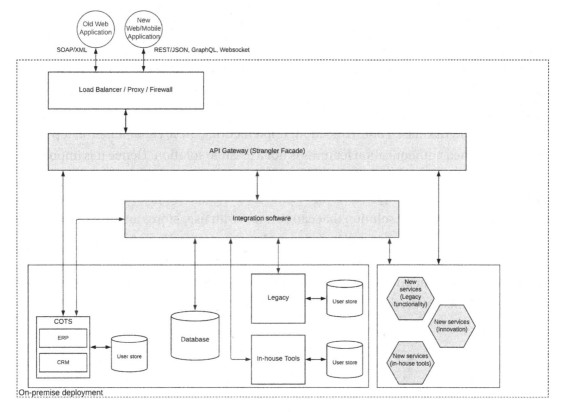

Figure 4-14. *Legacy platform modernization with API gateway and integration software*

In the figure, the older ESB is replaced with an integration software that is capable of doing the required transformations for API gateway as well as supporting the existing integration requirements with a more futuristic feature set. As an example, the integration tool should be capable of deploying in cloud-native infrastructure, and it needs to provide more friendlier development tools such as low-code and web-based environments.

Consolidating User Identities with Centralized IAM Solution

Most of the legacy systems and applications use built-in user authentication capabilities to provide application level security. This results in multiple user stores attached to the applications and the users have to create multiple accounts in those systems and keep track of their usernames and passwords. A more modern application level security provides capabilities such as single sign on (SSO), multi factor authentication (MFA), social logins and risk-based authentication. Implementing these capabilities on top of the self contained authentication features is not a feasible solution. Hence it is important to consolidate different security implementations to a standards based authentication and migrate users into a single or multiple user stores without duplication. This can be achieved using an IAM solution that can connect with user stores and migrate those users into a single user store. It also provides a centralized location to configure advanced authentication features and enable applications to provide more secure and easy to use authentication for the users. Figure 4-15 depicts how an IAM solution can integrate the different users and applications to implement modern authentication.

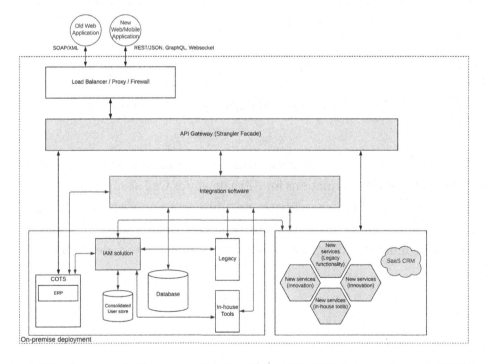

Figure 4-15. *Legacy platform modernization with API, Integration and IAM solution*

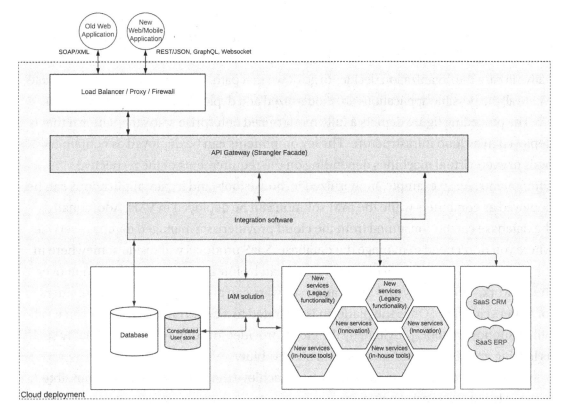

Figure 4-16. *Legacy platform modernization with cloud deployment*

The figure depicts a state of the enterprise software system that has migrated all the individual user stores into a single user store and all the applications are utilizing the IAM solution for authentication. This will make sure that implementing SSO, MFA and social logins is possible and users do not need to create multiple user accounts to access different systems. IAM solutions provide different options to migrate users from existing user stores to the consolidated user store. The preceding figure also depicts the introduction of SaaS CRM to replace the on-premise, COTS CRM which was there before. These SaaS applications as well as modernized microservices can also utilize the IAM solution for authentication purposes.

Infrastructure Modernization

Once the legacy applications and the in-house applications are fully migrated into a microservice architecture and the COTS applications are replaced with SaaS alternatives, the only remaining monolithic component would be the database which we cannot modernize unless the vendor supports it. The final phase of the modernization effort is to migrate from on-premise infrastructure to a cloud environment based on modern infrastructure solution such as containers. This will help the enterprise software system to be cloud-ready and cloud-native in case the organization decides to go down that path. The figure below depicts a state where all the possible applications are modernized and deployed in a cloud environment.

The preceding figure depicts a fully modernized enterprise software platform that is deployed in a cloud infrastructure. These components can be deployed as containers, pods or even virtual machines depending on the requirements of the respective components. As an example, modernized in-house tools and legacy applications can be deployed as containers while the IAM solution can be deployed in VMs. Additionally, the database can be consumed from the cloud provider as a managed database service where you don't need to manage the database. SaaS products will reside somewhere in the cloud which is outside of our control and can be integrated with IAM solution over the network. API gateway and integration software can also be deployed as containers for better scalability. Once the platform is migrated to a cloud environment, it can easily utilize supportive tools provided by the cloud provider for supportive functionality such as logging, monitoring, automation and observability.

Once the modernization is done, you can achieve the goals that were not possible with the legacy enterprise platform.

Summary

In this chapter we discussed about building enterprise software systems by using hybrid integration platforms. We started the chapter by identifying the key requirements of enterprise application integration and there we discussed about data integration, application integration, business integration and consumer integration in detail. Then we moved into discussion about API management which is an unavoidable component of an integration platform. There we discussed different components of API management and how those components interact with each other. After the introduction of integration and API management concepts, we moved into discussion about designing an enterprise software system using an API-led approach by utilzing both API management and integration technologies. Then we moved on to discuss one of the most important, yet complicated topic of service governance with the usage of SOA governance and API management platforms. Finally, we discussed about modernizing a legacy enterprise software system using an integration platform and an IAM solution.

CHAPTER 5

Designing Enterprise Platforms with Event-Driven Architecture Patterns

Enterprise software systems use messages to share data between systems. Users of enterprise systems use different types of client applications such as web, mobile, and terminal applications to exchange data with the system. Sharing of data always happens between two or more systems. There are two types of communication patterns we can identify within enterprise software system:

- Synchronous communication (request-response)

- Asynchronous communication (publish-subscribe)

Synchronous communication is the more common pattern of data sharing that is used in enterprise software systems. It allows applications to work with each other in real time. One challenge with the synchronous communication model is that both the sender and the receiver need to be available at the time of the communication to avoid data loss. If any of the component is not available, the communication becomes a failure. Asynchronous communication model provides a solution for such scenarios by introducing an intermediate message broker to control the communication from the sender to the receiver. In this chapter, we are going to focus our attention on asynchronous communication model where the message sender is decoupled from the message receiver. This model uses an event-driven communication model to share data between applications and services. It allows supporting senders and receivers to

© Chanaka Fernando 2023
C. Fernando, *Solution Architecture Patterns for Enterprise*, https://doi.org/10.1007/978-1-4842-8948-8_5

communicate at their own pace without losing messages or data. As an example, a sports website that provides live updates on scores (e.g., cricket, tennis) uses an asynchronous communication mechanism to receive the updates from the server by subscribing to a topic that publishes live scores. On the other hand, if you perform a search on Google, you send a request to the Google search engine and receive a response in a synchronous manner.

Message broker plays a pivotal role in event-driven architecture where it acts as the common component that decouples the sender and receiver. But it is not the only option to implement asynchronous communication. In this chapter, we will discuss the following topics:

- Introduction to event-driven architecture

- Kafka-based event-driven architecture for enterprise

- Change data capture pattern

- Asynchronous APIs' pattern

- Improved event-driven architecture

Let us first understand the fundamentals of event-driven architecture and the asynchronous communication model.

Introduction to Event-Driven Architecture

Enterprise software systems send data from one system to another over a network such as local area network (LAN) or wide area network (WAN). This data is bundled as messages according to a certain protocol or standard and shared between systems and applications within the enterprise software system. This message may contain data which can worth millions of dollars in case of a sales deal. On the other hand, it can also contain some invalid data that is submitted by a fraudulent user. It is important to understand the value of data and design the system so that it caters to the expectations of the business needs. In the first case, losing that message (data) means a huge loss to the enterprise. But in the second case, it is not an issue at all. What this means is that we need to identify the data guarantee when designing an enterprise software system. Synchronous communication can tackle the data guarantee requirements by implementing retries on the client side. But it makes the clients' implementation complex. Instead, asynchronous communication model can solve this problem in a much simpler manner by introducing a message broker and decoupling the client (sender) and the server (receiver). In this model, messages are referred to as events and that is why it is called as event-driven architecture. Let us first identify some common event-driven communication models used in enterprise software.

Asynchronous Messaging Models

Asynchronous communication model can be used for different use cases, and these use cases require slightly different approaches to implement the data sharing. The following list is a common set of asynchronous communication patterns used in the enterprise software systems:

- Topic-based publish-subscribe pattern

- Queue-based publish-subscribe pattern

- Store and forward pattern

Let us take a closer look at each of these patterns in the following section.

Topic-Based Publish-Subscribe Pattern

This pattern is used to decouple the sender from the receivers with the use of a message broker. It uses an entity called "topic" to share data from the publisher to the subscribers. This topic can be implemented with advanced features such as partitions, replicas, and durability through the message broker technology that is used to host it. Some example message brokers are Kafka, RabbitMQ, and NATS. Figure 5-1 depicts this communication pattern.

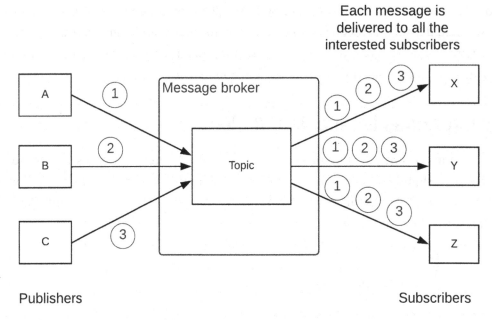

Figure 5-1. *Topic-based publish-subscribe pattern*

As depicted in the figure, publishers send messages to the topic using some unique identifier such as "subject," and the subscribers who are interested in that topic can subscribe to the same. Once the messages are received to the topic, those messages will be distributed to all the subscribers who have subscribed. In a case where the subscriber is not available during the time of the message arrival, the message brokers can keep the message for some configurable time period within that the subscriber can come back online and consume the message from the topic.

Shared Subscriptions (Durable and Non-durable)

A slight variation of the topic-based publish-subscribe model is the shared subscription model where the work of receiving messages on a topic is shared across multiple consumers. In this model, only one consumer in the shared group receives a particular message on the shared subscription. A given topic can have both shared and non-shared subscriptions such as the one we discussed in the previous section. In that kind of a situation, all the non-shared subscribers will get a copy of each message, while the shared subscribers also get a single copy that would be delivered to one of the consumers in that group. Additionally, these subscriptions can be durable or non-durable depending on the requirements of the system. A durable shared subscription holds the messages even when the consumers are not available during the message publishing time.

Queue-Based Publish-Subscribe Pattern

Sometimes there are use cases where the publishers are sending events at a higher rate than the subscribers can process. In such a scenario, the messages need to be distributed across multiple subscribers in a load balancing manner. That is where the queue-based publish-subscribe pattern can be useful. Figure 5-2 depicts this pattern.

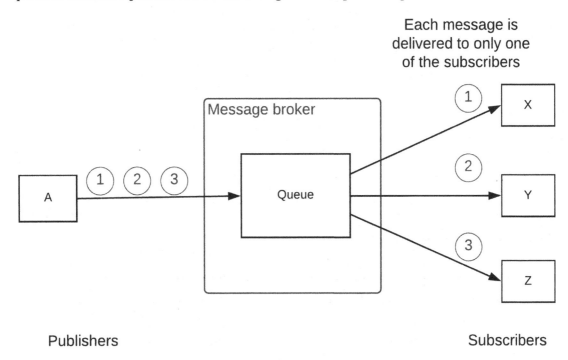

Figure 5-2. *Queue-based publish-subscribe pattern*

As depicted in the figure, the messages that are sent by the publisher are delivered to the interested subscribers in a load balanced manner. In the case of the unavailability of the respective subscriber, the message can be persisted for a given time period until the subscriber comes back online.

Store and Forward Pattern

In both of the topic- and queue-based patterns, both publisher and subscriber need to be available in general. Even though there are features in the message brokers to handle situations when the subscriber is not available, it is not the primary use case those patterns are implemented for. The store and forward pattern is designed to support such a requirement natively. In this model, the message will be stored in a persistent storage regardless of the availability of the subscriber or the target system. In this model, there is a message processor that takes the message from the message store and forwards that message to a target system. Figure 5-3 depicts this messaging pattern.

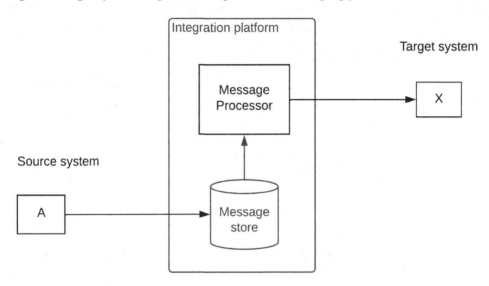

Figure 5-3. *Message store and forward pattern*

This model is supported through most of the integration tools out there in the market. As depicted in the figure, source system will send the message to the integration platform which will store that message in a persistent message store. Then the message processor will take the message from the message store and send it to the target system based on the configured rate. This model can be really useful when you have two systems that operated at different rates. As an example, the source system may send messages at a rate of 200 messages per second, while the target system can only process messages at a rate of 100 messages per second. We can use the store and forward pattern to integrate these two systems without losing any messages in an asynchronous manner.

Streaming Data Processing

In addition to these asynchronous communication models, there is a new model of data processing evolving around the event-driven architecture which is the streaming data processing. In this model, a continuous stream of messages (events) is processed at an intermediate layer before connecting with target systems. In this model, the individual messages are not necessarily targeted towards the target systems. Instead, these streams of messages are generated from source systems, and the intermediate processing layer does the processing and generates valuable results before sharing with the target systems. There are two main types of processing models to work on event streams:

- Real-time stream processing

- Batch processing

Let us discuss these models in a bit more detail in the following section.

Real-Time Stream Processing

There can be situations where we need to make real-time decisions based on events or messages that are generated from certain activities. As an example, let's say we need to identify fraudulent activities on a bank account based on the transactions that are performed in the account. The way to do this is to push all the transaction details as events to an event-processing component and continuously analyze the patterns to identify the fraudulent activity. Similarly, there can be situations where a set of IoT devices generating a continuous event streams as outputs and you need to measure the statistical values of these outputs such as min, max, and average in real time and communicate that back to a controller that can change the conditions of the environment. In addition to these simple use cases, many artificial intelligence (AI)-related operations can be done by processing events in real time. Figure 5-4 depicts a simplified view of a real-time processing pattern.

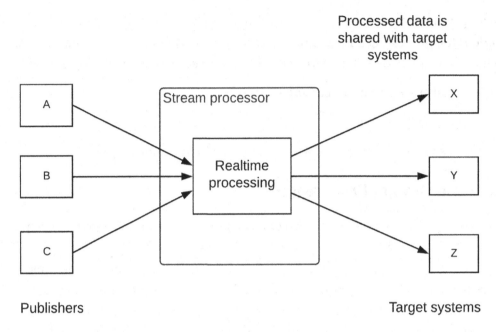

Figure 5-4. *Real-time stream processing pattern*

As depicted in the figure, there are multiple event publishers who publish events to the stream processor where it collects, process, and output the results to the target systems. The results can be stored in databases, sent as notifications, or sent to other systems for further processing. The important point to note here is that these events are not isolated events; rather they are a continuous stream of events related to each other. Once these event streams are received at the stream processor, they will apply real-time stream processing techniques such as filtering, cleansing, summarizing, and joining to these streams.

Batch Processing

There can be another set of use cases where processing events need to be done separately and produce results so that they can be consumed at the will of the target system. A simple example of this is a monitoring component of an API gateway which collects information from multiple APIs deployed in gateways and processes them separately and stores statistical results in a separate database so that monitoring applications can consume this information at the discretion of the user. Another example is a standard ETL job where data is extracted, transformed, and loaded into a target system in batch mode at a given time of the day. Figure 5-5 depicts the batch processing pattern.

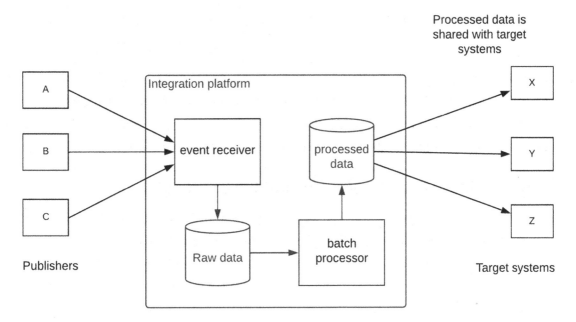

Figure 5-5. *Batch processing pattern*

As depicted in the figure, event publishers publish events continuously to the enterprise software system where it has an event receiver which collects the raw events into a persistent storage such as database. Then a separate component called batch processor reads the raw data and executes different batch processing tasks such as transformations, statistical calculations, and machine learning on top of this data and publishes the results to a processed data store. Then the target systems will retrieve this data as per the interfaces provided by the solution. This can be over a REST or a GraphQL interface.

Now we have an understanding of different event-driven messaging patterns available to us for processing messages. Let us design an enterprise software system based on event-driven architecture by using this knowledge.

Designing an Event-Driven Architecture for Enterprise

Event-driven architecture pattern is not a new concept for enterprise software systems. If you have used an integration platform or a message broker within the enterprise architecture, you are already using event-driven architecture. In this section, we are going to design a modern enterprise software system with the usage of event-driven architecture. The easiest way to design a solution is to start with a problem statement.

Let us consider a scenario where we need to design a robust messaging solution for an e-commerce website. This is a perfect example where each event or message is highly critical and important for the business. Hence, we need to design the system in such a way that there won't be any message loss. That is the reason why we go with an event drive architecture instead of the standard request-response type of model. This does not mean that we are completely removing the synchronous communication model from the solution. Instead, it won't be the only communication pattern in this architecture.

Common Requirements of an E-commerce Website

Let us first define the requirements that need to be fulfilled by the solution that we design. The following is a list of a few requirements for an e-commerce website:

- Guaranteed message delivery

- Scalability

- Availability

- Performance

- Data analysis

Messages need to be delivered end to end without any loss of data from the customer order until the package is delivered successfully to the customer. The solution should also need to scale with the popularity of the website. The system needs to be available all the time since any unavailability can cause a loss of business and bad customer experience. The website should present information to the users without any major latencies. Additionally, system should also allow the business teams to analyze the customer purchasing patterns and trends.

Solution Architecture

Based on these requirements, we can clearly see that there is an opportunity to use event-driven architecture pattern to cater to them. Figure 5-6 depicts an architecture that can be used to build the e-commerce website that can cater to the requirements mentioned in the preceding section.

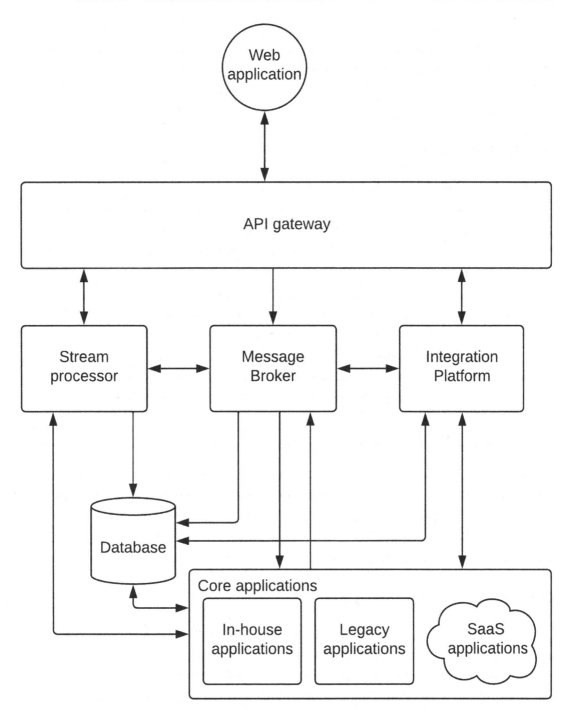

Figure 5-6. *Event-driven enterprise-based architecture*

The figure depicts a solution architecture that we can use to build an event-driven enterprise software system for an e-commerce website. Every connecting line in this diagram depicts an important communication link that defines the characteristics of the overall system. Let us go through these connections so that we understand the architecture properly.

Web Application and API Gateway

The line connecting the web application to gateway represents the requests made by the web application to retrieve data and update data. This communication can happen in a synchronous (request-request) model for simple HTTP-related operations. As an example, if the website needs to showcase the available products for a particular "search" term, that operation will be executed through a synchronous communication. In addition to that, this line also represents asynchronous communication over a protocol such as WebSockets. As an example, once the order is placed by the customer, subsequent updates on the order can be delivered to the website in an event-driven manner using WebSockets protocol. This improves the user experience and avoids unnecessary HTTP polls towards the system. The backend of such a WebSockets call can be the stream processor or another in-house built WebSockets application.

API Gateway and Integration Platform

This communication mainly happens in a synchronous manner over HTTP. Any CRUD operations on data can go through this communication link. Additionally, if the API gateway does not support communicating with the message broker over native protocol of the broker, the integration platform can act as the intermediary between API gateway and the message broker and make that communication successful.

API Gateway and Message Broker

This is an asynchronous communication where API gateway sends the events to the message broker and message broker distributes those messages to backend services in an isolated manner. A typical example would be a client ordering an item through the web application. This message will be stored in the message broker for further processing, and eventually, the client will be updated asynchronously via the web application once the order is processed and moved to the next stage of its life cycle.

API Gateway and Stream Processor

If we take the order placement example mentioned previously, API gateway needs to get the updates about the order life cycle (e.g., accepted, packaged, shipped, delivered) in an asynchronous manner. The stream processor can help the API gateway by listening to the respective event producers such as topics or databases and expose these events to the API gateway through a protocol such as WebSockets. The stream processor can listen to different types of events such as file changes, database changes (through change data capture), topics, queues, and events coming from other sources and convert them into an API gateway compatible service such as WebSockets.

Message Broker and Integration Platform

Integration platform can act as an event producer as well as event consumer to the message broker. It can receive synchronous messages from API gateway and put them into the message broker to process them later. In case the API gateway does not support connecting to the message broker using its native protocol, integration platform can mediate those messages and act as the intermediary between API gateway and message broker.

Message Broker and Stream Processor

Stream processor communicates with message broker to process messages that are stored in the broker. It can be a stream processing use case where messages are first stored in the message broker and then applied stream processing by connecting to the broker. It can be a case where API gateway needs to be notified over WebSockets for certain events or updates. Additionally, the stream processor can also publish real-time results to the message broker so that those results are distributed to the required audiences.

Database and Stream Processor

There can be situations where we need to update other systems when the data is changed in a particular database. The typical approach of getting this done is to poll the database periodically. But it is highly inefficient. Instead, we can use the concept of "change data capture" or CDC to automatically listen to the changes happening in the database and notify other systems about these changes. We can use stream processor to achieve this requirement with a CDC connector that is configured at the stream processor side. Also, stream processor uses the database to store intermediate and final results of real-time stream processing tasks so that other systems can access these results at their will.

Database and Message Broker

Message brokers use a persistent layer such as a database or a file system to store the messages for a longer period of time. The connection from message broker to the database can happen for such a requirement. This could improve the reliability of the message persistence when compared with file-based approach.

Database and Integration Platform

Integration platform can hide the database details from the database users by creating data services that expose the required data over a secured access point such as an API gateway. This is a common requirement in enterprise applications where API gateway cannot directly talk to the database as a backend system. Integration platforms can generate different types of data services to do all kinds of operations that are required to be executed on the database without actually getting direct access to the database. It also avoids the chance of getting the DB credentials and details exposed to outside users.

Database and Core Applications

There will be core applications such as microservices and COTS applications that require connecting to the databases to store and retrieve data related to those applications. There can be different types of databases such as relational databases as well as noSQL databases depending on the use case of the application.

Core Applications to Integration Platform

The actual backend or the source of truth for most of the data resides in the core applications layer. Hence, it is an essential that the integration platform must communicate with these core applications. These applications may expose different protocols and data formats which the integration platform will understand and integrate with the other applications.

Core Applications and Message Broker

These core applications can be the subscribers of the messages that are published into the message broker by client applications over API gateway and integration platform. In case these core applications cannot directly communicate with the message broker, it will route through the integration platform to make the connection feasible. But there can be many core applications such as microservices that directly communicate with the message broker.

Core Applications and Stream Processor

There can be use cases where stream processor needs to publish the real-time stream processing results to these core applications so that these applications can act accordingly. A possible example is when there is a notification about any failure or a fraudulent activity is detected in the real-time processing, this notification can be sent to the core application that is handling customer care so that the respective agents are aware of the failure.

That sums up the solution architecture that we can use to build an event-driven enterprise software system that can cater to an e-commerce website. The same architecture can be utilized to support many other use cases with minor modifications. As an example, instead of the web client, this architecture can easily support other types of clients such as mobile and terminal apps since the services are exposed over standard protocols such as HTTP and WebSockets. It can also extend to support more modern protocols such as GraphQL or gRPC if required. Also, if the APIs need to be exposed to third-party developers, we can bring in the developer portal which comes with API management tools. We can introduce security and observability components to this architecture to make it a more generic and complete architecture. The improved architecture is depicted in Figure 5-7.

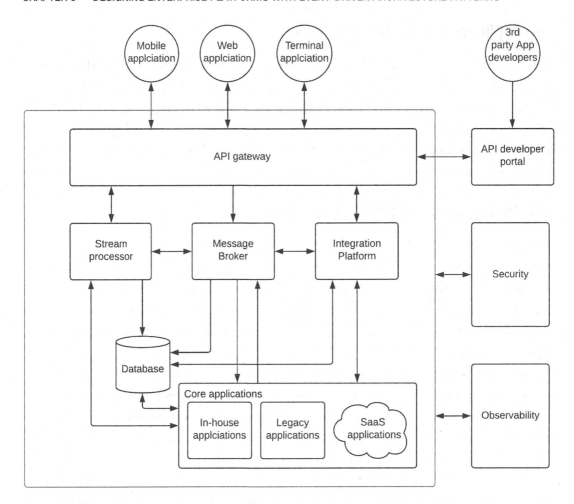

Figure 5-7. *Event-driven enterprise software reference architecture*

The figure depicts a reference architecture based on event-driven approach for an enterprise software system. In this diagram, we have added the security and observability components as common components that are utilized by almost all the other enterprise software components that we discussed in the preceding section. We will be discussing these aspects in detail in the upcoming chapters of this book. Additionally, the developer portal is added to integrate third-party application developers to the system. This architecture can be used to build enterprise software systems that provide an improved user experience by utilizing both synchronous and asynchronous communication models.

Implementing a real-world enterprise software architecture is more challenging than designing the reference architecture. It requires a special set of skills to identify the correct vendors for each functionality by considering the requirements, vision, future, ROI, TCO, and pricing. In this book, we are not going to teach you with the vendor selection since it comes with the real experience. Instead, we will discuss certain technologies that you can use to build the reference architectures that we discuss here. We have made every effort to use only the standard features provided by a certain vendor in such scenarios so that you can replace the vendor easily.

Kafka-Based Event-Driven Architecture for Enterprise

Apache Kafka is one of prominent vendors in the market that supports building event-driven enterprise software systems. It can act as the message broker that can work with many other integrations, API gateway, and stream processing technologies out there. Hence, we have decided to use that to showcase a reference implementation of the aforementioned architecture. Before we jump into the architecture, let us first get a basic understanding of Kafka and its features.

Brief Introduction to Kafka

Kafka is simply a message broker that provides the performance, reliability, and scalability that is required by modern enterprise platforms. It provides a unique yet simple architecture to decouple the message producers from the message consumers. Kafka uses topics to store the messages and deliver them in a reliable manner to the subscribers. Kafka provides many benefits that are found in several other message brokers with its unique design. Some major advantages include the following:

- Excellent scalability allows building cloud-scale applications with fault tolerance.

- Message persistence and durability with a configurable retention time allow consumers to process message at their own rate.

- Provides message order guarantees within a partition.

- Distributed deployment with clustered nodes allows replication to make it more robust so that failure of a given node does not cause message loss.

- Exposes a streams API with a native Kafka Streams library to build real-time applications.

- Ability to deploy across multiple data centers for high availability using clusters.

There are many advanced features available in Kafka that are outside the scope of this book. Figure 5-8 depicts the Kafka architecture and the interfaces it exposes in a summarized figure.

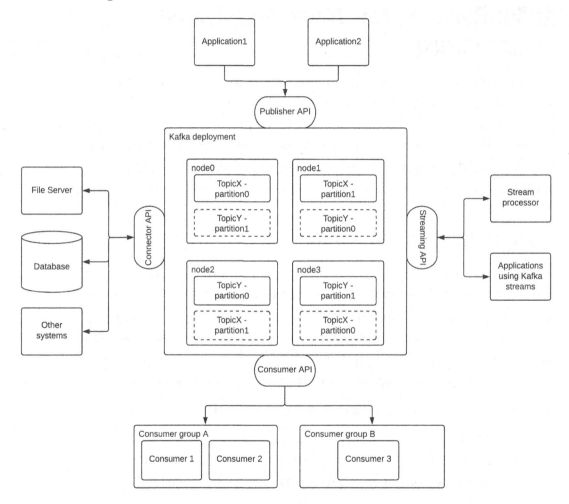

Figure 5-8. *Kafka architecture in a nutshell*

The figure depicts a Kafka cluster running on a four-node deployment. It shows two topics named TopicX and TopicY which has two partitions (parition0 and parition1) each. These partitions are located in separate nodes, and both partitions have one replica each on a separate node. There are four different APIs offered by Kafka to interact with any of the Kafka nodes. Those APIs and their usage are as follows:

- Publisher API – This is the event publishing API used by applications or the event sources. Kafka uses topics to store these events. Each topic can be partitioned into more than one and stored across multiple nodes with replication to make sure that a failure of a single node does not cause message loss. These events are stored for a duration that is configurable by the user. Events will be available for the consumers within this time period. Publishers can specify the topic and partition when publishing events.

- Consumer API – The consumers who are interested in receiving message on a given topic can subscribe to these topics and consume the events once available. The difference with the Kafka consumer API is that these events can be consumed at the will of the consumer and messages won't be removed from the topic until the persistent time is elapsed. What this means is that consumer can retrieve the same message any number of times within the configured persistence time. Consumer can also specify which message needs to be retrieved by specifying the offset. In case you need to share the load among multiple consumers similar to a queue, Kafka supports the concept of consumer group where each consumer in the group received messages in a load balanced manner. These individual consumers are bound to a given partition in a topic. That means there cannot be more consumers than the partitions in a topic within a consumer group. There can be multiple groups connected to the same topic, and each group will receive a copy of the same message.

- Connector API – Kafka can be integrated with many other systems than the client applications. Some examples are databases and file systems that need to be integrated with Kafka for processing data in these systems. You can build a connector for these integrations using the connector API.

- Streaming API – As we discussed in a previous section, the messages stored in a message broker can be processed through a stream processor for generating valuable outputs from the data. The streaming API allows such streaming systems and applications to connect with Kafka and consume messages for streaming use cases.

With the brief introduction to Kafka, let's move into designing an event-driven enterprise architecture with Kafka. Let us take a hypothetical order processing use case where the customers can place orders using mobile, web, and terminal client applications. Given that there can be thousands of orders coming at a given time, we decided to decouple the order placement from the order processing since order processing takes more time to complete and doing that in a synchronous manner does not work well here. Hence, we decided to use Kafka as the message broker. At the same time, we decide to go with a few other open source and commercial vendors for other components as depicted in the following:

- Kafka – Message broker

- WSO2 API Manager – API gateway and developer portal

- WSO2 Micro Integrator – Integration platform

- WSO2 Streaming Integrator – Stream processor

- Okta – Security platform

- ELK – Observability solution

- MySQL – Database

- SAP – ERP system

- Salesforce – CRM system (SaaS)

- Spring Microservices – Order management

The preceding list is a sample set of vendors that we have selected to showcase the given use case. You can select any alternative vendor that supports similar capabilities in your scenario. Given that we decided to implement the enterprise software system in an event-driven model, we must decouple the publishers from the subscribers whenever possible. Figure 5-9 is a diagram that depicts the implementation approach of an order management system using an event-driven architecture.

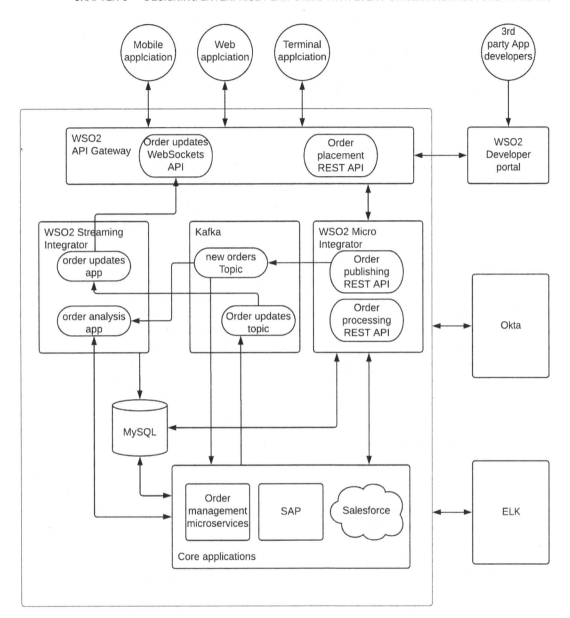

Figure 5-9. *Event-driven enterprise software system with Kafka*

The figure illustrates how an order management use case can be implemented using an even-driven architecture using Kafka as the message broker. The figure depicts the actual APIs, topics, and services that are used to implement the use case. Let us go through these artefacts in detail:

- Order placement REST API is exposed through the API gateway so that client applications can send an order placement request once a customer confirms an order from the applications. This API connects with the order processing REST API that is running on the integration platform.

- Order processing REST API receives the data from the API gateway and publishes the event (message) to a Kafka topic named "new orders topic." This would complete the order placement process, and the customer is notified with a response saying order has been accepted.

- Order management microservice and the order analysis app consume this order via Kafka consumer API.

- Order management microservice receives the message and starts processing the order by updating the required details on SAP and Salesforce systems by calling the order processing REST API which is running on the integration platform.

- Order analysis application which is running on stream processor analyzes the order and does real-time analysis as well as statistical analysis and updates the required systems as and when required. As an example, it sends a special notification to order management system if the order is beyond a certain threshold so that special attention is given to high-value orders. It also updates the statistical tables on MySQL database related to order counts, sales numbers, average sale size, etc. so that dashboard can be updated with the details.

- Once the order status is changed across other stages such as packed, shipped, and delivered, the "order updates topic" will be updated from the order management microservices.

- Order updates application which is running on the stream processor listens to the events published into order-updated topic and pushes these events to the clients through the WebSockets server interface.

- Order updates WebSockets API running on API gateway pushes these updates to the client applications over the WebSockets protocol.

While executing these tasks, this platform utilizes Okta as the security layer for authentication and authorization with standard security models such as OAuth2, SAML, and OIDC. For observability, it utilizes elastic search/log stash/kibana (ELK) stack to capture logging events and produce outputs that are useful to troubleshoot failures. The WSO2 developer portal is used to expose the APIs to internal and external application developers to find the available APIs and use them in their applications.

The architecture described previously can be used to implement any event-driven enterprise software system. It has the ability to support both synchronous and asynchronous communication models. It also can support high-capacity requirements with a proper API gateway, Kafka broker, and other components.

Change Data Capture (CDC) Pattern

If you have observed our event-driven enterprise architecture closely, you may notice that the database is an extremely important component that connects with almost all of the other systems. The reason is that the databases are considered to be the place where all the data stored at rest. Most of the other systems help with moving data from these databases to the client applications. When data moves across systems, there is a possibility that there can be different versions of the same data used in different systems. In such a scenario, we need to define one system as "source of truth" to make sure there are minimum confusions when using dynamic data. In our order processing example, once the order is placed via the client application, that will be retrieved by the order management microservice and store that in the orders database. This data is called source data. The other applications such as order processing REST API can read this data and apply transformations and store with own representations to serve their needs. This data is called derived data. A few examples are search index, cache, and data warehouse which can have the source data in a derived format for application level use cases.

When there are multiple versions of data stored in different places, it is important to synchronize these different data sources to offer a consistent experience to the users. This has been done manually with the usage of tools such as ETL or ELT tools where data is periodically transferred between different data sources. But this is not suitable for real-time application requirements such as indexes and caches. For these use cases, we need a real-time mechanism to capture database changes and move them to target systems without a periodic polling mechanism. The change data capture or CDC is the pattern that allows us to achieve these requirements.

A typical CDC system has three main stages of capturing the changes and propagating these changes to the target systems. Those stages are

1. Change detection

2. Change capture

3. Change propagation

Change detection is the method of identifying that there has been a change to a database. This can be done using one of the following methods:

- Periodically polling the tables for LAST_UPDATED column

- Using database triggers to capture changes

- Monitoring the transaction log of the database

Depending on the use case, you can use either of the aforementioned methods to detect the database changes. Once the change is detected, it needs to be captured and propagated to the target systems using an intermediate component. In a typical CDC system, change detection happens at the database level with a tool such as Debezium, and these changes will be pushed toward the change capturing component as events. This component will capture the events and then propagate to the target system natively or apply transformations as and when required. This process is described in Figure 5-10.

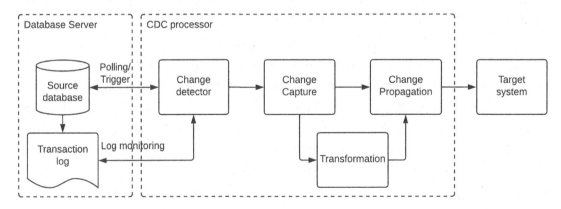

Figure 5-10. *Change data capture working model*

As depicted in the figure, the source database updates the transaction log for each and every change that happens in the database in the respective order. These log entries are listened to by the change detector through log mining, polling, or using database triggers that are converted into events and pushed them to the change capture component of the CDC processor. Then these events are propagated directly or transformed into the target system.

Let us see how we can use this pattern in a real-world enterprise software system with real components. Let us consider an example use case where we need to update a data warehouse for analytics purposes when there is a change in an RDBMS database. Figure 5-11 depicts a possible solution with Kafka to achieve this requirement with CDC pattern.

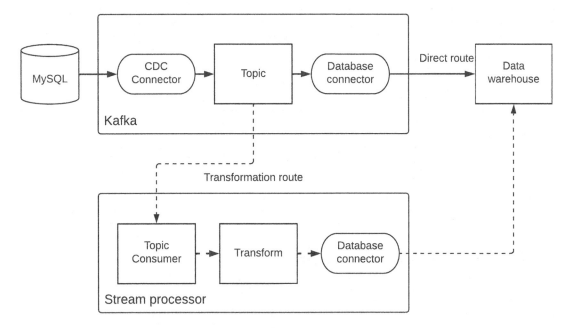

Figure 5-11. *CDC pattern with Kafka*

The figure showcases moving data changes from a MySQL database to a data warehouse in a real-time manner with the usage of Kafka and a stream processor. It shows two possible data migration options:

1. Migrating data directly

2. Migrating data with transformations

The first option of migrating data directly is depicted at the top of the diagram where the data changes are read from the CDC connector of the Kafka broker and stored in a topic. Then this topic is consumed by the database connector that is provided by the Kafka connector API and pushes these changes to the data warehouse.

The second option uses a stream processor to read the change event from the topic using a Kafka consumer and then applies transformations and sends them to the data warehouse using the database connector of the stream processor.

If required, we can completely get rid of the Kafka broker and use the stream processor to implement the CDC pattern as depicted in Figure 5-12.

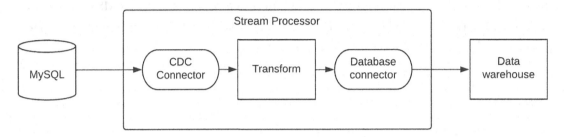

Figure 5-12. *CDC pattern with stream processor*

The figure depicts a scenario where we use a CDC connector provided by the stream processor to capture the database changes. It uses a stream processing techniques to transform the data and push it to the data warehouse using the database connector of the stream processor.

Asynchronous APIs' Pattern

In the order management system example, we discussed the usage of WebSockets API to provide updates on the order status to the client applications. A WebSockets API is somewhat different than the standard REST API since it allows asynchronous communication from the server to the client. In a standard REST API, there needs to be a request to get a response from the server. But WebSockets allows the server to send messages to the client without a request, and it happens in an asynchronous, event-driven manner through the usage of WebSockets frames. WebSockets is an example of an asynchronous API where clients and the server can communicate in a decoupled fashion. But in this case, we are not using an intermediate message broker. WebSockets is not the only mechanism to implement asynchronous APIs.

Asynchronous APIs are also known as event-driven APIs, streaming APIs, or reactive APIs since these APIs allow client and the server to communicate in an event-driven manner. There are many use cases we can use this concept to improve the user experience instead of using standard REST APIs. Some examples are as follows:

- Sending a notification for an instant message received from another person on a chat application

- Updating a live score of a sports event through mobile and web application

- Updating a news feed on a news website based on live events

- A stock ticker displaying price changes in a stock within a trading application

There can be hundreds of different use cases that we can use asynchronous APIs within enterprise software systems. It also allows the event-driven architecture to directly interact with external communications instead of staying within the boundaries of the enterprise networks. Asynchronous APIs' specification is a key component of implementing this model, and it allows us to expose asynchronous APIs for different types of backend systems that supports this sort of communication model. This specification is similar to Swagger or OpenAPI Specification for REST APIs. It is essential to learn and understand the specification if you are implementing asynchronous APIs. More details can be found at the official website: www.asyncapi.com/.

We already mentioned that asynchronous APIs can be implemented with different types of backends. The following is a list of backend protocols that we can use to build asynchronous APIs:

- WebSockets

- WebSub

- GraphQL subscriptions

- Server-Sent Events (SSE)

WebSockets is a protocol defined to allow web applications to maintain bidirectional communication. It allows servers to communicate with clients without a request as and when data is ready. WebSockets uses HTTP to initialize the connection with a handshake and afterwards uses the WebSockets protocol over TCP for communication. It uses subprotocols to define the message formats such as JSON, XML, and other formats. WebSockets does not use an intermediary hub or broker to decouple the client from the server.

WebSub is a protocol that allows publish-subscribe type communication over HTTP. It was designed as a replacement for HTTP "long-polling" that required a long-standing connection to send frequent updates from the server to the clients. WebSub uses a publisher-hub-subscriber model to communicate from publisher to the subscribers similar to the message broker-based model. In a typical message exchange, the publisher publishes new content to the hub, referencing the HTTP headers that contain the topic's information. Then the subscribers who are subscribed to the topic via hub get the content securely through HTTP POST call from Hub. The subscribers need to share the HTTP endpoint to the Hub at the time of the subscription.

GraphQL is a query language for APIs to retrieve data. It uses HTTP protocol under the hood. A client would send the query to fetch the data or change (mutate) the data as the payload in a POST request. The GraphQL server will parse the request and provide only the requested data based on the query. GraphQL subscriptions are used to deliver real-time updates from the server to the clients. The client subscribes to a server-side event using the subscription query. This request will open up a long-lived connection to the server. This request uses a WebSockets to send the subscription query. Once there are updates on the related query, updates are sent over WebSockets to the client.

Server-Sent Events or SSE is a subscribe-only protocol that allows clients to receive data from servers after an initial connection has been established. It is a simple protocol and uses standard HTTP instead of a separate protocol such as WebSockets. With SSE, the client can subscribe to a stream of events generated by the server. A connection over SSE starts with a client-initiated communication over HTTP, and the client passes the URL of an endpoint to the server. The server leaves the HTTP response open until it has no more events to send.

In addition to these asynchronous protocol-based systems, we use message brokers heavily in enterprise software systems for asynchronous communication. Asynchronous API specification allows message brokers as the backend servers when implementing asynchronous APIs.

Now we have a better understanding of the various asynchronous protocols that we can use to build asynchronous APIs. Let us design an event-driven platform using asynchronous APIs. From what we have discussed in the preceding section, we can identify that there are multiple client protocols that support asynchronous APIs. We need to have a supported backend service for the respective client. Similar to what we did with REST APIs, we can use an API gateway to implement quality of services capabilities such as security, rate limiting, and monitoring. It is essential to select an API gateway that supports synchronous (REST) APIs as well as asynchronous APIs. Figure 5-13 depicts a solution architecture that can be utilized to build asynchronous API-based enterprise software system.

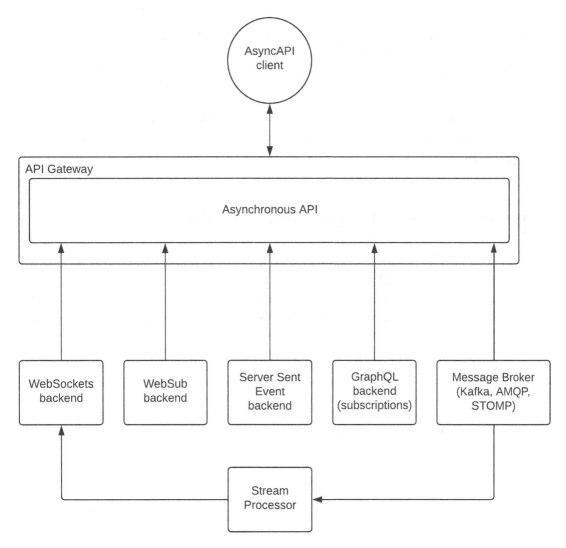

Figure 5-13. *Asynchronous APIs with API gateway*

The figure depicts how we can use an API gateway that supports asynchronous API specification to build asynchronous APIs. The figure illustrates how the AsyncAPI specification allows client applications to easily consume asynchronous APIs with a single specification regardless of the backend implementation. The API gateway provides the capabilities such as security, rate limiting, and monitoring through configurations to apply on top of the asynchronous API. In addition to the protocols we discussed in the preceding section, message broker protocols such as JMS, Kafka, and AMQP can also be used as the backend for asynchronous APIs. In case the API gateway does not support these native broker protocols, a stream processor or an integration platform can translate these native broker events to a supported protocol such as WebSockets and expose it as an asynchronous API.

Now we have discussed beyond the standard event-driven architecture that we initially discussed and expanded it based on the use cases such as Kafka-based use cases, CDC pattern, and AsyncAPI pattern. Let us use this knowledge to improve the initial version of our event-driven architecture to an architecture that can support these different use cases.

Improved Event-Driven Architecture

A typical enterprise software system needs to support both synchronous and asynchronous use cases. Hence, it is important to design the solution with the support for both of these communication styles consistently. Figure 5-14 is an improved version of our event-driven enterprise architecture that we defined in a previous section of this chapter.

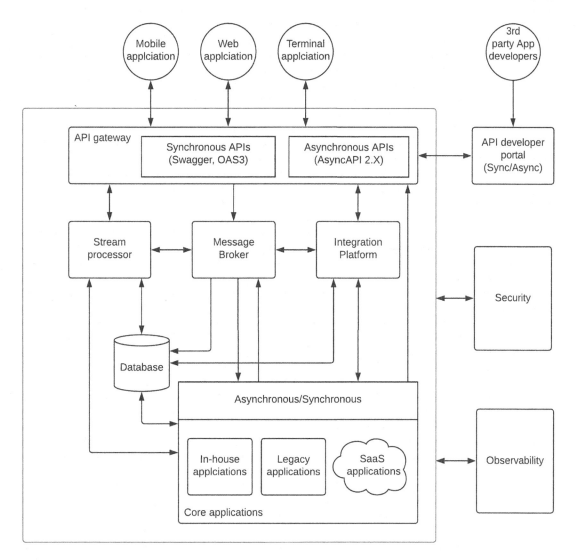

Figure 5-14. *Event-driven enterprise architecture with sync/async APIs*

As per the figure, API gateway exposes both synchronous and asynchronous APIs using standard specifications such as Swagger and OAS 3.0 for synchronous APIs and AsyncAPI 2.2 for asynchronous APIs. The various backend systems including the message broker, integration platform, stream processor, and the core application layer can expose either synchronous or asynchronous interfaces for API gateway as backends. Additionally, the database layer can integrate with stream processor for CDC use cases. The API developer portal also showcases both types of APIs for developers to build their applications. We can realize this architecture with the usage of Apache Kafka and other software components as depicted in Figure 5-15.

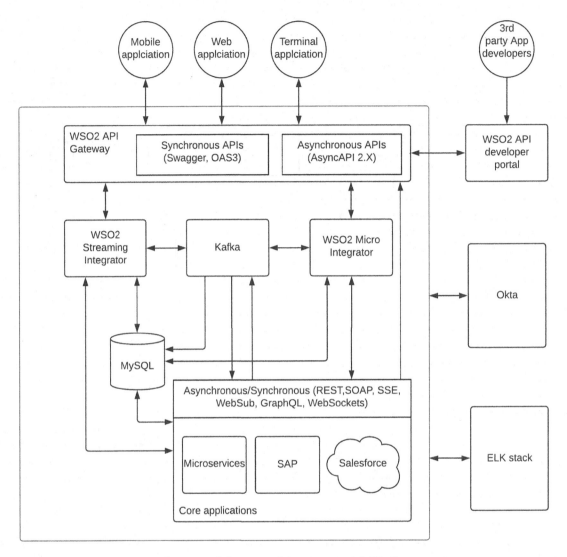

Figure 5-15. *Improved event-driven architecture with Kafka*

As per the figure, we can utilize Kafka as the message broker while using WSO2 platform for API management, integration, and stream processing. The backend services can be implemented with both synchronous and asynchronous protocols while using Okta for security and ELK stack for observability. MySQL is used as the database. The same architecture can be realized with many other alternative vendors as per your need. It is up to you to decide which vendor is suitable for which component as per your requirements and capacity to spend.

Summary

In this chapter, we have discussed about asynchronous messaging models and streaming data processing models before moving into designing an event-driven software system architecture for enterprise applications. We discussed the details of event-driven solution architecture and how different use cases are supported through various interactions between components. Then we discussed a few real-world examples of using event-driven architecture in enterprise software systems. We went through an introduction to one of the most popular message broker solutions in Kafka which is used heavily in real-world examples. We discussed how to use Kafka to realize the solution architecture that we discussed in the preceding section. Then we discussed the CDC pattern which is another real-world example of event-driven architecture where data is moved from the source system to a target system via an event-driven approach. We also discussed the latest addition to the API landscape which is asynchronous APIs that play an important role in designing modern event-driven software architectures. Finally, we discussed an improved version of the original event-driven solution architecture with the learnings from the example use cases. We also discussed about a realization of the improved architecture with the usage of sample vendors at the end of the chapter.

CHAPTER 6

Securing Enterprise Software Systems

The consumer-driven economy has made the enterprise software systems exposing more and more enterprise assets (data and systems) to external parties and hence increased the attack surface. The proper solution to handle this situation is to implement suitable security controls at each level of the enterprise to secure its assets. These security controls span across network layer, application layer, transport layer, and physical security layers. In this chapter, we will be mainly focusing on the application layer security. One of the main challenges we have in the online world (or metaverse) is the validation of digital identity. In the physical world, it is not that hard to validate the identity of a person since we have unique characteristics of individuals such as face and fingerprints. But in the metaverse, it is much easier to imitate someone else and fool the system since there is no real person in the metaverse except some digital tokens or keys. Anyone who possesses these digital identities can act as the physical person who created the identity. Not only that, these virtual users or clients can send different types of attacks to the system since accessing the system over the network does not require an actual human being. It only requires a few lines of code running in a computing device. Hence, security is an essential part of any enterprise software system that we design. We can use some of the physical characteristics such as face and fingerprint for securing access to enterprise software systems with the usage of the digital technology and biometric devices. When implementing security for enterprise software systems, we can use the following mechanisms to validate the identity of a user:

C. Fernando, *Solution Architecture Patterns for Enterprise*, https://doi.org/10.1007/978-1-4842-8948-8_6

- A physical characteristic of the user (e.g., face, fingerprint, biometrics)

- A physical item owned by the user (e.g., device, card)

- A digital token acquired by the user (e.g., username/password, token, key)

We can use one of these options or many of these options depending on the client that needs to be validated. As an example, the client can be an actual human being who needs to do a bank transaction using their mobile phone. In such a scenario, we can validate the user with biometric information and a digital token such as an OTP for advanced security. If the client is a program that is accessing the system to cater to a request made by an already validated user, we need to go with a digital token only since there is no physical person directly involved in the communication. On the other hand, we need to make sure that the customer experience is not compromised badly due to the advanced security measures we implement in the system. Securing enterprise software systems is a vast field that deserved several books on its own. In this chapter, we are trying to cover some of the common patterns that can be used to implement security for enterprise software systems. This chapter includes the following subsections:

- Introduction to security of enterprise software systems

- Centralized IAM pattern

- Cloud application security pattern

- Security federation pattern

- API security pattern

- Microservices security pattern

Let us first identify the common security requirements of an enterprise software system and how we can design an enterprise software architecture to support these requirements.

Introduction to Security of Enterprise Software Systems

In a broader sense, enterprise security includes the techniques, processes, and strategies that secure data and IT assets from unauthorized access and prevent risks that may interfere with confidentiality, integrity, and availability (CIA) enterprise security of the system. It is a combination of technology, people, and processes that secure the most valuable asset of an enterprise, which is data. In a typical enterprise software system, we can identify two main components that we need to secure against unauthorized access in order to prevent attacks:

1. Data

2. Applications

You may wonder why we consider data separate from the applications since applications are the users of data. We have separated out the data security from the application security since the techniques we use are a bit different from each other.

Data Security

Data contains the value of the business. It is stored and retrieved from the systems based on the needs of the consumer. Once it is stored in a system such as a database or a file server, we call that as data at rest. When the data is requested by a user and transferred through the network, we call that as data in transit. It is essential to secure data both at rest and in transit in an enterprise system. Let us discuss how we can secure data in these situations.

Securing Data at Rest

Think of an enterprise software system that is designed for a bank. This system contains highly confidential information such as bank account numbers of individuals that should not be exposed to anyone other than the individual customer and the required employees of the bank who work with the individual. This data is stored in a database or a file system. To prevent anyone else accessing this data, we can use techniques such as encryption to secure data at rest. In encryption, we transform the content to a form that is unreadable without a secret key to decrypt the content. Another technique used to secure data at rest is tokenization in which the actual data is represented as a token that is unusable without the context. As an example, you can represent a credit card number with a token so that other people cannot recognize the credit card number other than the system that is capable of detokenizing the data. Additionally, the database system or the file server can be protected with advanced security measures such as strong authentication.

Securing Data in Transit

The data stored in the storage systems need to be retrieved by the user via the applications or systems. Usually, data transmits through the network, and we need to prevent network-based attacks such as man in the middle attacks. The solution for securing data in transit is to use transport layer security protocols such as SSL and TLS for communication of data from data store to the consumer. By implementing a proper secure key and certificate management system, we can implement transport layer security and encrypt the data while in transit.

Data Privacy

Another critical aspect of data security is the privacy. What this means is that the data that we collect from the users (e.g., customers, partners) needs to be used according to the data privacy laws applicable to the specific region that these users are pertaining to. As an example, for European countries, there is a data protection law called the General Data Protection Regulation (GDPR) which all the organizations need to follow when dealing with data related to users from that region.

Application Security

Each and every software component that you run within the enterprise platform can be considered as an application. These applications need to be prevented from unauthorized access and risks. Application security is a responsibility that is shared by the entire IT team of an organization. It requires a collective effort to implement proper security measures for applications. The end goal of the application security is to avoid any risks that can cause damage to the system and the organization. Figure 6-1 depicts how the terms threat, vulnerability, and risk correlate to each other.

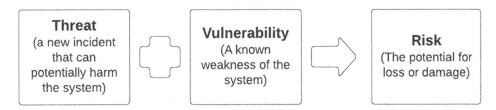

Figure 6-1. *Threat, vulnerability, and risk correlation*

As per the figure, a threat is a newly identified incident that can potentially harm the system such as newly released mobile application. A vulnerability is a known weakness of the system such as usage of eight-character passwords to protect logins. The risk is that potential hackers would guess the passwords of users and get access to their valuable personal information that can damage the reputation of the organization. It is the task of the enterprise team to prevent this risk by handling threat properly and removing the vulnerability. As an example, a proper security audit of the mobile application release would uncover this threat and avoid the vulnerability by enforcing strong authentication with strong password and multifactor authentication.

Enterprise application security needs to be implemented with a coordinated approach between people, processes, and technology. We can identify a set of basic principles that we can adhere to when implementing security for enterprise applications. Those principles are as follows:

- Build a strong identity foundation.

- Adhere to security best practices and automate them.

- Follow zero-trust architecture for application security.

- Prepare for security events.

Let us discuss these principles in detail in the following section.

Build a Strong Identity Foundation

Enterprise platforms need to deal with different types of users. We can categorize the users based on different criteria depending on the industry or domain. But a more generic categorization that is applicable across the industries is based on the association of users. Those categories are

- Customers

- Employees

- Partners

Having this sort of a categorization makes it easier to implement security measures according to the role they play within the enterprise ecosystem. Based on these user categories, we can identify certain security use cases defined so that we can identify the common requirements for each use case. Those use cases are

- Business to customer (B2C)

- Business to employees (B2E)

- Business to business (B2B)

In addition to these main use cases, there are certain derivates of these use cases such as government to citizen (G2C) and business to business to customers (B2B2C) also identified in certain enterprises. Let us discuss these primary use cases in detail so that we get a better understanding of the security requirements of an enterprise.

Business to Customer (B2C)

This is the most common and highly demanding use case within enterprise platforms. This covers the interaction between the customer and the enterprise software systems. This is also called as customer identity and access management or CIAM. This is the most challenging and complicated use case since most of the risks are associated with this use case. At the same time, we need to build a security foundation for this use case that is secure as well as easy to consume since it directly impacts the user experience. Most of the modern security features are produced to cater to this particular use case. Some examples are

- Single Sign-On (SSO)

- Passwordless authentication

- Multifactor authentication (MFA)

- Bring your own identity (BYOI)

- Multi-option authentication

- Delegated authentication

- Adaptive authentication

These new security features try to strike a balance between the security and the user experience. We will talk about these features in detail in a subsequent section of this chapter. A derivative of B2C security is the G2C use case where a government provides services to their citizens. In this case also, we can utilize the aforementioned features to provide greater experience to the citizens while maintaining the security of the systems.

Business to Employee (B2E)

Enterprises can be so large that they need to manage the employees as a separate user base. That is where the B2E security becomes a requirement for the enterprise security team. This is sometimes called workforce identity since it deals with the workforce of an organization. The interaction between an employee and the enterprise systems focuses more on security rather than the ease of use. The reason being that employees can access highly confidential and important information that is not possible for the customers. On the other hand, employees are trained to use these systems, and hence, security comes ahead of the user experience. As an example, if an employee needs to use a physical device such as a key or a card to log into their office workstations, they will not have any other option than to log into the system. In contrast, for a customer, we will provide multiple options to login into the system in case they forget one method of authentication. In addition to the application-level security controls, we need to use network security controls such as VPN-based access for employees when they access enterprise software systems over the Internet.

This use case can have different variations depending on the industry. As an example, an organization that deploys sales teams to remote areas may allow their employees to access the systems over the Internet, but they will restrict access only through the special devices that are given to them so that they can keep track of all the activities. Another scenario would be that a call center team might need to access multiple systems to help customers on their queries and might require SSO to these applications to provide better experience to the customers. In such a scenario, the security team will allow these call center associates to use SSO while they are on duty. Similarly, there can be situations where B2C-related features are utilized for B2E use cases as and when required.

Business to Business (B2B)

Another common requirement of enterprise security is providing security for third-party businesses or organizations that an enterprise works with. Sometimes this requirement is called organization management since it deals with the security of third-party organizations. Here the requirement is not simply to authenticate a few users from the third-party organization to provide access to enterprise systems. It is not B2B use case, rather a B2C use case. Think of a scenario where you are a manufacturer of some equipment and you work with third-party dealers to sell your products. In this scenario, these dealers have their own workforce, and each and every dealer needs to control how their employees access the systems that are implemented on your enterprise. To support this requirement, we need to have a hierarchical user management so that each of these dealers can have administrators who can do certain activities such as user creation, role creation, and permissions management without contacting your enterprise security team. This way, you can onboard any number of dealers to the system without having an additional overhead of managing the users of these dealers. This is a unique security model that deals with a hierarchical security model.

A variant of this use case is the B2B2C use case where we need to provide security for the customers of these third-party businesses. As an example, let us assume that the dealers that we discussed in the preceding section allow their customers to access your enterprise's retail website as a customer of that dealer. In this case, the enterprise software system, which is the retail website, needs to rely on the authentication done by the dealer on their system and provide required access to the user based on the permissions associated with that user. It is a complicated use that involves sharing user details between systems over standard protocols and implementing required security controls at each point without disrupting the user experience.

With that understanding of the use cases that are common in enterprise software systems, let us take a closer look at the main requirements of an identity platform within an enterprise ecosystem. There are three main aspects that we need to cover when building a strong identity foundation for your enterprise:

- Authentication – identifies who the user is

- Authorization – identifies what the user can do

- User management – controls the user lifecycle

All the implementations we do related to security within the enterprise ecosystem connects with the aforementioned core concepts. Let us discuss these in detail in the following section.

Authentication

There will be different types of users (clients) who need access to enterprise software systems to perform their day-to-day tasks. It is the responsibility of the enterprise system to validate the authenticity of these clients before granting them access to the applications. Authentication is the process of validating the identity of the user based on the credentials that user provides at the time of requesting access to the application. These credentials can come from different forms such as

- Username/password

- Access token (JWT)

- Hardware device

- Biometrics (fingerprint, face)

- One-time password (OTP)

Once these credentials are presented by the client, the system needs to extract the information that is stored in the credentials or contacts the required servers and gets those details and takes the decision on whether the client is valid or not. If the client is valid only, the authentication process is successful, and the client will be granted access to the system.

Authentication process involves multiple systems, and these systems need to share these details in a secured manner over the network. We use different authentication protocols to make this work. Examples of such protocols are SAML, OIDC (on top of OAuth2), and LDAP. It is essential that the systems that involved in the authentication process agree on a protocol before communicating to make the process successful.

Authorization

Knowing who the user is sufficient for simple applications that do not provide advanced capabilities. But most of the enterprise applications offer different types of services, and these services need to be controlled with a set of permissions. Authorization is the process of validating the user's permissions so that once authenticated, the user is capable of doing certain actions but not others. As an example, an employee from the HR department should be able to access the salary details of the employees, while a regular employee should be blocked from accessing the same information. In such a scenario, even though the regular employee can access the HR system and see the other employees' basic information such as department, phone number, and location, they should be avoided from accessing the salary details of other employees.

Authorization is always a secondary step after the authentication, and we can use different mechanisms to implement it based on the need. If we need to control access based on user groups, we can use a mechanism such as role-based access control (RBAC) where the users are assigned to a group (role) and this group is granted with a set of permissions for the application. In this case, any user pertaining to the same group has the same level of access. This is called coarse-grained access control since we give access to a group of users at once. Another mechanism that we can use to implement authorization is attribute-based access control (ABAC) in which case we check one or more attributes of the user from the authentication response and provide access based on these attributes. This is a fine-grained access control mechanism since we consider the attributes of each and every user before making the decision.

User Management

Every action that we perform related to the enterprise security involves a user. So it is essential to manage the users in the platform so that we can implement different types of authentication and authorization mechanisms. The main tasks of the user management include user provisioning, permissions management, and user convenience.

The user provisioning is the process of onboarding users into the enterprise system. These users can be customers, employees, or business partner users. Depending on the user type, we might need to store them in different user stores or to the same user store. If we consider a scenario where we acquire another organization and we need to onboard all the users from their system to our enterprise user store, we need to migrate the users with a bulk import mechanism and ask all the users to reset their passwords at the first login. Another use case would be to provide a self-sign-up portal to the users so that they can register to the platform by themselves. In this scenario, we can implement a user onboarding workflow to validate the user details prior to provisioning the users into the enterprise user store.

Once the users are onboarded, we need to assign these users with different roles depending on their position and responsibilities. Managing these roles and permissions is also a requirement that we need to fulfill with the user management component. Creating the roles and assigning roles to the users can also be implemented with a workflow so that we have visibility over these actions.

Consent Management and Privacy

A common requirement for B2C use cases would be to allow the users to control their passwords and consents that they have given to the applications through a user portal. This can provide the users with the convenience to change their profile information, security questions, and privacy settings by controlling the consents. Consent management is a critical requirement specifically for use cases on financial services, banking, and healthcare domains where there are strict regulations around privacy. As an example, if the system is capturing user's personally identifiable information (PII) data in the system, the user must give the consent (agree to share the data) to store that information. Also, if the user decides to revoke the consent, the system must provide mechanisms for the user to revoke the consent, and it will eventually remove all the PII data from the system.

With that foundation knowledge on identity and access management of enterprise applications, let us build a common framework to implement application security for the enterprise.

Key Components of Strong Identity and Access Management for Enterprise

We can identify the following main components for building a strong enterprise identity management framework:

- Utilize a centralized identity and access management solution.

- Use strong authentication with flexibility to provide multiple options.

- Use standards-based authentication.

- Use scalable user stores to securely store the users and credentials.

- Use groups and attributes to implement authorization.

- Audit the user actions and user management with proper workflows and logging mechanisms.

We will discuss these points in detail when we discuss the practical usage patterns of the identity and access management in the upcoming sections of this chapter.

Adhere to Security Best Practices and Automate Them

Enterprise security involves people, processes, and technology. Hence, it is essential to define a set of security best practices so that we can identify how people can use processes and technology to build a secure enterprise for customers, employees, and business partners. It is always good to have a dedicated security team to research on latest security trends, threat models, and vulnerabilities in the system. This team can provide security guidelines for the enterprise so that they can follow the guidelines when they operate in their respective areas. The following is a list of areas that we can consider for adhering to security best practices within an enterprise:

- Secure software engineering process

- Vulnerability and risk management process

- Security reward and acknowledgement process

Let us a take a closer look at each of these processes to get a better understanding of security best practices in an enterprise.

Secure Software Engineering Process

We use different types of software systems within the enterprise ecosystem. Some systems are developed within the enterprise teams, and some systems are brought in and installed within the enterprise ecosystem, while others are purchased as SaaS services. Each of these applications needs to be properly handled with security best practices. Let us take the example of in-house applications and see how we can implement a secure engineering process.

A typical software application goes through three main phases regardless of the development process that you follow (e.g., agile or waterfall). Those phases are

1. Design phase

2. Development phase

3. Release phase

In addition to these phases, once the software is released, it needs to be managed so that no new security vulnerabilities are discovered. In each of these three phases, we need to do certain activities to make sure that no vulnerabilities are released to the end users of the application. Figure 6-2 depicts a secure software engineering process with high-level details.

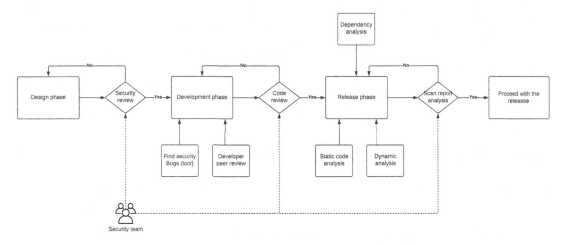

Figure 6-2. *Secure development process for enterprise*

The figure depicts how a software application can be developed with proper security practices within an enterprise. The process starts at the beginning of the application design phase where security team will join the design review meeting and clarify the need of the application and any security-related questions that need to be answered by the development and architecture team. If there are any remaining questions or clarifications, the development team can work on those items and get back to the next phase with the go-ahead from the security team.

The next phase of process is the development phase where developers start building the application using the technology stack they have chosen. In this phase, the developers can use automated code scanning tools to identify security bugs in the code. Additionally, they can also do peer reviews with co-developers to identify any security problems in the code. Once the code is ready to be reviewed, the developers can call for a code review meeting with the participation from the security team. During this review, the security team will identify any vulnerabilities and security weaknesses in the code by questioning the code segments at a deeper level. Given that this is the last chance to get the code to be reviewed, these code reviews will be highly argumentative and might need a several iterations to get the code approved by the team. After a rigorous review, the code becomes ready to be released.

Once the code is reviewed and approved, it will be merged with the release code base and the release process will kick off. During this phase, the security team will use different tools to perform static code analysis, dynamic analysis, and dependency analysis to make sure the code does not contain any vulnerabilities. These scanning tools will generate reports with different levels of vulnerabilities, and depending on the scale, the developers need to fix these critical vulnerabilities and do the scanning process again before releasing the code.

The final stage of the development process is to release the code to the runtime environments such as staging, QA, and production.

Vulnerability and Risk Management Process

No matter how rigorous your security testing process during the development process, there can be situations where certain vulnerabilities go undetected and result in major problems. This can happen in third-party dependencies that you use as well in the code that you write. The reason for this is that the scanning tools go through continuous improvements and the vulnerabilities that were not detected before can be detected in a later version of the tool. In such a scenario, we need to have a mechanism to handle these vulnerabilities and risks with the minimum impact towards the customers. Figure 6-3 depicts a vulnerability and risk management process for an enterprise.

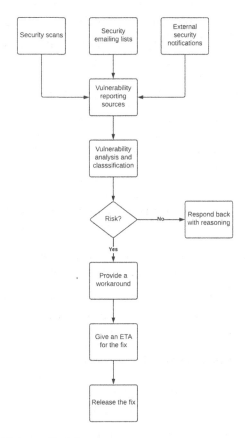

Figure 6-3. *Vulnerability and risk management process*

As depicted in the figure, the process starts with the vulnerability reporting sources that capture the vulnerability through a test scan, via an email from a user, or through a security notification from an external party who manages a dependency that we use in our code base. The process that follows this initial reporting is depicted in the figure.

Security Reward and Acknowledgement Process

Security vulnerabilities can cause severe damage to the brand of an enterprise if not handled properly. It is important to implement processes to capture these vulnerabilities as soon as possible. Security reward program is a mechanism that can be used to motivate genuine developers and security researchers to report these critical vulnerabilities to the enterprise first rather than publicly exposing the details. This allows the enterprise to fix the issues quickly without damaging their brand. As a token of appreciation, the enterprise can reward these reporters with a gift and a certificate so that they are recognized for their effort. Such a program can contain details on the following aspects:

- Products and services considered for the program

- Details on qualifying criteria

- Rewards and acknowledgement details

- Any exceptions

We can open a private emailing group that can be used by the reporters to send their vulnerability reports.

In addition to these processes, an enterprise can maintain a security space in its knowledge base to maintain all the resources related to the security best practices for the enterprise. Having a frequent training sessions on security best practices is also a useful mechanism to keep everyone up to date on the processes.

Follow Zero-Trust Architecture

The software components that run within internal local area networks (LAN) or militarized zones (MZ) are considered as trusted subsystems by most teams within the enterprise except the security team. Given these applications are not exposed to the outside world and protected with network level security, when these applications communicate with each other, most of the development teams tend to go with less-secure approaches when compared to the communication with external users. But the security teams will prove that this argument is no longer valid and there can be threat coming from external as well as internal sources in a real-world scenario. Hence, they propose this model called "zero-trust architecture" where no system is considered trustworthy when communicating with another system. It eliminates the implicit trust that was there in the trusted subsystems model and continuously validates every interaction within the system. It uses the mantra of "never trust, always verify" in communication between systems in an enterprise. There are three main principles of zero-trust architecture that needs to be considered when implementing it:

1. All entities are untrusted by default.

2. Least privilege access is enforced.

3. Comprehensive security monitoring is implemented.

These principles pave the way to build a proper zero-trust enterprise. The concept of zero trust needs to be implemented at each of the following components:

- Users

- Applications

- Infrastructure

Users need to be validated with strong authentication mechanisms such as MFA while implementing "least access" policies for authorization along with verification of user device integrity. Applications need to be secured with authentication for all the interservice communications, and any implicit trust models need to be removed. Infrastructure components also need to be secured with the available security models when communicating within the networks as well as communicating with the external parties.

Prepare for Security Events

Even with the utmost security models and best practices implemented within your enterprise, there can be situations where the systems become vulnerable and pose risks. In such a situation, you need to have a mechanism to respond to these events to control the damage that could otherwise occur. It is important to prepare for such incidents with proper planning and resources in place. This requires having the following aspects in place:

- Identify the responsible persons and their roles.

- Develop incident management process.

- Deploy the necessary tools for monitoring and reporting.

- Provide necessary access to the responsible persons ahead of time.

- Prepare forensic capabilities and processes.

The first step in preparing for security events is to identify the responsible individuals in the team and their roles during an incident. These individuals might span across multiple team such as support, engineering, legal, and leadership. Once the individuals are identified, the next step is to develop an incident management plan with clear steps on how to deal with an incident. When doing this, the security team will recommend certain tools for monitoring and reporting the security events so that the respective individuals get notified as soon as the incident occurs. When these notifications are received by the individuals, they must have the required permissions to do certain things such as shutting down a server. Hence, these access privileges need to be provided ahead of time. Finally, there should be a mechanism to collect the details on what went wrong during the incidents and any possible root causes so that the teams can take actions to prevent such incidents in the future.

Now we have a good understanding of securing enterprise software systems. Let us take a look at some of the example use cases that can be used to implement security for enterprise software systems. We are going to use an identity and access management (IAM) platform as the centralized identity provider (IDP) for our sample use cases.

Enterprise Security Use Cases

Enterprise platforms contain different types of applications that are developed by different vendors. These applications may use different approaches to implement security. As an example, some applications may use built-in user stores for managing users, while other applications may use an external user store for the same functionality. Another example is the protocol that is used to authenticate users for the application where one application may use SAML while another application may use OpenID Connect (OIDC). Due to these differences, we need a centralized component that can deal with these differences and provides a unified user experience to the users. That is the task of an IAM platform. Let us discuss a few use cases that we can identify in enterprise platforms that can be implemented using an IAM platform.

Single Sign-On (SSO)

Have you ever thought about how you log into the Gmail and then access Google drive or Google Calendar without ever asked to log in again? These are entirely different services offered by Google, and they have their own security implementations. But you can access many services that Google offers with a single login. This is achieved through the concept of Single Sign-On or SSO. In an enterprise environment, there are many different services (service providers) that are developed by internal teams, partners, or third parties. It is a bit challenging than a Google scenario since Google can control which protocols their applications use for authentication. But in an enterprise setup, these heterogeneous applications may use different authentication protocols to provide access to these systems. That is where we can use a centralized identity platform to integrate with these different protocols and build a unified SSO experience to the users. Figure 6-4 depicts this use case.

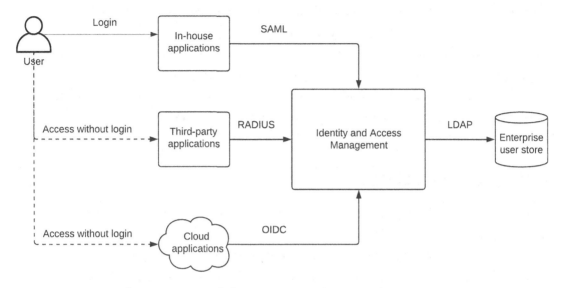

Figure 6-4. *Single Sign-On with heterogeneous protocols*

The figure depicts a typical enterprise software system that has different types of applications such as in-house, third-party, and cloud applications that use different authentication protocols such as SAML, RADIUS, and OIDC in each of these applications. The centralized IAM platform acts as the authentication server for these applications. When a user needs to access any of the systems (e.g., in-house applications), the user will be redirected to the IAM platform for authentication. The user will provide the login credentials in the login page, and the user will be authenticated against the enterprise user store that is connected to the IAM platform via LDAP protocol. Once the authentication is successful, the IAM platform will store the cookies of the user in the user's browser session and redirects the user back to the original application. The in-house application uses the security token that is provided by the IAM platform to validate the user information and let the user access the application resources. Now let us imagine that this user needs to access the cloud application and they type in the URL of the cloud application in the browser. At this moment, the cloud application will use OIDC protocol to call the IAM platform via a redirect. The IAM platform will check the request and identifies that the user is already authenticated based on the browser cookies and send the authentication token back to the cloud application. Then the cloud application will use that token to verify the user, and the user is automatically logged into the system and granted access to the resources. Similarly, if the user tries to access any other application during this session, they will be able to access the applications without a separate login.

This process makes it easy for the users to access multiple applications simultaneously without remembering usernames and passwords for different applications to login into each and every time. The IAM platform makes it possible for enterprise teams to bring in new applications into the system without interfering with the user experience.

Strong Authentication

One of the key requirements mentioned in the zero-trust architecture is the strong authentication. What this means is that instead of providing a simple authentication step such as username/password, the users are prompted for multiple (typically two) authentication steps to validate the user identity before accessing the system. This is sometimes called two-factor authentication (2FA) or multifactor authentication (MFA). There are applications that implements strong authentication only on certain scenarios while allowing simple authentication for other use cases. This type of a model uses certain factors such as the location of the user, the device used to access the system, or some other factors to determine whether the strong authentication is required or not. This is called adaptive authentication. Figure 6-5 depicts how the strong authentication works in an enterprise environment.

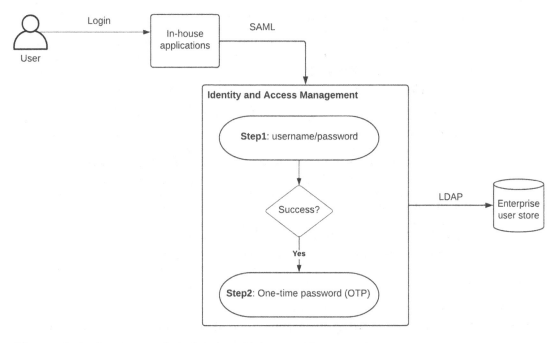

Figure 6-5. *Strong authentication for enterprise security*

The figure depicts a scenario where the user tries to access an in-house application that uses SAML for authentication. The user is redirected to the IAM platform by the application, and then the user is prompted with the login prompt to provide username and password as the first step. If those credentials are valid, then the user is prompted to provide the second factor to complete the authentication process. In this example, we have used an OTP as the second factor, and this OTP can be received via an email, SMS, or even generated from an authenticator application in the user's phone. The user will get access to the OTP in one of the previously mentioned methods and type in that code in the second authentication step that is prompted by the IAM platform. If the code is valid, the user is authenticated and redirected back to the application where the user is granted to access the resources of that application. In an adaptive authentication scenario, the second factor will only be prompted based on a certain property of the authenticated user such as the location or device. In addition to the OTP that we used in this example, we can use several other mechanisms as the second factor for strong authentication:

- Security questions – A few questions you can set up during the sign-up process to verify the identity. This is not secure as the other options.

- TOTP – Time-based one-time passwords can be generated by authenticator applications in your mobile device.

- Physical keys – We can use a physical device such as a USB device or a key card that contains a private key that is secured by an asymmetric encryption algorithm can also be used as the second factor.

- Biometrics – The user's physical properties such as fingerprint, iris, or retina can be used as the second factor. This is highly secure but can cause privacy issues.

- Cryptographic challenge response – The server sends a challenge to the client and they need to respond appropriately. This method is highly secure.

Having strong authentication is really important for enterprise applications since the data that are accessed over these applications can be highly sensitive. If you are planning on getting any security compliances such as FEDRAMP, FISMA, or ISO, having a strong authentication is a must.

Multi-option Authentication

If you are building a consumer-focused software system such as an e-commerce website, which is accessed over the Internet frequently, you need to make sure that as many users are allowed to access the system. If you design the system in a way that a new user has to create a user account and remember another set of username and password pairs, there is more chance that certain percentage of users will go away without accessing the system. Instead, if you can provide multiple options to the user to log into the system with some of their existing credentials such as Google, Facebook, or GitHub, that would make life easier for the user and more users will be able to access the system without creating new credentials. This use case is called multi-option authentication. If you are willing to implement strong authentication along with multi-option authentication, you can implement the multi-option method for step1 and keep the step2 of the authentication as a single option since it needs to be more restrictive than the first option. Figure 6-6 depicts the multi-option authentication in an enterprise software system.

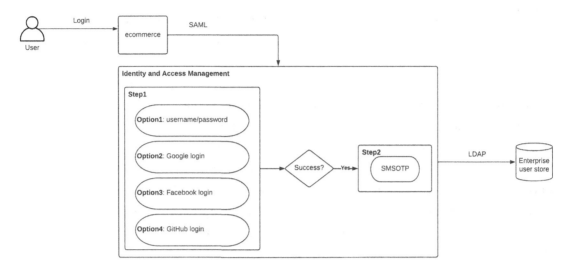

Figure 6-6. *Multi-option authentication for enterprise security*

The figure depicts a use case where a user tries to access an e-commerce website by log in the application. The application redirects the user to the IAM platform, and the user is prompted with a login page that contains multiple options to log in. Depending on the user's preference, they can log in with one of their Internet accounts such as Google, Facebook, or GitHub or a username/password pair that they used to create an account in the e-commerce website in the past. A new user will most probably go with the social login option. If required, we can implement strong authentication with a second factor such as an SMSOTP so that users are protected against any identity theft. Once the user is authenticated, the IAM platform will redirect the user back to the e-commerce web application, and it will use the user details received in the authentication response to create the user profile within the system.

Federated User Provisioning

It is common in enterprises to work with partners and deal with mergers and acquisitions. In such a scenario, these partner systems or the acquired companies might have their own identity providers that they have been using for ages to store the users and authenticate these users. At the same time, as the parent company, your enterprise needs to allow these external users to access the services that are offered by you. There are multiple ways to handle this kind of a scenario. One would be to recreate all the users in the parent enterprise user stores by importing the users via a manual process. Another option would be to provision the users to the parent user store via a federated user provisioning method. We will go with this second option since it is easier to implement and will not disrupt the behaviors of existing users and systems of parent enterprise as well as child enterprises.

To achieve this requirement, we need to configure the IAM platform to consider the IDP of the child enterprise as a trusted IDP for federated authentication. Once the user logs into the application, the user will be redirected to this trusted IDP by the IAM platform, and the user will perform the authentication there. Once the authentication is successful at the trusted IDP, the enterprise IAM platform will retrieve the user details and provision the user into the enterprise user store. This is called the Just-in-Time (JIT) provisioning. During this process, we can offer multiple options to the user to provide a new password and get the user consent for storing user information. This use case is depicted in Figure 6-7.

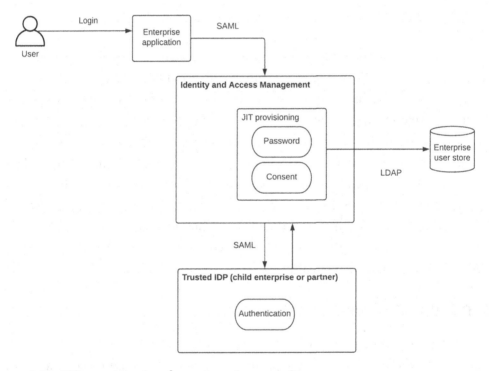

Figure 6-7. *JIT provisioning for enterprise security*

As depicted in the figure, the user who wants to access the enterprise application will be redirected to the enterprise IAM first and then again to the trusted IDP that is running in the child enterprise or partner ecosystem. Once the user is authenticated based on the option provided there, the user is taken back to the enterprise IAM platform and the user will be asked to provide an updated password and updated consent to use the services offered by the enterprise. Once this is successful, from next time onward, the user can directly access the services without federating into the trusted IDP. This mechanism can be used to migrate users from the trusted IDP to the enterprise IAM platform in a seamless manner. It is also possible to provision users to different user stores and domains based on the attributes of the user.

Delegated Access Control

A common problem faced by the web and mobile applications (clients) in the past was that when such a client needs to access a resource (e.g., image) that resides in an external server on behalf of a user (human) who owns the resource, the client needs to prompt the user for credentials again and again. This was not a good user experience to the user. The delegated access control based on Open Authorization 2.0 (OAuth2.0) is the solution for this problem. With this model, the client can acquire a token that is approved by the user to access the resources owned by the user without prompting the user to approve again and again with credentials. This model paved the way for a much improved user experience for mobile and web applications since these tokens can be refreshed automatically by these applications so that clients can use these applications for a longer period without needing to re-login. Figure 6-8 depicts this use case.

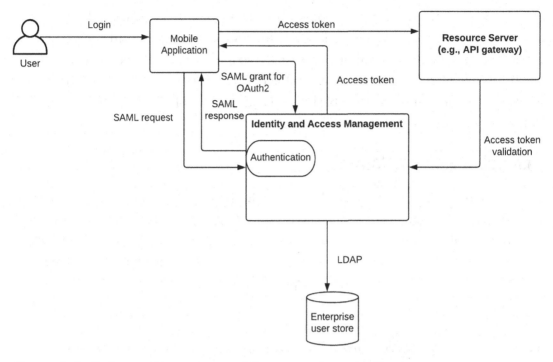

Figure 6-8. *Delegated access control for enterprise security*

The figure depicts a use case where a user tries to log in a mobile application and subsequently access the resources that are residing in a resource server through the same mobile application. The user is first redirected to the IAM platform, and the required authentication steps are completed by the user for a successful authentication. Once that is done, the mobile application will receive the authentication response and uses that response to request an access token from the IAM platform. The IAM platform will exchange the SAML token with the access token and response back to the mobile application with this access token. Then the mobile application will use this access token to access the resources that are residing in the resource server. Once the request is reached to the resource server with the access token, the resource server will validate this token by itself or by calling the IAM platform. If the access token is a valid one, the mobile application will be granted access to the resources residing in the resource server on behalf of the authenticated user.

This mode of delegated access control is becoming the standard for modern web and mobile applications since it reduces the user interference and let the applications run seamlessly.

User Management with Approvals

When we talked about enterprise security use cases, we discussed about different types of users such as customers (B2C), employees (B2E), and partners (B2B). Given that these users need to be managed with their own set of rules and regulations, we need to have a proper mechanism to govern the user onboarding and role assignments. We can use an approval process with the usage of a workflow solution to support this requirement within an IAM platform. There can be workflows defined for different user management tasks such as

- New user creation

- New group creation

- User information change

- User deletion

- User group assignment

- Group information change

- Group deletion

These workflows can be assigned with multistep approvals so that multiple stakeholders need to approve certain user management tasks such as group deletions and group creations. Figure 6-9 depicts the user management workflow in an enterprise environment.

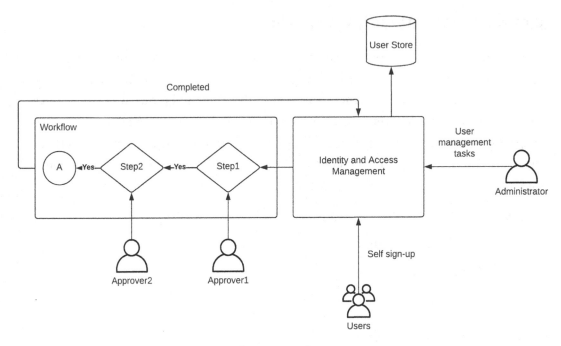

Figure 6-9. *User management with approvals*

As depicted in the figure, the users can be onboarded to the system through a self-sign-up portal or through a manual process that is executed by the system admins. The system admins will execute other user management tasks such as user deletion, user updates, and group creations. The IAM platform can be configured to work with a workflow engine to initiate a workflow for each and every operation such as user creation or group creation. Then this workflow needs to be completed by the respective approvers to finish the workflow, and once it is done, the user management operation will be completed (e.g., user will be created in the user store). Having this kind of a governance process can be really useful since it makes sure that any operation related to the identities and the permissions is properly monitored and managed.

There can be many other use cases and derivatives of these use cases in a real-world enterprise software systems. The use cases that we discussed in the previous section are the most common use cases that you would find across many industries and domains. In the next section, we will discuss a few common security patterns that can be used in enterprise software systems.

Centralized IAM Pattern

Enterprise applications are designed to fulfill a specific set of business use cases such as customer relationships management (CRM), enterprise resource planning (ERP), and human resource management (HRM). Each of these applications must probably be developed by different vendors, and there is a good chance that these applications might use different mechanisms to implement security. Figure 6-10 depicts a typical enterprise software system with different applications that use their own authentication mechanisms for security.

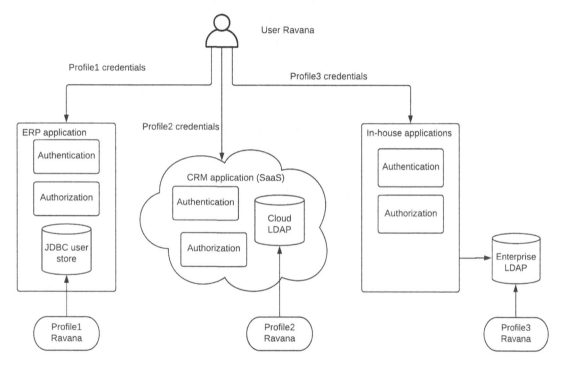

Figure 6-10. *Enterprise security with application-specific security*

The figure illustrates an enterprise where three different applications developed by different teams use in-built security mechanisms to authenticate users to grant access to each application. The figure depicts a user called "Ravana" who has three separate user profiles in three different user stores of the applications. When the user needs to access a specific application, Ravana needs to remember the username/password for each application and provides that to authenticate with the specific application. This approach has many challenges when providing a compelling user experience:

- The user needs to remember multiple usernames and passwords.

- The user needs to log into each application separately.

- Creating, updating, or deleting the user requires updating multiple user stores.

- Implementing modern authentication mechanisms such as strong authentication, social logins, and multi-option authentication requires changes to individual applications.

Due to these challenges and the lack of ability to implement modern authentication and security capabilities, enterprise architecture teams explored possible solutions. This problem was not new in enterprise architecture since these challenges were similar to the challenges faced in integration applications for data sharing. The solution for integration challenge was using a centralized integration component such as an enterprise service bus or ESB. Due to the similarity of application integration and security integration, enterprise architects recognized that using a similar approach would resolve these challenges. It became clear that centralized IAM solution can resolve most of the challenges while allowing the enterprise teams to implement modern security requirements. Figure 6-11 depicts this architecture with a full list of capabilities.

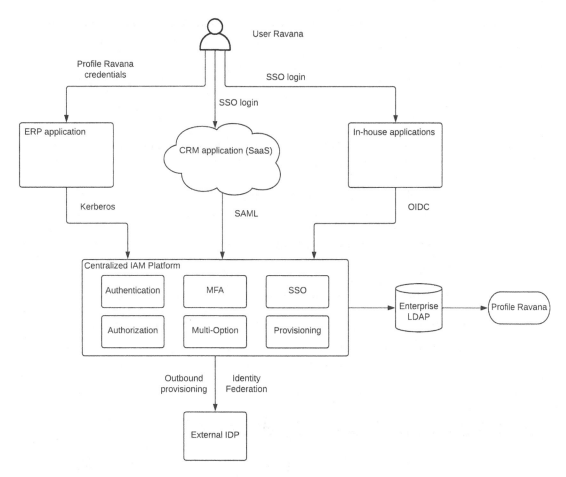

Figure 6-11. *Centralized IAM pattern for enterprise security*

As depicted in the figure, the enterprise applications are connected with a centralized IAM platform. This IAM platform provides the authentication, authorization, and user management capabilities that were implemented within the applications before. There can be challenges when integrating these applications with the IAM platform in case these applications use nonstandard authentication mechanisms. As long as they use standard authentication protocols such as SAML, OIDC, or Kerberos, the integration would be much easier. A flexible IAM platform can cater to nonstandard integrations via extension points so that no application is left behind. In addition to supporting these existing security requirements of these applications, this IAM platform can provide many advanced and modern security features such as SSO, strong authentication, multistep authentication, and inbound/outbound user provisioning to name a few. All of these capabilities can be configured through a centralized component without needing to change the applications drastically. It also supports different IAM use cases such as B2C, B2E, B2B, and other variants of these use cases. A few notable advantages of this architecture includes the following:

- Ability to implement standards-based security for the enterprise software system

- Ability to enhance the user experience through SSO, social logins, and passwordless authentication

- Ability to implement strong authentication with MFA and adaptive authentication

- Ability to support security compliance requirements such as GDPR and FISMA

- Ability to support different use cases such as B2C, B2E, and B2B

In addition to these advantages, this architecture also resolve the challenges we experienced with the previous security model where each application had its own security.

Cloud Application Security Pattern

Enterprise platforms are evolving from using strictly controlled, on-premise applications to more and more cloud-based applications in the recent past. Enterprises are considering a "cloud migration" of enterprise applications to gain benefits that are offered by the cloud platforms. These benefits include

- Cost reductions (operational, infrastructure, and human resources)

- Scalability

- Availability

These benefits are highly enticing for enterprise architects and business leaders given that these are the aspects these leaders always wanted to improve in enterprise software systems. Even though there are practical challenges when achieving these benefits, there are more success stories than failure stories with respect to the benefits achieved with cloud migration.

It might be inevitable that your enterprise goes with the cloud migration route and brings in more and more cloud applications by replacing the existing on-premise applications. As enterprise architects, you should be able to handle these sort of changes through technical solutions. No matter what approach we take to build the enterprise software system, we need to make sure that security of the applications and enterprise data is not compromised. With the onboarding of cloud applications into the enterprise platform, we may experience a new set of challenges that were not there before. These challenges include

- Individual cloud applications have their own mechanisms to authenticate users.

- Creating multiple user accounts and remembering username/ password pairs for each application would be cumbersome for the users.

- Different cloud applications may come with different levels of security (e.g., simple authentication, strong authentication).

- Keeping user profiles at each application level can be challenging when it comes to managing users.

Dealing with these challenges require a mechanism to delegate the authentication, authorization, and user management to an enterprise-controlled IAM platform. We can utilize a cloud-based IAM platform in this scenario since this particular enterprise is going through a cloud migration. But it is not a must since on-premise IAM solution can also handle the challenges mentioned previously. The choice is within the enterprise architecture team. Figure 6-12 depicts a use case where a list of cloud services is configured through a cloud IAM platform to implement security.

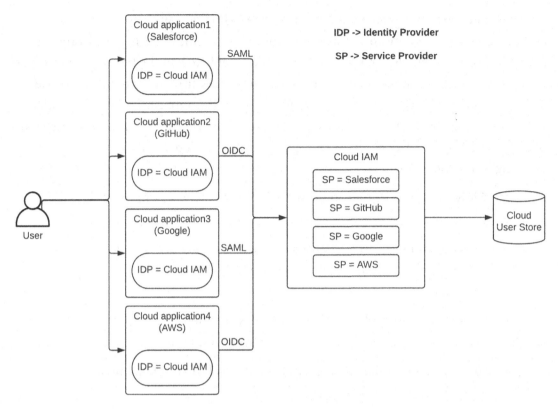

Figure 6-12. *Cloud application security pattern*

The figure depicts a solution that can provide a seamless login experience to the user who needs to access multiple cloud applications securely. This solution has two main components as depicted in the figure. Those are the cloud applications (service providers) and the cloud IAM platform (identity provider). The service providers use the cloud IAM solution as the identity provider and delegate all the authentication and user management tasks to it. This is achieved by configuring the cloud IAM as a federated IDP at each cloud application level. At the same time, cloud IAM platform is configured to consider individual cloud applications as service providers. Each of these applications can have their own security features such as MFA, multi-option login, and adaptive authentication through the configuration of the service provider. Once the configurations are done on both components, the enterprise users could access these applications securely by using their enterprise credentials, and they no longer need to remember different credentials and log into applications separately. All the cloud applications can be configured with SSO and required strong authentication mechanisms. The user management also becomes much easier since users are managed through the cloud IAM. This solution allows the enterprise to onboard more and more cloud applications without worrying about the security and compliance requirements.

Security Federation Pattern

Enterprise platforms need to scale along with the business expansions. As an example, if a particular enterprise is growing fast through a disruptive product innovation or through mergers and acquisitions, the amount of users that needs to be handled by the enterprise platforms becomes a challenge. Instead of onboarding all the users into the enterprise platform, we can think of delegating some of these user management tasks to the respective business partners while controlling the overall security of the enterprise. It will ease out the burden of storing thousands or sometimes millions of external users within your enterprise user store, which would decrease the performance of these user stores significantly. If there is a definite need to migrate these external users to the enterprise user store, then we cannot use this approach. But there can be many situations where the users coming from these third-party businesses or business partners do not need to be added to the enterprise user store. Using an external identity platform to authenticate users is called federated security. Figure 6-13 depicts an example of security federation pattern.

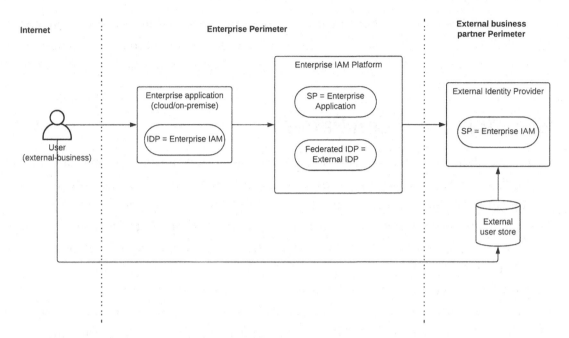

Figure 6-13. *Enterprise security federation pattern*

The figure depicts a use case where a user from an acquired business entity or from a business partner tries to access one of the enterprise applications. In this scenarios, the user has not been moved into the enterprise user store, and the user resides within the external party user store. Once the user tries to log into the application, the user will be redirected to the external IDP through the enterprise IAM. The user will not see the enterprise IAM interaction since it will happen under the hood without notifying the user. Depending on the provided authentication options, the user can log into the system by providing the credentials they had used before. With this model, this user will be able to access new enterprise applications without changing any of their credentials, which is a good user experience.

Configuration-wise, the enterprise application needs to configure the enterprise IAM platform as the identity provider, and the authentication request (e.g., SAML, OIDC) will go to the IAM platform. On the enterprise IAM platform side, we need to configure the enterprise application as a service provider. Under that service provider, we also need to configure the external identity provider as a federated identity provider. That will make sure that the authentication request will be relayed to the external IDP without the user actually seeing it. Finally, on the external IDP side, we need to configure the enterprise

IAM as a service provider so that the relayed authentication request is properly handled and the authentication process executes properly.

Once all these configurations are done, the entire user base that is coming from the business partner becomes an extended user base of the enterprise platform. The enterprise team can decide on which applications need to be granted access to these partners and configure the respective applications accordingly.

API Security Pattern

Application programming interface or API is becoming the de facto standard of exposing business capabilities to client applications such as web applications, mobile applications, and terminal applications. These APIs need to be exposed securely to these client applications since these applications are consumed by both internal and external users. Instead of implementing security for each and every API, most enterprises go with the option of using an API gateway to handle the security for all the APIs. But these API gateways cannot live without an IAM platform or IAM component since authentication, authorization, and user management tasks are too much of a task for an API gateway. In this section, we are going to discuss how an IAM platform can work together with an API gateway or API platform to implement security for enterprise applications that are based on APIs.

API gateways hide the implementation details of the business services such as microservices or integration services from the client applications and provide a standard interface to them so that they can access these APIs without worrying about the internal implementation details. The standards such as Swagger, OpenAPI Specification (OAS), GraphQL, and AsyncAPI are a few examples of standards used by API gateways to expose services. On top of these standards, enterprise teams can use different types of authentication mechanisms to implement security for these APIs. Some common API security mechanisms are

- Basic authentication

- API key-based authentication

- OAuth2-based authentication

Let us discuss these options in detail.

Basic Authentication for API Security

The simplest and most primitive authentication mechanism that can be used for API security is the basic authentication. In this model, the API consumer, which is an application, provides the username/password pair of a user in a Base64-encoded string as the authentication header in the request to the API gateway. Then the API gateway validated these credentials using its built-in authentication component or using an enterprise IAM platform. Figure 6-14 depicts this use case in which an enterprise IAM platform is used to manage the users.

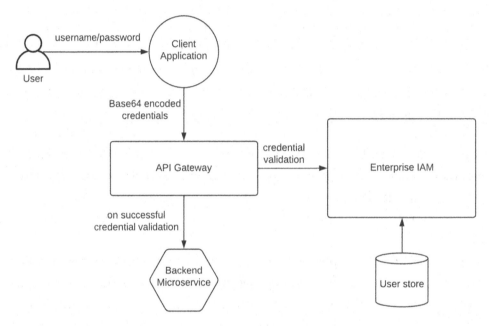

Figure 6-14. *API security with basic authentication*

As depicted in the figure, the client application collects the username and password from the user and uses that credentials to call the API gateway. Once the request with basic authentication details in authorization header comes to the API gateway, it will verify the credentials by calling the enterprise IAM, and if the validation is successful, the request will be allowed to go through to the backend microservice.

This solution is not the most secure approach since collecting user credentials directly from applications is not a recommended due to the fact that these applications can be hacked and the credentials can be leaked. But it is simple to implement, and for an internal application that is running inside an enterprise, this method would be sufficient.

API Key-Based Authentication for API Security

Given that the basic authentication mechanism raises concerns over credential leakage, the API key-based authentication provides an alternative approach while keeping the simplicity to a certain extent. Instead of using the end user credentials (e.g., username/password), this method uses an API key that is provided by the API owners to the client. This key is just a random number sequence, and it does not have any context outside the API gateway and the IAM solution. Any leakage of a key will not leak the actual user credentials. But it can allow an intruder to access the APIs for a given time, which can be avoided by properly protecting the API keys. Figure 6-15 depicts this use case.

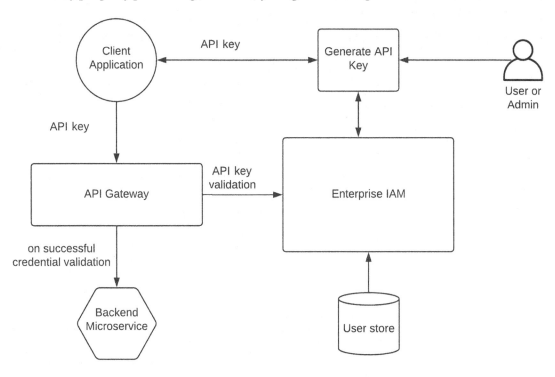

Figure 6-15. *API key-based security for enterprise APIs*

As depicted in the figure, the user or an API admin will generate an API key by logging into the IAM platform and then handing it over to the client application. This key typically contains a random character sequence (opaque token) that does not have any meaning unless it is deciphered by the IAM platform that generated the token. When the client application requires to access a backend microservice via the API gateway, it will send the API key via an HTTP header to the API gateway, and it will connect to the IAM platform and validate the API key. If the key is valid, the request will be allowed to pass through to the backend microservice.

Delegated Authentication with OAuth2 for API Security

Both the previously mentioned mechanisms require a credential to be given to the client application through a manual process. This can cause security issues when storing the credentials within the source code of the client application. We can get rid of this manual intervention by using OAuth2-based delegated authentication for API security. With this model, the client application does not need to store the credentials of the user such as username/password or an API key. Instead, it can dynamically retrieve a token that is generated with the user consent. These tokens can have a predefined expiration, and the client application can automatically refresh the token whenever necessary. Figure 6-16 depicts the usage of delegated authentication for API security.

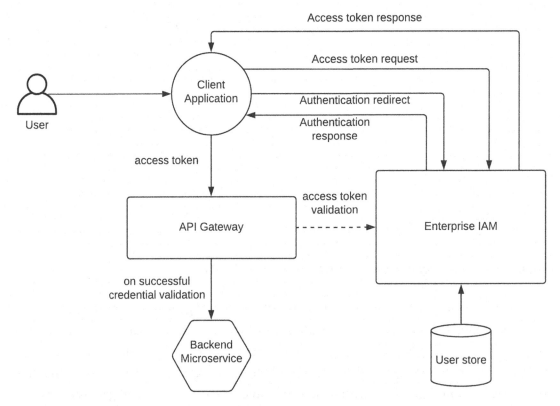

Figure 6-16. *API security with access delegation using OAuth2*

As depicted in the figure, the user is first authenticated with the IAM platform, and the client application will retrieve the authentication response with the details to get an access token. Depending on the OAuth2 grant type in use, the details on the authentication response are used to request an access token from the IAM platform by the client application. Once the client application received this access token, it will use that token to call the API gateway with the access token included in the "Authorization" header. Depending on the access token type (e.g., opaque JWT or self-contained JWT), the gateway will either contact the IAM platform to validate the credentials and grant access to the backend microservice from the client application.

This solution has several benefits over the other two methods mentioned previously:

- Authentication of the user can be done with more flexibility (e.g., strong authentication, MFA) since the authentication happens through the IAM platform.

- User credentials are not directly shared with the client application.

- No need to store static API keys in the source code.

- Leakage of a token can be mitigated with best practices such as short token lifespan, token revocation, and access controls at the API gateway level.

In general, OAuth2-based delegated authentication is becoming a best practice within the industry given that the client applications can support such a model. The enterprise architects need to evaluate the client applications that are going to access the APIs and make the decision on which approach they are going to use to secure the APIs. We only discussed about the security at the gateway layer. The zero-trust architecture suggests security at services layer as well. In the next section, we will discuss the security of microservices.

Microservices Security Pattern

Microservice architecture suggests a decentralized architecture where individual microservices are developed, deployed, and maintained independently. Implementing security for microservices can also be done within each microservice. But implementing the same capability repeatedly within each microservice can be an overkill and a waste of engineering resources. Hence, we can use a dedicated security component to provide security for microservices. In the preceding section, we discussed about securing the communications coming from outside (north-south traffic) using an API gateway. In this section, we are going to focus on implementing security for interservice communication (east-west traffic) within a microservice architecture. This interservice communication can utilize different protocols such as HTTP and gRPC for synchronous communication and Kafka and NATS for asynchronous communication. The security architecture that we design should cater to any of these communication models.

The real challenge here is that the microservices promote the decentralized architecture, while IAM platform that we discussed so far promotes the centralized architecture. Let us discuss both the centralized and decentralized security architectures for microservices.

Security with Centralized IAM

Let us start with the centralized IAM architecture that we utilized so far in this chapter. In a typical interservice communication scenario, we need to focus on securing the microservices by passing the user context among microservices in a secured way. During the API security section, we discussed about using OAuth2-based access tokens (JWT) to secure the edge of the microservice architecture at the API gateway. This access token contains the contextual information related to the user within the JWT. We can use that to pass the context to the individual microservices layer as depicted in Figure 6-17.

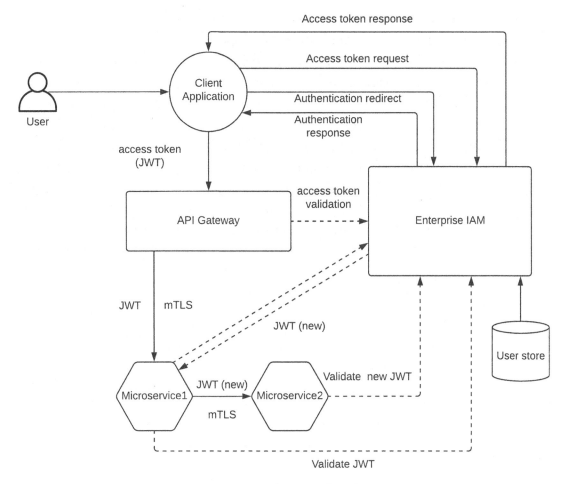

Figure 6-17. *Microservices security with centralized IAM*

The figure depicts a scenario where the client application has presented an access token (JWT) to the API gateway to access the microservice1, which will eventually access the microservice2. Here, we have used mutual authentication (mTLS) for certificate validation at the API gateway to microservice and inter-microservice communication as an additional security measure. This measure is taken to enforce the zero-trust architecture and make sure the client who is accessing the microservice is a trusted client. Once the API gateway validates the JWT received from the client application, it will pass that JWT token or generate a new JWT token with the user context and pass it to the microservice1. In the scenario depicted in the figure, the API gateway passes the same JWT to the microservice1. Then this microservice will validate the JWT by calling the centralized IAM component, and then when it needs to call microservice2, it can also pass the same JWT or generate a new JWT. In this case, we are generating a new JWT by calling the IAM component and then pass it to the microservice2. Then the microservice2 will talk to the IAM component and validate this new JWT for authentication and authorization before allowing the access to the data. That will conclude the end-to-end communication from the client application to the microservice1 and microservice2 in a secure manner.

We can improve the overall latency of the flow by using a self-contained JWT at each level so that the microservices and the API gateway can validate the token itself without calling the IAM platform. But it comes with its own limitation such as complex implementations at the microservices level. But it is an option if you have problems with the latency of the overall security validation process. One solution to handle complexity of token validation at the microservice level is to use a service mesh technology with a sidecar proxy as depicted in Figure 6-18.

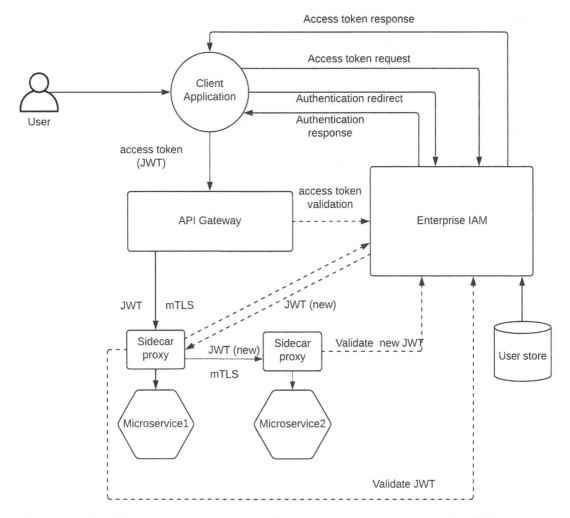

Figure 6-18. *Microservices security with sidecar proxy and centralized IAM*

The major difference in the figure from Figure 6-17 is that the security-related interactions are done at the sidecar proxy level since all the incoming and outgoing traffic is passing through it. Most of the service mesh implementations such as Istio and Linkerd provide a separate control plane component to configure the security policies at the sidecar proxy layer without changing the microservice implementation. Even though this solution adds a bit more complexity to the overall solution, if you are looking for a way to offload the security handling outside of the microservices, this is a viable solution.

Security with Decentralized IAM

The true nature of the microservice architecture is to have a decentralized components at each layer and make every microservice an independent unit that can be developed, deployed, and maintained separately. Having a centralized IAM solution in such an architecture can be an anti-pattern for some of us. That is where the concept of decentralized IAM pattern comes into rescue. Instead of using an IAM component that is deployed in a monolithic pattern, we can run micro-IAM component along with the microservices to implement security. The Open Policy Agent (OPA) project tries to implement such a solution for microservices security. Figure 6-19 depicts this architecture.

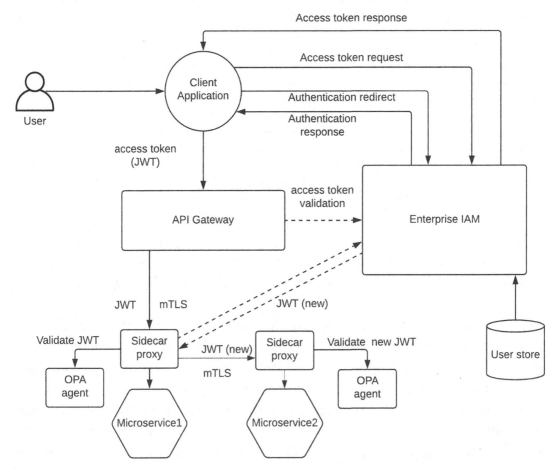

Figure 6-19. *Microservices security with OPA agent*

The figure depicts how we can use OPA agents to implement the security validations at each microservice level instead of contacting a centralized IAM platform. Here the user will log into the authentication system (e.g., LDAP/AD or IAM platform) and generate an access token that can be utilized by the client application. Then the client will pass that JWT token to the API gateway, and it will pass it back to the microservice1. Then the microservice1 will have a sidecar proxy that will receive the request and call the OPA agent to validate the JWT token for authentication and authorization. Here we have removed the need for having the centralized IAM component for JWT validation. If the JWT is valid, the microservice1 will either pass the same JWT or generate a new JWT by contacting the centralized IAM and pass the new JWT to microservice2. Then the sidecar proxy running alongside the microservice2 will validate that new JWT token with the OPA agent running alongside the microservice2. In a Kubernetes environment, all three components (microservice, sidecar proxy, and OPA agent) will run on the same pod so that they can communicate over localhost network interface. OPA agent can be configured through an external CLI tool using the REST interface exposed by the agent. Figure 6-20 depicts how this model works in a Kubernetes architecture.

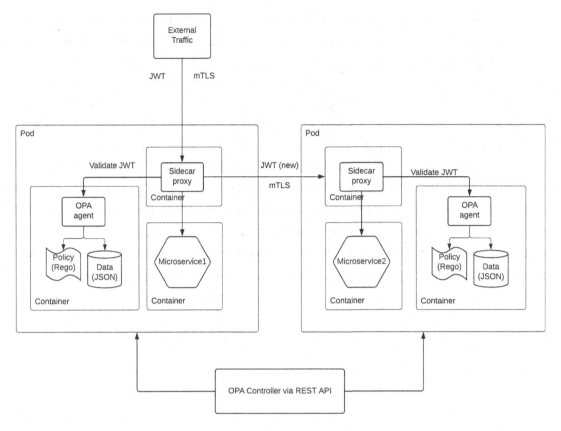

Figure 6-20. *Microservices security with OPA in Kubernetes*

The figure depicts how OPA-based security can be used to implement security for microservices in a Kubernetes environment. Here the microservice, sidecar proxy, and the OPA agent run on their own containers within the same pod. This pod can be used to replicate the same microservice and scale it based on the demand. OPA stores its policies and data as separate entities in the file system to isolate the policy from the OPA agent. These policies and data element can be updated through the REST API exposed at the OPA agent through a REST client such as Postman and SoapUI or through the CLI tool provided by OPA framework itself.

In addition to the aforementioned deployment model, OPA agent can also be integrated to the microservice itself as a library, and we can get rid of the sidecar proxy to simplify the deployment architecture. This mode of deployment is depicted in Figure 6-21.

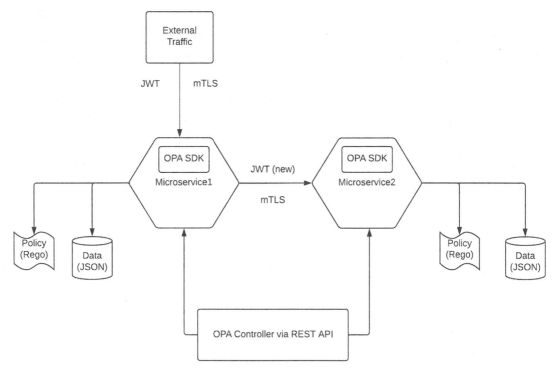

Figure 6-21. *Microservices security with OPA SDK*

The figure depicts a scenario where we have used the OPA SDK to embed the security capabilities provided by OPA within the microservices itself. With this model, we can reduce the deployment complexity since the token validation happens inside the microservice itself. One important point to note here is that still the policy and the data reside outside of the microservice so that we can control them without changing the microservice code. OPA provides SDKs for different languages and a lot of popular tools such as Kubernetes, Docker, Envoy, and Kafka.

Summary

In this chapter, we discussed the importance of security in an enterprise ecosystem and how to implement security for different use cases that we come across within those environments. We started the chapter by introducing the security requirements within the enterprise software systems and discussed about key aspects of data security and application security. Then we moved on to discussing some of the common use cases of enterprise security with examples. We discussed about the centralized identity and access management pattern and the benefits of using such a model. We also discussed about securing cloud applications within the enterprise environments with an enterprise IAM platform. Then we moved on to discussing security federation, which is a key requirement for enterprises that work with business partners and do mergers and acquisitions. We then discussed one of the hottest topics in the security industry, which is API security. There we discussed about different mechanisms we can use to secure the ever-growing API ecosystems. Finally, we discussed about another popular and demanding security topic, which is microservices security. There we discussed about implementing interservice security within a microservice architecture.

CHAPTER 7

Implementing Observability for Enterprise Software Systems

Distributed computer systems increase the number of communication links required to perform a certain computing task. These communication links can fail due to many reasons such as hardware failures, firmware bugs, or software bugs. Hence, the more distributed the system is, the more chance that a particular component can fail, and hence, the overall system stability is impacted. But this is not something we can avoid since the benefits of distributed systems outrank the challenges they pose. Instead, we can design these systems to withstand failure and continue. There are three main aspects that we need to deal with when implementing and maintaining distributed systems in a robust manner:

- Make the system observable.

- Monitor the system continuously.

- Take remedial measures to fix the failures.

If the failure is inevitable in a distributed system, we can make the system observable so that we can measure the external outputs of the system and decide on the internal state of the system. Observability is a characteristic of the overall system that lets system owners understand the internal states of the system by examining the external outputs it produces. We need to have proper mechanisms to monitor these external outputs so that when there is a failure, we can derive the internal states of the system and identify

© Chanaka Fernando 2023
C. Fernando, *Solution Architecture Patterns for Enterprise*, https://doi.org/10.1007/978-1-4842-8948-8_7

the root cause of the failure. Once the root cause is identified, we can take corrective measures to keep the system running. We can go a step further and make sure that failures are detected earlier through proactive measures such as defining threshold values to certain parameters that can cause system failures. With that, we can take corrective measures before the actual failure and avoid as many failures as possible. In an enterprise landscape, handling failures and avoiding every possible failure are critical to the overall business success.

In this chapter, we are going to discuss the importance of having proper observability measures in an enterprise software system. We will cover the following topics in detail in this chapter:

- What is observability?

- Tools available for observability

- Observability reference architecture for enterprise

- ELK, Jaeger, and Prometheus-based observability pattern

- Grafana, Tempo, and Prometheus-based observability pattern

- Let us start with an introduction to the concept of observability and the importance of observability in an enterprise ecosystem.

What Is Observability?

Observability is not a new concept in the world of technology. It is a term used in control theory to describe a property of the system that is defined as how engineers can infer the internal states of a system by examining the system's external outputs. We say that a system is observable if its current state can be derived using only the external outputs of the system. If the external outputs of a system are not sufficient, we cannot derive the internal states of the system, and the system becomes hard to observe and recover during failures.

Let us try to adopt the control theory definition of observability to the enterprise software domain. In a distributed enterprise software system, we have heterogenous systems that are developed by different vendors and teams. These systems generate external outputs in the form of log files such as access logs, audit logs, error logs, and application logs. Producing these outputs into log files and other output devices such as terminals from the application is called instrumentation, and the data that is produced is called telemetry data. In typical enterprise software systems, observability uses three types of telemetry data:

- Logs

- Metrics

- Traces

Logs are the data events produced by applications during the execution of their functionality. Typically, log events are published to log files, and these files can be categorized based on the data type included in the log entry. As an example, if the log event contains an error that just occurred in the application, the log entry would go to a dedicated error log file. Another example would be a log event that contains a login attempt by a user. Such a log event would publish data to a separate audit log file. Using logs for observability is the most common approach followed by many enterprises and cloud platforms out there. We will talk about using log-based approach for observability in detail in this chapter.

Metrics are a mechanism to understand the behavior of the system by examining the statistical information about it. There are different levels of metrics used by the SRE teams to determine the current status of the system. An example is the infrastructure level details associated with the application such as CPU usage and memory usage. Continuously capturing this information and monitoring it via a network operations center (NOC) would help the enterprise teams to identify possible failures ahead of time.

There can be situations where we need to identify what exact message has caused the failure of the system. By using standard application logs, we can identify which component the issue has occurred and the location of the source code. But to find the actual data that caused the issue, we need tracing of messages to be enabled. Tracing allows us to keep track of data that flows through a system. Tracing is a bit costly operation since it requires us to clone the messages and store them in a secure place. It would reduce the performance of the system due to the time it takes to build the actual messages inside memory before pushing into trace logs or tracing databases. Most systems implement tracing as an optional feature so that users can enable and disable it as and when required.

Modern enterprise systems are becoming more and more complex and distributed with the introduction of new applications and systems that are running on-premise, cloud, and hybrid infrastructures. A single query that is originating from a client application such as a website can traverse through multiple applications and systems within the enterprise system. In such a scenario, a failure can happen in any of these applications and systems. Without a proper observability solution, finding the root cause of such a scenario can be difficult, and hence, the recovery can be highly costly for the entire organization. Hence, it is obvious that having a proper observability foundation in your enterprise software system is really important.

Benefits of Observability

The following is a list of advantages we gain by designing an observable platform:

- Ability to provide better user experience by mitigating failures quickly and avoiding possible failures of the system

- Ability to allow teams to improve the efficiency of the system and fuel innovation and growth using metrics

- Ability to keep operational data in one place so that audit and compliance requirements can be met without much hassle

Let us discuss these benefits in detail so that we understand the value of observability properly.

Observability allows developers and architects to create improved user experience by collecting, analyzing, correlating, and alerting based on the captured data. We can identify the gaps in user experience using the telemetry data captured through observability tools and make the necessary changes to the applications to fill these gaps. With a proper alerting mechanism, we can identify the failures ahead of time and take necessary actions to avoid such failures. Also, in case an error occurs, we can automatically notify the relevant stakeholders and perform the remediation as soon as possible without waiting for customer complaints. The metrics and insights into the application usage allow the development team to scale the required services effectively and innovate new services based on the user demand. In addition to improving user experience, observability helps internal teams to improve the efficiency of their daily operations as well. These teams can observe the time taken to retrieve a response from an internal microservice and work on improving the performance of the backend microservice so that the overall response time of the application is improved. Additionally, with tracing enabled, we can keep track of all the data that is flowing through the system during a given time period (e.g., 3 months) and use this data for audit and compliance purposes, which otherwise would be a tedious task to recover this data.

Observability vs. Monitoring

One of the common misconceptions in the world of enterprise software is "observability is same as monitoring." But in reality, these two are separate yet interconnected concepts. The following is a comparison of observability and monitoring:

Observability	Monitoring
Property of the system (noun)	Action perform on the system (verb)
Produces data	Consumes data
Implemented internally in each system	External tool to capture data
Allows you to find out the root cause	Lets you know if the system works

Even though observability and monitoring are two different concepts, they are related to each other. Monitoring of a system relies on the observability features of the system. As an example, a performance monitoring dashboard relies on the performance data published by the application through the observability tools.

Let us take a look at how we can implement observability within an enterprise software system.

Implementing Observability

Implementing observability requires a change in mindset in your developers. Most of the time, developers write code that is less verbose, and understanding such a program requires a significant time. The solution for that is adding comments and documentation annotations to the source code so that anyone who has access to the source code can easily understand what is actually going on inside the code. Similarly, if we are to implement observability for any application, developers need to change their mindset to instrument the code with proper telemetry events. Once the code is instrumented properly to reflect the internal state of the application from the external outputs, we can use external tools to capture these events and troubleshoot issues properly. We can identify four main aspects we need to deal with when implementing observability:

- Instrumentation
- Correlation
- Automation
- Insights and predictions

Let us discuss these aspects in detail.

Instrumentation

Applications need to generate the telemetry data within the source code and publish them to output channels such as log files and APIs so that external tools such as log scrapers or client applications can collect this information. Using an open standard for data publishing lets external tools collect this telemetry data easily and process them without needing additional customizations.

Data Correlation

Once the telemetry data is published through the instrumentation, this data needs to be collected and analyzed to derive the context and correlation data. Let's say we identified that a system is not responding and we need to go through the log files of multiple applications to identify and trace the execution path of a certain request (message), which might have caused the problem. In such a scenario, having the correlation across applications is important to trace that particular request and find out the root cause of the failure.

Automation

Systems fail at unexpected times and situations. Having people monitoring each and every log file in the system is a costly operation that would not be welcomed by business leaders. But they need the system to be up and running without problems. The way to achieve both these requirements is to implement proper incident management solution with automation using thresholds and alerts. We can use observability monitoring tools to capture the failure events and automatically filter them and generate alerts to the respective stakeholders without any delay so that they attend to these failures. At the same time, we can also put preventive measures with proper threshold to identify the possible failures ahead of time and send notifications to the respective individuals to take the necessary actions.

Insights and Predictions

We can use the observability data to not only respond to failures and avoid such failures but also to improve user experience and innovate. The mechanism to achieve the latter is to generate insights and predictions based on the telemetry data captured from the observability tools. We can use metrics to understand the usage patterns and performance details of the services so that we can make the right decisions when scaling the components and developing new services. With the usage of artificial intelligence and machine learning techniques, we can make predictions based on the collected data and offer unique value to the customers ahead of competitors.

It is evident that we need to build an architecture to implement observability for a software system. The major functionality that is required includes the following:

- Event (data) publishing

- Data collection

- Data analysis

- Alerting

Figure 7-1 depicts how these functional components work together to implement an observability solution for an enterprise software system.

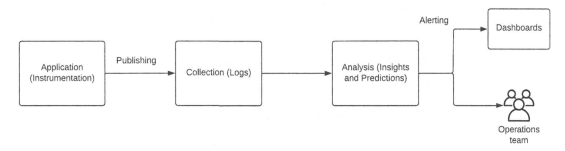

Figure 7-1. *Implementing observability – functional components*

As depicted in the figure, the applications are the sources of events that publish telemetry data through instrumentation. These events are collected by monitoring tools for further processing. These event collectors can be log aggregation systems or some applications that extract statistical data from the APIs exposed by the application. Then this collected data is analyzed to generate insights and predictions as well as alerts based on certain thresholds and conditions. This information is then published to a set of consumers such as dashboards or operations team members depending on the context of the data.

Based on the points that we discussed so far, it is clear that we need to use proper tools to implement a proper observability solution for a software system. Let us discuss these tools in the next section.

Tools Available for Observability

Observability of an enterprise software system depends on the application source code, the monitoring tools, and the analytical capabilities of these tools and the users who use these tools. In this section, we are going to discuss about the tools that we can use to implement an observability solution for an enterprise software system.

Observability with Logs

The first step in implementing observability is to instrument the application source code so that the relevant telemetry data (events) are published from the application into the observability backend systems (collectors). If we think about a modern enterprise platform, we can identify different types of software components such as

- Operating systems (e.g., Linux)

- Virtualization software (e.g., VMware)

- Containerization software (e.g., Docker)

- Container orchestration software (e.g., Kubernetes)

- Application software (e.g., on-premise, SaaS, hybrid)

  - Core business applications (e.g., microservices)

  - Commercial off-the-shelf applications (e.g., SAP)

  - Integration/API applications (e.g., API Manager)

  - Software-as-a-service applications (e.g., Salesforce)

To design an observability solution covering all types of applications is a challenging task since these applications are developed by different teams. Having said that, almost all of these applications produce logs that contain data related to the application execution. We can start with these logs and aggregate these logs into a single platform. Figure 7-2 depicts an architecture where we collect application logs from different software components and use that information to derive context and insights related to overall system behavior and performance.

238

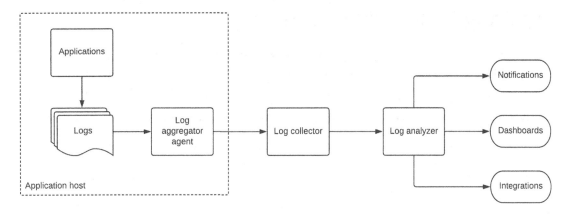

Figure 7-2. *Observability with logs*

As depicted in the figure, different types of applications expose the internal states of those applications as external outputs using logs. These logs can be aggregated or read by an agent, which is running alongside the application. The task of this agent is to read the log entries and publish them into the log collector, which will collect these log entries and pre-process them for further analysis by the log analyzer. Through the log analyzer, the users can either directly analyze the logs with some query language or use an external dashboard component to analyze the logs. There are many open source and proprietary solutions available for implementing a solution that is depicted in this figure. Some popular tools are

- ELK (Elasticsearch, Logstash, and Kibana) stack

- Grafana Labs

- Splunk

- Dynatrace

- New Relic

- Sumo Logic

In addition to these tools, if you are running your entire application stack within a cloud infrastructure such as AWS, Azure, or Google Cloud, those platforms offer native log monitoring tools for implementing observability on their respective infrastructure. The solutions mentioned previously can run in almost any type of infrastructure such as on-premise, cloud, or hybrid. Out of the aforementioned solutions, both Elastic (ELK) and Grafana Labs offer open source solutions in addition to commercial offerings. We will be talking about these two tools in a bit detail in the following sections.

Log-Based Observability with ELK

Elasticsearch, Logstash, and Kibana are a set of tools that we can use to implement observability for a software system based on log files. It consists of these three components which read log files, collect and aggregate them and index them for further analysis and exploration. Figure 7-3 depicts how these components work together to implement observability.

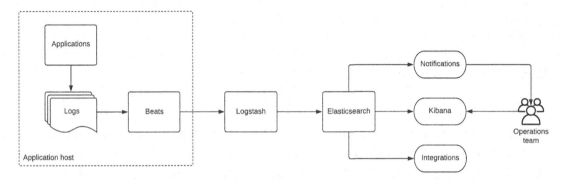

Figure 7-3. *Log-based observability with ELK*

As depicted in the figure, the beats agents running alongside the application read the log files and push those log entries toward Logstash, which acts as the log aggregator. Then Logstash stores these aggregated logs into its unique storage and does the indexing, search, and analysis of the data stored in the log files. Kibana lets users interactively explore, visualize, and share insights and monitor the system in a visual dashboard. Elasticsearch is a powerful tool that can analyze different types of data such as structured, unstructured, numerical, textual, or geospatial data so that users can derive valuable insights and contextual information from the data.

Log-Based Observability with Grafana

Another popular tool for implementing observability with logs is Grafana Loki. It also provides a set of tools to collect, analyze, and represent data stored in log files. It uses a trio of components called Promtail, Loki, and Grafana to perform this log-based analysis. Figure 7-4 depicts how these components work together to implement observability based on log files.

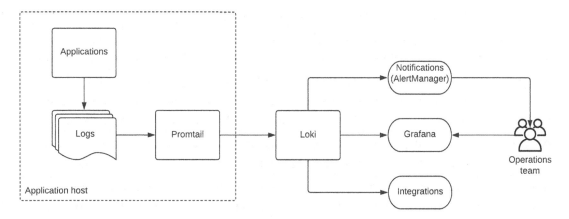

Figure 7-4. *Log-based observability with Grafana*

As depicted in the figure, Promtail collects logs from the application log files and pushes these log data to Loki, which acts as the log aggregator and stores these log entries into a group of streams with labels used for indexing. Here, Promtail can perform additional tasks such as labeling, transforming, and filtering before publishing log events to Loki. The log data that is stored in Loki can be queried directly using a powerful query language called LogQL. You can run these LogQL queries from the Grafana or using LogCLI, which is a command-line interface to interact with Loki. Finally, we can use Grafana to interactively search, explore, and analyze the log details with LogQL or create dashboards.

Observability with Traces

Implementing log-based observability is a good starting point, and that is the maximum we can do without changing the applications that are running inside an enterprise software system. With the power of the analysis tool, we can derive valuable insights on what has happened during a failure and understand the internal states of the application with the log entries. But due to the inconsistency of the data published by different applications, sometimes, finding the root cause of a failure can be difficult due to the lack of context propagation across these tools. As an example, to identify a particular message that traverses through multiple applications within an enterprise software system, we need to use some sort of UUID that is included in all the log entries from different applications. But sometimes, some of the applications may not print this detail in their log entry, and hence, it becomes a tedious task to identify that particular message from that log file, and hence, the entire troubleshooting can become much complicated.

What this means is that we need to have a common way of publishing observability data from applications so that we can correlate that information when needed. There have been several libraries and frameworks used in the past to standardize the logging, but those libraries were specific to a certain framework or programming language. As an example, for Java, people used Log4j as a common logging framework. But if you have applications developed with .Net or Python or Go, you cannot use the same library. Hence, enterprise teams decided to come up with a common framework to instrument applications and publish telemetry data from applications. That is where the OpenTelemetry standard was created.

OpenTelemetry for Distributed Tracing

Due to the lack of standardization in the applications and log monitoring tools, the technology community came up with two open source projects called OpenTracing and OpenCensus. These projects were designed to complement each other to provide a vendor neutral mechanism to publish telemetry data.

- The OpenTracing project was targeted to develop a vendor-neutral API for publishing telemetry data over to an observability backend.

- The OpenCensus project was designed to provide a set of language-specific libraries to instrument code and publish telemetry data to one of the supported observability backends.

Given the fact that both these projects were trying to achieve the same goal through a complemented approach, the community decided to merge these two projects into a single project called OpenTelemetry (OTel). It provides capabilities such as

- Language-specific libraries to instrument application code automatically and manually

- A common collector binary that can be deployed in the infrastructure of your choice

- A complete, standard process to produce, collect, and process telemetry data

It is not that easy to get the support from different open source and proprietary vendors to support such a new standard given the competitive nature of the observability landscape. But OpenTelemetry has been embraced by the observability community better than expected. There are observability backends developed to receive OTel instrumented events by major vendors including the following:

- Splunk

- Zipkin

- Jaeger

- Prometheus

- Elasticsearch

- Google

- AWS

- Azure

OpenTelemetry allows publishing telemetry data through "signals." There are four main types of signals supported by the specification as of this writing:

1. Traces – Details of a message and the activities happening around that message

2. Metrics – Statistics or measurements about a particular service

3. Logs – Textual record with a timestamp in a structured or unstructured format

4. Baggage – Additional contextual information passed between spans

These signals allow us to implement a full observability solution using the OTel standard, and if we are to change the observability backends in the future due to some reason, we can migrate the observability solution across different vendors without much hassle. Let us discuss how we can implement an observability solution with OTel using some of the open source tools available.

OpenTelemetry with Jaeger

Jaeger is a distributed tracing platform that is open source and used to implement observability solutions for modern cloud-native applications. It helps operations teams to capture traces across multiple applications and use that information to troubleshoot issues and improve the performance of the system. Before jumping into the solution architecture of Jaeger, let us define some key terms used in distributed tracing.

Span

A span represents a single operation related to a request. It captures specific tasks related to the operation for that request and provides a complete picture of what has happened during the time of the operation. It contains a name, start and end timestamps, structured log messages, and other metadata to describe the operation. Spans can be nested in a parent-child relationship to represent suboperations. Figure 7-5 depicts a span with a few child pans.

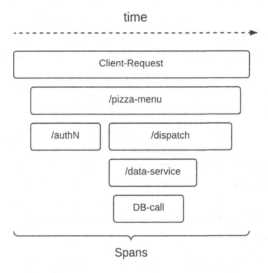

Figure 7-5. *Spans in a distributed tracing scenario*

The figure depicts a sample use case where a client makes a request to an API to get details of a Pizza menu. The parent span is the client request that invokes a child span that has details on the API call to the /pizza-menu endpoint. This call then invokes two more child spans for authentication and dispatching to the backend data service. Then the /dispatch endpoint will call the /data-service endpoint, and it will eventually call the database to get the details of the available pizzas during that time of the day.

Trace

A trace or a distributed trace tracks the paths executed by a request as it traverses through multiple services in an enterprise platform. It provides us the overall picture of what actually happened for a given request in a distributed system. Tracing helps us to troubleshoot failures and identify performance bottlenecks. Figure 7-6 depicts a trace of the pizza menu example we discussed in the preceding section.

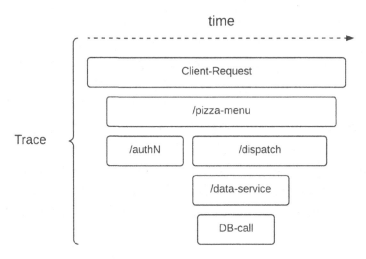

Figure 7-6. *A trace in a distributed application*

As depicted in the figure, a trace consists of one or more spans. The first span is the root span that represents a request from start to end. The child spans provide in-depth information about the operation.

Now we have an understanding of the main concepts used in Jaeger with OpenTelemetry for capturing observability data. Let us discuss how this can be implemented with a real-world use case. Figure 7-7 depicts a sample use case where an application uses OpenTelemetry Protocol (OTLP) to publish observability data to a Jaeger-based observability backend.

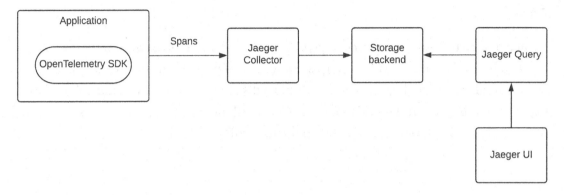

Figure 7-7. *Observability with a Jaeger example*

The figure depicts a use case where an application is utilizing OpenTelemetry-based SDK to instrument the application and publish telemetry data as spans to the Jaeger collector, which will validate and transform the data before storing that in a storage backend. The storage backend can be an in-memory store, Elasticsearch, Kafka, or a database. Once the data is stored in the storage backend, the Jaeger query component will execute search and query operations to retrieve the traces, which will be visualized in the Jaeger UI.

Observability with Metrics

Measuring the systems state using metrics is another important aspect of implementing observability. The logs and traces that we discussed in the preceding section capture textual, verbose information about the system, and that information helps immensely to identify the root causes of failures. The metrics provide a numerical representation of the current state and the behavior of the system over a period of time. They allow the enterprise teams to tune up the system to provide better performance and avoid any failures in the future. Even though OpenTelemetry Protocol (OTLP) provides the ability to publish metrics-related data from applications in a vendor-independent manner, it is not yet optimized for metrics. Prometheus has become the popular choice for implementing metrics-based observability at the time of this writing. Hence, we are going to talk about Prometheus-based metrics capturing in this section.

Prometheus for Metrics-Based Observability

Prometheus is an open source system for collecting and storing metrics as time series data. In simple terms, metrics are numeric measurements of a system such as the uptime, response time, or transactions per second (TPS). The data collected by Prometheus are stored with the timestamp at which it was recorded, along with optional key-value pairs called labels. Prometheus uses a pull model to collect the data from the applications. It also supports a push model with the usage of an intermediary gateway. The applications that Prometheus needs to connect with (called targets) can be configured statically or can be discovered dynamically using a service discovery mechanism. The data stored in Prometheus can be queried through a query language called PromQL, and it can be consumed by various data visualization tools such as Grafana and other API-based clients. The stored data can also be used to generate real-time alerts based on thresholds to avoid possible failures via the AlertManager component, which can send notifications via emails, pagerduty system, and other mechanisms. Figure 7-8 depicts the architecture of using Prometheus to capture the metrics from applications.

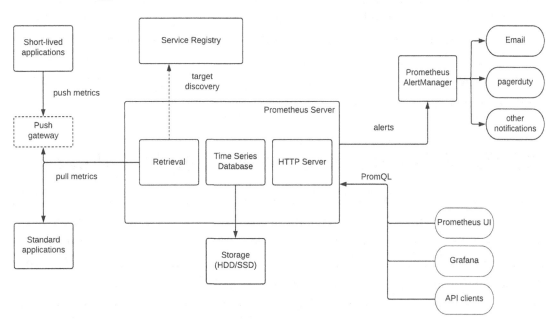

Figure 7-8. *Prometheus component architecture*

The figure depicts the high-level components of Prometheus metrics-based observability solution. The default mode of capturing metrics information is using the pull method where Prometheus is configured statically or dynamically with the target applications, which exposes metrics endpoints. Prometheus provides a set of client libraries to instrument the applications to expose metrics data through APIs so that Prometheus can pull data from. In addition to that, Prometheus also provides a set of exporters to popular systems such as databases, message brokers, proxy servers, and many other applications, which would collect the existing metrics and expose them as Prometheus metrics in case we cannot modify the application with Prometheus instrumentation. This is really useful in enterprise systems since there are many applications that we cannot change the behavior by injecting code. Additionally, if there are short-lived applications that complete the execution within a given time duration, those applications can push metrics at the end of the execution, and a push gateway can be used to capture that information and relay it to the Prometheus server via the pull method. Once the metrics data is received, it will be stored in the time series database model, which will eventually store the data in a disk that is connected to the same server that the Prometheus is running. This stored information will be exposed through an HTTP server so that interested client applications can consume it via PromQL interface. These clients include Prometheus Web UI, Grafana, and API clients. Additionally, you can configure alerts through the Prometheus Server configuration, which will push these alerts to the Prometheus AlertManager component, which can disburse these notifications via different channels such as email and pagerduty.

Observability Reference Architecture for Enterprise

Enterprise software systems consist of heterogeneous applications and systems that are developed by different development teams. In any given enterprise platform, there will be some applications and systems that are developed by internal teams unless it is a small enterprise with few team members. Also, there will be some applications that are developed by third-party vendors. When we are designing an observability solution, we need to include all these applications since these applications usually integrate with one another during the business operations. Hence, it is important to understand how we can include these different types of applications into our overall observability solution without disrupting the applications unnecessarily. Let us start with a typical enterprise platform that has all kinds of applications in it. Figure 7-9 depicts such a platform.

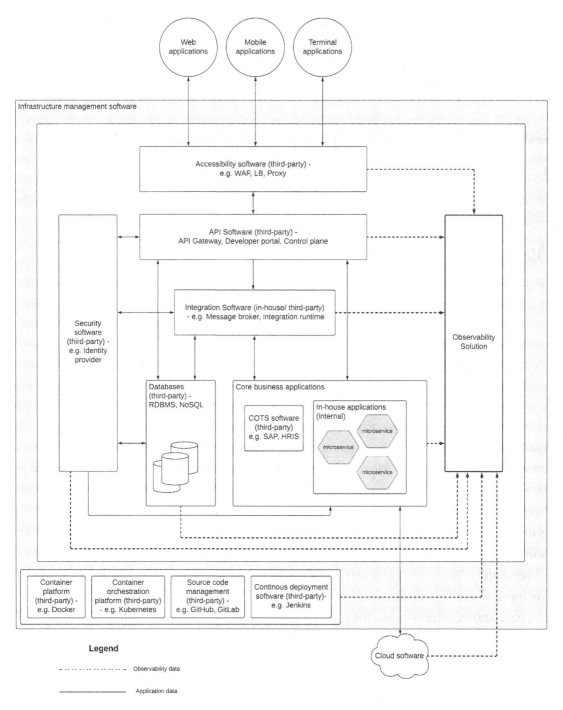

Figure 7-9. *Heterogenous components of an enterprise software system*

As depicted in the figure, an enterprise software system can contain different types of applications to cater to the requirements of the business operations. Most of the systems depicted in the figure are developed by third-party vendors. As per the figure, all these components are connected with the observability solution.

Component-Specific Observability Approach

Let us discuss how each of these components can be implemented with observability and finally design the components that need to be configured inside the observability solution box in the figure.

Accessibility Software

The outermost software layer that interacts directly with the external clients is the accessibility software components. This layer includes software such as

- Proxy servers

- Load balancers (LB)

- Web Application Firewalls (WAF)

The main responsibility of accessibility software is to act as an entry point or gateway to the clients who need to access the enterprise system over the Internet or another external network. Most of the time, these software components are developed by external vendors, and the enterprise teams will either purchase the commercial version of the software or use an open source version of the software within the enterprise software architecture. It is not so common that enterprise teams modify these software components and customize the behavior such as adding instrumentation for observability. We need to rely on the observability data that are exposed by these tools via log files, metrics, and traces. In most cases, these tools push observability data to log files, and in certain cases, the metrics-related data will be published through an accessible interface such as an API over REST or through a native interface such as JMX. We can use a log monitoring tool such as ELK stack along with a metrics exporter such as Prometheus exporter to capture this information and derive useful insights to troubleshoot problems and make better business decisions.

API Software

Once the requests from external clients are entered through the accessibility layer, then it hits the API management layer for which it provides application-level security, rate limiting, and monitoring for internal APIs and services. The main components of an API software are

- API gateway
- Developer portal
- API control plane

Out of these components, API gateway is the most critical and highly utilized component, which receives all the traffic that is coming from the external client applications. The developer portal is only used by people who want to use these APIs and build applications on top of it. Hence, it is the component with the least amount of interaction when compared with the other two components. The API control plane interacts directly with the gateway during the traffic flows to check the security tokens, rate-limiting policies, and development of the APIs. Hence, it has a moderate level of traffic. There are many open source and proprietary software tools available in the market to fulfill the needs of API management software. In most cases, enterprises rely on API management software that is developed by an external party. Hence, it is highly unlikely that enterprise teams go and change the code and instrument the API software to publish observability data. Instead, some of these tools support standards-based observability integrations and direct integrations with popular observability tools. As an example, there can be tools that expose observability data over OpenTelemetry Protocol (OTLP) so that users can capture this data through popular observability tools such as Jaeger. Additionally, these tools also provide metrics data over compatible interfaces over REST APIs so that tools such as Prometheus can directly consume this data. In addition to that, there will be different types of log files to capture important observability data related to system failures, state changes, and other critical notifications. When you are selecting a vendor for API software, it is important to look for observability features that it supports so that you can have freedom over which observability tool is used instead of tying into the vendor-specific, basic observability tools.

Integration Software

After the request has been authenticated and authorized to access the API resources, it will come inside the enterprise network and hit the integration layer, which will execute functions such as data transformations, service orchestrations, and protocol translations so that the request can retrieve the required data from the core business applications. Given that the integration layer consists of implementing a certain level of business logic, it can be implemented with a programming language and a framework without seeking assistance from a third party–developed integration software. But it can be a challenging task when you need to deal with different types of systems, protocols, and messaging patterns as the enterprise grows. Hence, it makes more sense to utilize an open source or proprietary, vendor-developed integration software to implement the integration services. If your enterprise follows the in-house developed integration software path, you can instrument these integration services with OTLP using the language-specific SDK and publish metrics data to be compatible with Prometheus. In case your enterprise decides to go with vendor-developed integration software, you need to depend on the observability features of the vendor. In case the vendor does not provide standards-based observability data, you can utilize a log monitoring tool to aggregate the logs and derive the insights using tools such as ELK or Grafana with Loki.

Database Software

One possible destination for an external request is the database software where it will directly be consumed by the integration software to execute CRUD (create, read, update, delete) operations. These databases can be either relational databases (RDBMS) or NoSQL databases. In most of the cases, database software is developed by an external vendor, and we do not get a chance to modify or change the implementation as we wish. Hence, we need to rely on the telemetry data that is published by the database software itself. Most of the time, databases use log files to push this information. Metrics data publishing also depends on the database that we select. There are several metrics data exporters developed by Prometheus to connect with these databases and expose metrics over Prometheus-compatible APIs.

Core Business Applications

Another destination for external requests is the core business applications layer that consists of different kinds of business critical applications. These applications can be categorized into three main categories:

- COTS applications (on-premise)

- In-house applications

- SaaS applications

COTS applications are developed by external vendors to fulfill specific business functions such as enterprise resource planning or inventory management. These applications are installed and configured within the enterprise-owned infrastructure such as on-premise data centers in most cases. These applications are not easy to customize or change due to the strict compliance and functional requirements of these applications. Hence, we need to utilize the log files mainly to capture the observability information. More modern COTS applications might expose metrics over REST interfaces, which we can utilize to capture through a metrics exporter.

In-house applications are fully owned and developed by the enterprise IT teams. Hence, these teams have the full control over the tools and standards to be utilized. It is essential to use a standard such as OTLP to publish telemetry data (instrument) using the relevant SDKs so that we can utilize observability tools such as ELK, Jaeger, or Prometheus to generate insights. These applications can be developed using microservice architecture or service-oriented architecture depending on the technical capabilities and the requirements of the enterprise.

SaaS applications are becoming an essential part of enterprise software systems. These applications let the enterprises execute business operations such as sales, marketing, and customer relationship management without installing and maintaining software in the enterprise-owned data centers. These tools are developed by third-party vendors. Most of these tools do not allow us to read the raw log files since those are managed by the vendors. But these SaaS applications have their own observability solutions and expose APIs to consume this information from the enterprise observability solution.

Security Software

While requests are passing through different layers of the enterprise software system, we need to check for the authentication and authorization of the requests that are coming into each layer. As an example, the API management layer (API gateway) needs to check the validity of the access token that is presented by the client. This security validation requires a security software to generate, manage, and validate the tokens. In the preceding case, the API gateway will contact the security software to validate the token if that token is an opaque token. Otherwise, the API gateway will use the trust relationship that has been built prior to the client request to validate the token within the gateway itself. Likewise, in a zero-trust architecture, each component validates the request that is coming into that component by either contacting the security software or using the pre-built trust relationship. This security software component can also be developed as an in-house application for smaller use cases. In such a scenario, we can use the standards-based instrumentation and metrics publishing to push telemetry data so that observability tools can directly consume that information. But if you are a somewhat larger enterprise with modern security requirements such as single sign-on, strong authentication, and multioption login, there is more chance that you will utilize a security software that is developed by a third-party vendor. In such a scenario, you need to use the logs and the metrics that are published by the application to capture observability information.

Infrastructure Management Software

All the software components that are managed and maintained by the enterprise team are running on top of the infrastructure layer. This can be physical servers, an infrastructure-as-a-service (IaaS) provider, or a platform-as-a-service (PaaS) provider. Additionally, the actual runtime environment can be virtual machines, containers, or serverless platforms. In addition to the computing infrastructure, we also use different tools to automate the software development, deployment, and maintenance tasks. That includes the following:

- Container management software (e.g., Docker)
- Container orchestration software (e.g., Kubernetes)
- Virtualization software (e.g., VMware)

- Source code management software (e.g., GitHub)

- Continuous integration software (e.g., Jenkins)

- Automated testing software (e.g., JMeter)

These infrastructure and software development life cycle (SDLC) management software components are mainly developed by third-party vendors. We can use the logs published by these applications to capture the observability data. In addition to that, we can utilize metrics exposed by these tools (if there are) using a metrics exporter to capture numerical data related to the application.

Vendor-Independent Reference Architecture

Let us put together all the component-specific observability solutions into a common architecture so that we can build a vendor-independent reference to build observability for enterprise software systems. We have discussed three main approaches to capture observability data in the preceding section:

- Using vendor-provided log files

- Using instrumented telemetry (logs, traces, and metrics)

- Using adapters (for metrics capturing)

Based on these three approaches, we can update our enterprise architecture diagram to reflect the observability solution components in detail. The updated architecture is depicted in Figure 7-10.

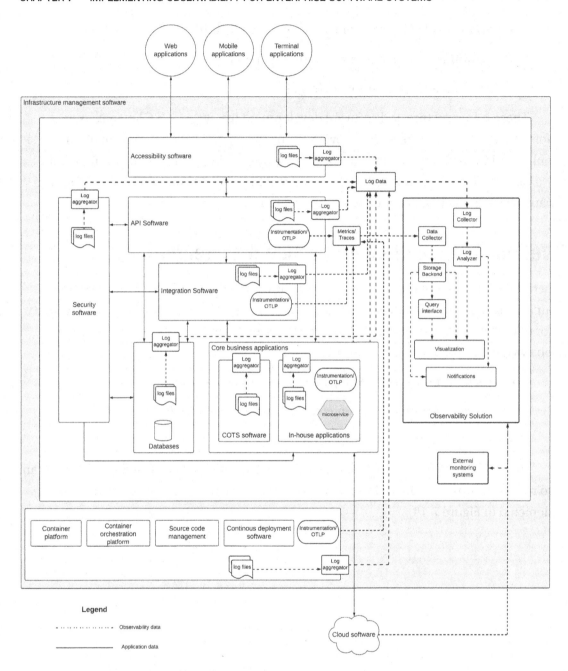

Figure 7-10. *Observability solution reference architecture*

The figure depicts the architecture that we can use to build a comprehensive observability solution for an enterprise software system. It shows different telemetry data publishers that we can configure on the software applications such as API gateways, integration software, microservices, databases, security software, infrastructure management software, and others. We can mainly identify the log-based data publishing as well as instrumentation and OTLP-based telemetry data publishing. The most important part of the figure is the updated observability component. It has two main data collectors that collect log data and metrics/tracing data. Let's discuss these two components in detail.

Log Processing Components

All the log file–related data that are published by the relevant log aggregators of each software application are collected by the common log collector. This allows us to process them as a unit and generate the correlations among the individual log entries during a root cause analysis. These log events are then indexed and stored in a way that it can be consumed by the log analyzer component. The log analyzer component processes these stored log data and allows users to explore the log files as per their need. Additionally, it will also connect with visualization systems to represent log events in a graphical mode to make more sense out of textual and distributed log events. These graphical representations can help the operations teams to troubleshoot issues, identify abnormal behaviors, detect fraud, and perform many critical tasks with the usage of advanced technologies such as machine learning and artificial intelligence. In addition to processing data for visualizations, the log analyzer can also generate real-time notifications to the relevant stakeholders to take immediate action based on certain scenarios. As an example, if there is a log that indicates an out-of-memory error, the operations teams need to be notified so that they can take the necessary action to prevent the application from failing or recover quickly after the failure.

Metrics and Traces Processing Components

There are software components that provide metrics and tracing information in addition to the logs. The in-house build applications and modern applications may expose this information over the standard OpenTelemetry Protocol (OTLP), which will be captured using a data collector. In case there are no standard metrics published, we can use a metrics exporter component to convert the existing metrics into standard metrics. The metrics information will be collected by calling the relevant metrics endpoint of the application or the related metrics exporter. The tracing data will be published by the application, and it will be collected by the data collector. In the figure, we have showed both metrics and traces under the same publisher and processing path. There are a couple of reasons for that:

- Both tracing and metrics data can be published using the same client if we use an OTLP-based client.

- To simplify the diagram that is already complex.

That means you can have a separate processing path for metrics while having a separate path for traces. We will showcase this when we talk about the vendor-specific reference architectures in the following section. The data collected by the data collector is then stored in a storage backend for further analysis. Then we use a query language to read the stored information and do various types of analytical tasks. Additionally, the visualization tools can also connect to the storage backend and retrieve the data to be displayed in dashboards for taking business decisions based on the metrics. Since this provides statistical information about the software applications, the technical leaders can make decisions on the usage of the services, failure rates, and latencies so that they can decide on where to invest on the infrastructure. Additionally, business insights can also be generated using this information so that business leaders can make decisions on innovations and the performance of existing services. In addition to the visualizations, it can also generate real-time notifications based on certain metrics data and limits so that relevant stakeholders can take the necessary actions. As an example, if a service is taking more time to respond than the agreed SLA for the customers, the system can send a notification to the relevant team members so that they can investigate the issue and provide a solution to the customers as soon as possible.

With this reference architecture, we can implement a robust enterprise software system that is capable of deriving the internal states of the system by examining the outputs that are available through the various interfaces. Let us see how we can use this architecture as a reference and build observability solutions with two examples.

ELK, Jaeger, and Prometheus-Based Observability Pattern

Elastic stack, which is commonly known as ELK, is one of the most popular open source observability solutions out there. It is used by many large enterprises as well as small to medium-sized companies across the globe. Let us discuss how we can realize the reference architecture that we discussed in the previous section with the ELK stack. In addition to Elasticsearch, Logstash, and Kibana (ELK), we will be using Jaeger to capture traces and Prometheus to capture metrics data. Figure 7-11 depicts a condensed version of the reference architecture diagram with additional details on the observability components with these tools.

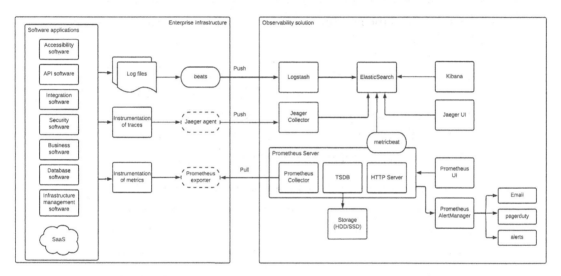

Figure 7-11. *Enterprise software observability solution with ELK, Jaeger, and Prometheus*

The figure depicts how an enterprise platform, which consists of different types of software components, can be observed with an open source observability solution using ELK, Jaeger, and Prometheus. In the figure, you can see that the applications are grouped into a single component to make the diagram less complicated, and these applications use three main mechanisms to publish observability data as external outputs:

- Log files – Consist of different types of log files that all the applications use to publish details about the application execution.

- Traces via instrumentation – There can be some applications that publish tracing information using standard protocols such as OTLP with instrumentation.

- Metrics via instrumentation – There can be applications that publish metrics data directly via standard protocols or in an application-specific manner.

Up to this point, the responsibility of publishing observability data is on the application side. After that, the observability solution takes over. The first task of the observability solution is to collect the information published by the applications via the aforementioned three mechanisms. For doing that, we can use the following components in this scenario:

- Beats – This is the component that reads (tailing) the log files and pushes the log events to the observability solution. It runs within the infrastructure of the enterprise platform along with the application as a separate agent.

- Jaeger agent – This is an optional component that can be used to publish tracing information if an application is using a protocol such as OpenTracing, which came prior to the OpenTelemetry Protocol. If you are using OTLP, you can skip this component and directly publish telemetry data from the application to the data collector.

- Prometheus exporter – This is an optional component that can be used when the application does not expose the Prometheus-compatible endpoints to retrieve metrics data. If the application supports Prometheus APIs, then we can skip this component.

Once the data is collected and published from these components, it is the job of the observability platform to receive this information and store it and process it for further analysis. From this point onward, the observability component we discuss here can be running on-premise or in a cloud environment that is offered by the vendor. It is up to you to decide how do you want to deploy these components. Let us discuss the three open source tools that we use in this scenario separately.

ELK for Logs

The log events published by beats agents are captured by the Logstash component, which is a data collection engine with real-time pipelining capabilities. It can read data from multiple sources and normalize the incoming data so that it can be sent to destinations such as Elasticsearch. It has three main stages in its processing pipeline:

1. Inputs – This is the source of the log data. In our example, this is the beats agent.

2. Filters – This is the processing component within Logstash that can do simple data transformations and filtering. This is an optional component.

3. Outputs – This is the destination that the collected, normalized data is pushed into for further processing. In our example scenario, output goes to Elasticsearch.

The logs coming from different applications need to be collected and normalized so that the analysis can be done properly. Logstash is the component that provides this functionality.

The next component in the log processing flow is Elasticsearch, which is a distributed search and analytics engine. It is capable of storing different types of data such as structured, unstructured, numerical, and geospatial data and indexing it so that users can search the required information fast. It is a highly scalable search engine that can store data across data centers and provide fast searching capabilities to the users. In this particular case, we are using Elasticsearch to store the normalized log data that are coming from Logstash. It provides a really powerful REST API for searching data that can be directly accessed from a simple REST client such as curl or use the language-specific clients to access this information programmatically. In addition to that, we can use Kibana to search data from Elasticsearch and visualize the information in a much powerful way. In our solution, we are going to use Kibana to consume data from Elasticsearch.

The final component of the log analysis process is Kibana, which is a powerful visual interface to analyze data. It provides capabilities such as searching, analyzing, and visualizing hidden data from complex data sources. In our observability solution, we use Kibana to connect with Elasticsearch and provide users with the ability to do fraud detection, root cause analysis, vulnerability detection, and many other troubleshooting and discovery tasks on your application logs.

Jaeger for Traces

As we discussed in the preceding section, Jaeger provides a standards-based approach to publish metrics and other telemetry data using the OpenTelemetry Protocol (OTLP).

The applications that support OTLP-based data publishing through instrumentation publish these events (spans) so that the Jaeger collector can capture this information for further analysis. In case the application does not support OTLP but supports some other protocol such as OpenTracing, Jaeger agent can collect the tracing information and publish that to the Jaeger data collector. Then the Jaeger data collector receives the spans and applies certain data validations and transformations before storing them into the storage backend. In our solution, we are using Elasticsearch as the storage backend.

The data stored in Elasticsearch can be retrieved using Jaeger UI over the Jaeger Query interface. This UI provides capabilities to analyze the spans and traces in a nice user interface. Since we are storing the data on Elasticsearch and Kibana is connected to that, we can use Kibana for further analysis of the traces that are captured through Jaeger. This architecture provides more power to analyze tracing data with Elasticsearch and Kibana.

Prometheus for Metrics

Even though we could use Jaeger with the OTLP to capture tracing, metrics, and log data, Prometheus has become the de facto standard when it comes to capturing metrics for distributed applications. Hence, we are using Prometheus in this solution for metrics data capturing. As depicted in Figure 7-11, the metrics data can be published directly from the applications if it supports the standards-based metrics APIs such as Prometheus APIs or OTLP APIs. In such a scenario, the Prometheus collector will directly call these APIs to capture the metrics data. There can be many scenarios where applications expose metrics data with their own format. In such cases, we can use the metrics data exporter to convert these application-specific metrics to standard metrics that can be collected from the Prometheus.

The Prometheus server is the consumer of the metrics data, which has a collector, a time series database, and an HTTP server. This Prometheus server is part of the observability infrastructure, and it can be deployed external to the enterprise applications. The Prometheus collector will read the metrics data from the instrumented APIs in the applications or from the metrics data exporter. This collected information is then stored in a time series database (TSDB), which will use a storage system that is connected to the server that is running the Prometheus. It can be a disk (SSD or HDD) attached to the server (node). Prometheus offers an interface called PromQL to access the data stored in the TSDB over the HTTP APIs. We can use the built-in Prometheus

UI to explore the metrics. In addition to that, it also integrates with the Prometheus AlertManager to send notifications for certain metrics-based events such as latency violations, system unavailability, and high memory consumption to name a few.

Given that we are already using the Kibana stack for data visualization, we can publish the metrics data that are captured in the Prometheus server using the metricbeat agent to Elasticsearch. Once this data is captured in Elasticsearch, we can use Kibana to create graphical representations and advanced searches against the metrics using the Elasticsearch APIs. Kibana is also capable of working with alerts, and if needed, we can completely drop the Prometheus UI and the AlertManager from this solution. But having them would be helpful since those components will provide unique capabilities related to metrics monitoring.

Kibana for Visualization and Analysis

As depicted in Figure 7-11, Kibana connects with Elasticsearch to provide the users with the ability to search, observe, analyze, and monitor the data there. Kibana is a platform for admins, analysts, and business users. Once the data is published into Elasticsearch from different sources such as Logstash, Jaeger collector, and metricbeat (from Prometheus), Kibana enables these different types of users to securely manage the data and use that to perform various tasks such as the following:

- Search for important data using the Elasticsearch backend.

- Monitor logs, traces, and metrics for operation purposes.

- Analyze the data using different mechanisms to find root causes of failures, troubleshoot issues, and identify fraudulent activities.

- Generate dashboards from the data by correlating data coming from different sources. These dashboards can be created by using Canvas to give a nice look and feel with better real-time data from Elasticsearch.

- Generate alerts based on conditions to take evasive actions for failures and provide remedial solutions when failures happen.

The aforementioned is a small list of capabilities that Kibana offers to the users. In a typical enterprise observability scenario, Kibana provides the end-to-end visibility of the platform using the logs, traces, and metrics published into it.

Grafana, Tempo, and Prometheus-Based Observability Pattern

The Grafana software stack is another open source observability platform that we can use to realize the enterprise observability reference architecture that we discussed in a previous section. It is another open source solution available for the users with adoption from large-scale enterprises to small and medium-sized enterprises. We will be using the three main components of the Grafana stack to capture logs, metrics, and traces:

- Promtail and Loki for log monitoring

- Grafana Tempo for traces

- Prometheus for metrics capturing

In addition to these components, we will be using Grafana for visualizations and graphical analysis of logs, traces, and metrics. Figure 7-12 depicts the component architecture of the Grafana-based observability solution, which is an extended version of our observability reference architecture.

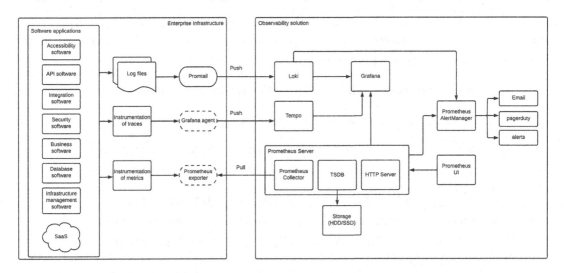

Figure 7-12. *Enterprise observability solution architecture with the Grafana stack*

The figure depicts how we can use the Grafana stack to implement an observability solution for an enterprise software system. The diagram depicts three main routes via we capture the logs, traces, and metrics using the Grafana tools. Let's discuss these routes in detail.

Promtail and Loki for Logs

Grafana provides a comprehensive log monitoring capability using Promtail and Loki. It allows users to read log files from different applications and systems that are running on the enterprise ecosystem. Promtail is the log aggregation agent that can read log files from applications running on on-premise infrastructure and cloud platforms (IaaS) and supports reading log files that store data in structured (e.g., JSON, XML, CSV) and unstructured formats. These log entries are labelled, transformed, and filtered by the Promtail agent before publishing into Loki. Promtail converts the log data into streams and uses an HTTP API exposed by Loki to publish these streams with associated metadata (labels). Loki is a unique log storing system that uses these labels related to the streams to index the logs without indexing each and every log message. This enables Loki to effectively index the log data without utilizing advanced computing resources for parallel processing. The stored log data can be read from Loki using the LogQL, which is a query language specifically designed for reading log data from Loki. Instead of reading the log data directly from Loki, the solution that we have designed here uses Grafana to read the log data and do advanced analysis of log data using its visual interfaces. With the usage of other observability tools such as Tempo and Prometheus integrated into Grafana, we can perform end-to-end analysis of the overall enterprise software system by correlating logs, traces, and metrics. Additionally, Loki can directly integrate with AlertManager, which is another component provided by the Grafana stack to generate alerts based on certain log events.

Tempo for Traces

As we discussed in previous sections, the OpenTelemetry Protocol (OTLP) is the current standard that is globally accepted for instrument tracing data. In the previous solution where we used ELK, we have discussed how to use OTLP with Jaeger. In this solution, we provide an alternative mechanism to capture metrics data using the Grafana-provided solution called Tempo. Given the fact that OTLP is a global standard, it is supported by many tracing solutions including Tempo. The first step in using Tempo is to instrument your enterprise application with one of the supported protocols. Since we need to design our system in a vendor-independent manner, we use OTLP to instrument the applications. Then we use an agent (Grafana agent) to read these traces from the applications and forward them to a storage backend. This is a component that runs closer to the application that may run in the same node or same cluster. In this agent, we can implement pipelines to offload the tasks such as batching and backend routing. Even though this agent is an optional component, it is better to use it if you are building a robust tracing solution. In case you don't use the agent, the application can directly send spans to the storage backend, which is Tempo.

Tempo is the storage backend that captures the tracing data published directly from the application or from the agent. It stores these traces efficiently so that the consumers can read tracing data for various purposes such as troubleshooting, root cause analysis, and metrics generation. In the solution that we proposed in this section, we use Grafana to read the tracing data from Tempo so that we can perform various analyzing tasks using the visual interfaces provided by Grafana. That allows us to correlate the tracing information with the logs to build the correlations and do complex analysis on the observability data.

Prometheus for Metrics

The Grafana team is supporting the maintenance of the open source Prometheus project and has built great integrations with Grafana. Hence, we can use Prometheus for capturing metrics data that are published via instrumentation from the applications. In cases where there are no Prometheus-compatible metrics published by the application, we can use an existing Prometheus exporter or build our own exporter to capture the noncompatible metrics and convert them into a compatible metrics API. Figure 7-12 depicts this approach. Once metrics data is available from the application itself or through the exporter, the Prometheus server can pull this data and store it in the time series database (TSDB) for consumption. In the Grafana stack, there is a dedicated storage solution called Mimir, which is available in case you need to store the metrics data for longer periods of time. Since the default storage option for Prometheus is the disk (SSD/HDD)-based storage, it will not be suitable for use cases where we need to store metrics data across multiple data centers and for longer durations. In such cases, we can use Mimir as the storage backend instead of disk storage.

Once the metrics data is stored in the Prometheus server, it can be accessed using the PromQL query language. We can use the built-in Prometheus UI component or the API client. Given that we use Grafana for visualizations in this solution, we can use Grafana to perform extensive analysis on the metrics. In addition to that, Prometheus can integrate with the AlertManager to generate alerts based on certain metrics and thresholds.

Grafana for Visualization and Analysis

Grafana is an open source tool to analyze and visualize data from different sources. It helps you to unify your data that are coming from multiple sources so that you can perform various analysis and visualizations that can reap great benefits for your organization. It provides the capability to query, visualize, and generate alerts based on the data that is coming from different sources. In this particular use case, we are using Grafana to build an observability solution for enterprise software systems. Grafana helps us to make correlations between data that are coming from log files, traces, and even metrics to derive the internal states of the system by looking at the external outputs, which is the definition of the observability.

Given the fact that we publish data from Loki, Tempo, and Prometheus to Grafana in this use case, we can analyze the data that are generated in the system via a single platform. This helps us to do the following tasks:

- Perform root cause analysis by going through the log entries, traces, and metrics. We can start with either data point and explore other correlated data points so that we can identify the root cause of a failure.

- Create dashboards for operations and monitoring teams to keep track of the overall system status. These dashboards can represent various details such as

  - System performance

  - System availability

  - Business insights

  - AI and ML-based predictions

- Generate alerts based on conditions to perform tasks such as the following:

  - Take necessary steps to avoid failure based on certain limits and thresholds.

  - Provide quick resolutions on failure.

  - Generate business alerts to notify business leaders on achievements.

The aforementioned is a small list of tasks that we can do with the usage of Grafana. It provides many more capabilities for users to keep track of the software system and perform necessary actions as and when required in a proactive and reactive manner so that the end users are given with the best experience.

Summary

In this chapter, we discussed the need for observability in an enterprise software system and how we can implement observability with a reference architecture and a couple of solutions using open source tools. We started the chapter with an introduction to the observability concept with respect to the enterprise software domain and discussed the benefits of it. We also discussed about the misconceptions around monitoring and observability and made it clear that those two concepts are not the same. Then we walked through the process of implementing observability. Next, we discussed various tools available to implement observability for enterprise software systems and covered the three main areas of logs, traces, and metrics. Then we moved on to discuss the design of a reference architecture for observability using a typical brown-field enterprise software system. Then we went through the observability capabilities of different types of applications and the tools that we can use to capture the observability data from those applications. We came up with a reference architecture that is independent of the applications that are present in the enterprise platform as well as the tools that are available for observability. Then we discussed two solution architecture patterns using the reference architecture to implement a real-world observability solution. We discussed a pattern using the ELK stack (Elasticsearch, Logstash, Kibana), Jaeger, and Prometheus and covered the main components and the interactions of these components according to the architecture we defined earlier. Finally, we discussed another pattern with the Grafana stack (Loki, Tempo, Grafana) along with Prometheus to showcase an alternative approach to the ELK-based solution. That concludes the chapter on observability.

CHAPTER 8

Designing Next-Gen Enterprise Software Systems with Cloud-Native Architecture

The emergence of cloud computing platforms such as Amazon Web Services (AWS), Google Cloud Platform (GCP), and Microsoft Azure (Azure) has changed the way enterprise software systems are designed, deployed, and managed. These platforms provide different types of services including

- Computing power (memory, CPU)

- Virtualization

- Storage services

- Middleware

- Containers

- Monitoring

- Security

- Application runtimes

- Networking

© Chanaka Fernando 2023
C. Fernando, *Solution Architecture Patterns for Enterprise*, https://doi.org/10.1007/978-1-4842-8948-8_8

These capabilities were the core requirements of most enterprise platforms that were designed, developed, and maintained by the enterprise teams. Instead of setting up servers, connecting them via networking, and installing the software components and then maintaining these different infrastructure and core software components, using an already-existing platform with such capabilities can save a lot of time and effort from the enterprise development teams. What this means is that they can spend more time on developing business applications and the required features and focus on innovation than dealing with the low-level infrastructure or middleware problems.

The term "cloud-native" is another term with thousand definitions but without a common definition. But in layman's terms, cloud-native computing is a mechanism used to build and run highly distributed, scalable applications by utilizing a cloud computing platform and its capabilities to the benefit of the application natively. As an example, if a cloud computing platform provides the ability to run the services in containers to efficiently use the computing power and if the application can utilize that feature and run on containers natively, we can call the application as a cloud-native application. Designing new applications in a cloud-native manner is not as difficult as migrating an existing legacy and monolithic application into the cloud. Most organizations have started migrating their workloads into the cloud and sometimes struggling to complete the migration due to many challenges. In this chapter, we are going to discuss the following topics, which cover the areas of cloud computing and its usage within the enterprise domain:

- Introduction to cloud-native computing

- Micro-architecture pattern

- Kubernetes-based deployment pattern

- Multi-cloud deployment pattern

- Cloud migration pattern

Let us first discuss what is cloud-native computing in a bit more detail.

Introduction to Cloud-Native Computing

What Is Cloud Computing?

Before we move into discussing the cloud-native aspect, let us first identify the characteristics of a cloud computing platform. In simple terms, a cloud computing platform offers on-demand access to computing services such as CPU, memory, and applications without the need to directly manage these services by the user. We can identify the main characteristics of a cloud computing platform as

- Globally available

- Automatically scalable

- Highly distributed and modular

- Managed by a vendor

- On-demand

Let us discuss these characteristics in detail to understand the cloud computing concept better.

Globally Available

The true value of a cloud computing platform resides in this characteristic where a person with an Internet connection can utilize the cloud platform from anywhere in the world. It provides global accessibility to computing power no matter where you live. With the globally distributed data centers and servers, users can experience better response times when using the services built on top of these cloud computing platforms. That would help businesses to grow customer loyalty without investing millions on infrastructure. It will be ideal if the actual computing resources can also be run globally. But there are practical challenges with infrastructure and regulations in certain parts of the world where setting up data centers is not possible. Hence, we might not find the actual computing environment is available in each country, but users from different countries can still deploy their applications and services on top of the cloud platform.

Automatically Scalable

One of main requirements of enterprise applications is the performance and the scalability. The cloud computing platforms allow the users to scale up their applications to global scale when there is high demand and scale down when the demand is low in an automatic manner. If we are to achieve this capability on a self-managed computing platform, it is a complex task that requires additional resources to be standby for scale-up, which is a waste of resources. On the other side, scaling down is not something common in self-hosted, on-premise environments where people tend to run computing resources that exceeds the real need of the system. A typical on-premise deployment will only utilize 50–60% of the resources that are available in the system, which is a huge cost for the organization. But with cloud computing, you can significantly reduce these costs by running only the required amount of computing resources at a given time.

Highly Distributed and Modular

Cloud computing platforms are perfect examples of distributed systems that have many different components working together to provide a unified experience to the users. As we depicted in Figure 8-1, there are servers, storage, operating systems, middleware, and different types of applications that are running to perform specific tasks within a cloud platform. These applications can be source code management, configuration management, billing and payments management, customer relationship management, and infrastructure management to name a few.

Managed by a Vendor

In most cases, cloud computing platforms are managed and maintained by a vendor such as a cloud service provider (e.g., Google, Amazon). These vendors allocate huge amounts of resources to keep these environments up and running across different geographical locations with global connectivity to make sure these platforms are resilient to natural disasters as well as accessible from different locations. These vendors also provide options to connect with user-managed applications and systems within the user's own data centers via virtual private network (VPN) connectivity as well as dedicated hardware components.

On-Demand

Even though cloud computing platforms provide a large number of services with highly sophisticated computing infrastructure, users can select which service needs to be consumed with which level of computing power. These decisions help the users save cost significantly when compared with self-managed infrastructure where we always provision resources for peak usage requirements. Whenever the users need to shut down a service or move away from a service, it is much easier with the cloud platforms than the on-premise, self-hosted models. In cloud platforms, it is just a matter of clicking a button or filling a form to either get a new service or remove an already-used service. Given that cloud platform allows us to scale up and scale down based on the demand from the consumers, we don't need to pre-allocate resources for our applications. On the other hand, we can always rely on the cloud platform to scale our solution indefinitely, which provides us great deal of flexibility to grow the customer base without worrying about the scalability.

From the user's perspective, it is easier to provision new computing resources and application instances with a button click or an execution of a command-line interface (CLI) tool from the user's computer. All the heavy lifting of installing the servers, networking the servers, installing base software such as operating system and application runtimes, and even installing and configuring the applications is done by the cloud service provider who manages the cloud computing platform. If we compare cloud computing with self-hosted computing, we can identify the difference clearly from the perspective of an enterprise user.

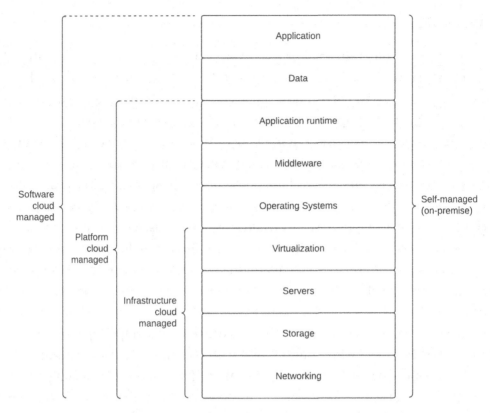

Figure 8-1. *Self-managed computing vs. cloud managed computing*

The figure depicts how the different computing capabilities are managed and maintained in a self-hosted and cloud-hosted computing environment. The figure depicts that in a self-hosted computing platform, the users need to manage all the hardware and software requirements from networking, storage, servers to application and data by themselves. In addition to that, it is the responsibility of the enterprise team to provide the space, security, and power to the infrastructure and keep the applications safe by installing patches and updates while maintaining the availability and scalability requirements from the business leadership.

In a cloud-hosted computing environment, certain functions are offloaded to the cloud provider, and the user does not need to worry about maintaining those aspects of the platform. As an example, an infrastructure cloud that is also called IaaS (infrastructure as a service) manages the underlying hardware components such as networking, storage, and servers as well as virtualization software while providing the space, security, and power required to keep the platform up and running safely. The user only needs to deal with the upper layers such as operating systems, middleware, runtimes, data, and applications. If your requirements are so that you don't even need to worry about operating systems, middleware, and application runtime maintenance, you can select a platform cloud that is also called PaaS (platform as a service), which provides those additional services in addition to an IaaS so that users can focus more on the application development and data management.

If your organization is operating in a non-computer-related industry such as construction, logistics, or even insurance, you might not even have time and resources to develop and manage applications. Rather, you might prefer using an already-existing application, which is accessible over the Internet. There are cloud computing platforms that provide even applications and data as managed services in addition to the PaaS capabilities. Such platforms are called application cloud platforms or SaaS (software as a service) platforms. These platforms allow the users to use the application by configuring its features over a web UI or a simple CLI tool. All the underlying capabilities from networking, storage, servers to runtimes, data, and application management and maintenance is done by the cloud service provider.

Another important aspect of cloud computing platforms is the deployment model. There are three main deployment models we can identify in cloud computing platforms:

1. Public cloud

2. Private cloud

3. Hybrid cloud

Out of these options, public cloud is the most popular deployment model where a third-party organization such as Amazon, Google, or Microsoft that has the resources and capacity to run and maintain a global cloud infrastructure such as IaaS, PaaS, or SaaS offers the different types of cloud computing services to the public in a shared infrastructure. Typically, each user or an organization gets a tenant from the cloud provider to consume the different types of cloud services offered by the platform. This model works well for many use cases where we can utilize a third-party, shared cloud platform without worrying about special security and data management requirements. It also provides better pricing options when compared to the other deployment models.

If your organization has strict regulations around data security and the location of data, you might need to go with the private cloud deployment model where you set up a dedicated deployment just for your organization with the required restrictions and features. As an example, if you need to make sure that the data that comes into the platform does not leave a certain geographical location (e.g., country or state), you can set up a dedicated deployment on that region either through a cloud service provider or by yourself. This option is costlier than the public cloud due to obvious reasons such as strict requirements, dedicated resources, and additional effort that the service provider has to put into to maintain such custom deployments.

If you need to reap the benefits of the both worlds, you can go with the hybrid deployment model where certain parts of the cloud platform are deployed in the public cloud and the remaining parts are deployed in a private cloud or on-premise deployment. This option is becoming popular in use cases where you need to have strict security and data compliance requirements as well as performance critical applications that need to be deployed closer to the core business applications.

Containers and Kubernetes

Even though the users of a cloud computing platform do not need to worry about setting up the software, hardware, power, and physical infrastructure, someone has to work on it. It is not a straightforward task to manage thousands of servers, storage devices, networking, and virtualization software on top of it. But these cloud service providers have the capacity to work on such large projects. The basic idea of a cloud computing platform is to hide the underlying infrastructure from the user and provide a higher-level abstraction such as a VM (IaaS), an application runtime (PaaS), or an application (SaaS) so that the user can focus more on innovation within the business landscape. Even with the cloud-based platforms that use VMs as application running components, sometimes, the resource utilization had not been optimal, and the automated scalability of the VMs was not good enough.

Containers allow users to run multiple applications as isolated processes similar to VMs without having the overhead of a host operating system. It also makes it possible to package the application and the required dependencies into a single unit called an image, which can be run in any environment that supports a container runtime. The user experience of the application would be similar regardless of the underlying environment. With the introduction of containers, cloud computing platforms also started adopting container-based deployments in addition to the VM-based deployment models. Figure 8-2 depicts the difference between VM-based deployments and container-based deployments.

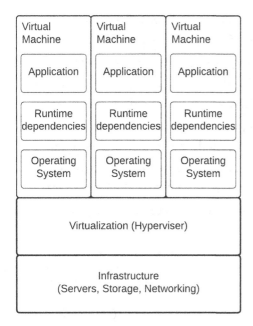 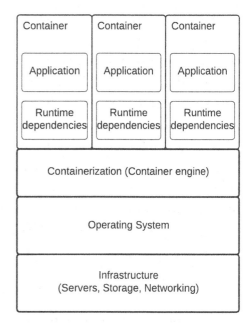

VM-based deployment   Container-based deployment

Figure 8-2. *VM-based vs. container-based deployment models*

As depicted in the figure, we need to have an operating system (guest operating system) on each virtual machine that we create to run the applications in the VM-based model. This operating system may consume memory, CPU, and storage for its functionality, which is not directly required for application execution. Hence, there is a considerable amount of resources allocated to the guest operating system with this model. In contrast, the container-based model does not require a dedicated guest operating system for each container. Instead, it uses the same host operating system that runs the container engine. The application container has the full quota of computing resources to use on application functionality.

Containers were a good idea on several fronts including resource utilization and application portability. But running containers on a large data center that contains thousands of servers required an additional functionality on top of containers to orchestrate the deployment of containers within the data center server pool. That is where the container orchestration platforms such as Docker Swarm and Kubernetes come into play. In addition to these two options, there are several other container orchestration platforms available in the market.

Kubernetes was initially developed at Google and later on adopted by large corporations and cloud service providers due to the flexibility and the functionality it offered on top of containers. In simple terms, Kubernetes is a container orchestration platform that hides the infrastructure complexity from the user and provides a high-level abstraction to the users to run their containers effectively. In other words, it converts an entire data center containing thousands of computers into a single computer that runs an operating system from the user's perspective. All the user needs to worry about is running the applications as containers and providing the configurations required to scale, run, and monitor the application state. Kubernetes made it possible to run cloud-like platforms within enterprises without ever going for a cloud service provider. The advantages that Kubernetes provides include

- Self-healing and automated scalability

- Automated rollbacks and rollouts

- Service discovery and load balancing

- Portability and flexibility (multi-cloud deployments)

- Optimizing resource usage

Due to these benefits, Kubernetes has become one of the most popular platforms for deploying container-based applications in public, private, and hybrid cloud environments. Most of the cloud service providers started offering managed Kubernetes services under their cloud service offerings so that users can run their applications on containers using Kubernetes in a cloud infrastructure. Additionally, enterprise teams also started setting up on-premise Kubernetes clusters to build their own private cloud environments so that the application developers can utilize these platforms similar to the way they use a public cloud platform purchased from a cloud service provider. With the introduction of containers and Kubernetes, Figure 8-1 can be updated to include these components as well. The updated figure is depicted in Figure 8-3.

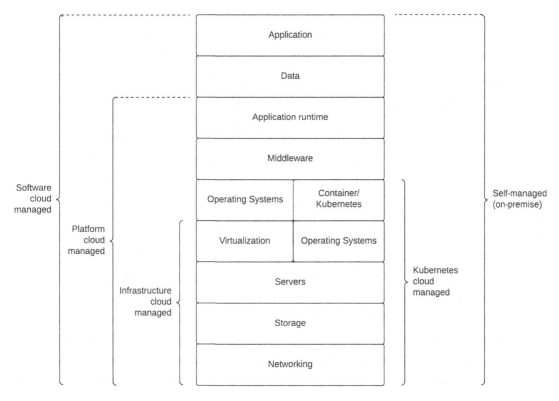

Figure 8-3. *Self-managed computing vs. cloud-managed computing with Kubernetes included*

As per the figure, the container and Kubernetes layer comes on top of the operating systems, and there is a new type of cloud offering provided by the cloud service providers, which is called KaaS (Kubernetes as a service). This service allows users to run their applications on top of containers and Kubernetes while utilizing a third-party cloud computing platform without worrying about setting up the infrastructure and the containers/Kubernetes components.

Cloud-Native Computing

The term "native" means something that is associated with the origins or the beginning of something. Accordingly, we can define the term "cloud-native" as a way of building software applications and systems that are associated with the origins of cloud computing. In other words, if we can utilize the full benefits offered by the cloud computing platforms by designing, implementing, and running a software application on such a platform, we can say that application is a cloud-native application.

Let's take a sample use case where we need to build an online education platform that provides access to courses from different universities across the globe to a global audience. We can always start small and set up the platform with the required software components such as a learning management system (LMS), video conferencing system, billing system, and other core components required for the solution. From the beginning, we can design the application in a modular manner so that each functionality is executed by independently managed software applications. We can deploy these applications in a containerized environment that is offered by a cloud service provider since managing our own container platform would be too much of work for a small organization. In cases where we have applications that do not provide container-based deployment options (e.g., images), we can run them with VMs that are provided by the cloud platform. Any new service that we developed can be developed as a microservice so that we can deploy, scale, and manage them independently. We can use a cloud-provided database to store the critical business information that is required for various operational tasks such as sales, marketing, and product development. In addition to the core components, we can use an integration component that supports developing integrations as microservices. Also, an API gateway component can be used to expose the services to external clients such as mobile and web over a secured interface. The API gateway also need to be deployed as microgateway as per the need of the application. We can also utilize certain SaaS applications for billing and CRM functionality since we don't need to manage them internally. Figure 8-4 depicts a solution architecture for an online education platform that is built utilizing the cloud computing capabilities offered by various cloud service providers.

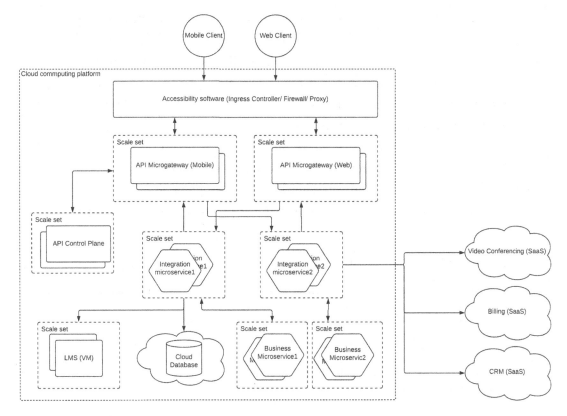

Figure 8-4. *Cloud-native online education platform solution architecture*

The figure depicts how we can architecture the online education platform so that we reap the full benefits provided by the cloud computing platforms. At the top, we have the accessibility software layer that is provided by the cloud service provider as a service. If we use Kubernetes as our deployment platform, we can use an ingress controller to allow the incoming traffic to the platform and have firewall and/or proxy server to filter the unwanted traffic. We don't need to worry about the availability or the scalability of those components since we are using them as services from the cloud provider. Then we have the API gateway layer that is deployed as microgateways serving for mobile and web clients separately. Each microgateway can be scaled independently. The control plane of the API gateway is deployed as a separate component so that it can scale independently. Then we have the integration layer that is also designed as separate microservices running as scale sets that can be scaled according to the capacity requirements of that given integration. These integration microservices integrate these SaaS applications with internal systems. Then we have the core business applications layer where we have the LMS, which is deployed in virtual machines in a scale set so that it can run and scale on its own. There can be such applications in real-world enterprise systems that we don't get much benefits by running on containers. It makes more sense to run those applications in VMs rather than in containers. For the database requirements, we will be utilizing a cloud-provided database service that can be an RDBMS or NoSQL-type database. These database services provide the required scalability, performance, and availability guarantees. Any new business service that is developed in-house is developed as microservices running on containers as depicted in the figure.

With this kind of solution architecture, we can gain the benefits offered by the underlying cloud computing platform while keeping enough flexibility on our side to innovate. This solution is designed in a way that it adheres to the basic principles of cloud computing:

- The solution is modular and highly distributed.

- Individual functional components can be scaled independently and automatically.

- Infrastructure is managed by the vendor in most cases.

- New services are provisioned on-demand without pre-allocating resources.

- System can be accessed over the Internet from anywhere in the world.

One important thing to keep in mind when designing solutions in a cloud-native manner is to use the right technology to the right component instead of going with all-in or all-out approach for a particular technology. We need to consider the factors such as data security, compliance, and international laws when dealing with these cloud platforms in addition to the technical capabilities.

Micro-architecture Pattern for Enterprise

Microservice architecture (MSA) is something that goes hand in hand with the cloud-native computing platforms. The reason being the characteristics of MSA such as modularized architecture, distributed nature, and scalability are similar to what we see in a cloud computing platform. This makes MSA a true cloud-native design pattern for building enterprise software systems. One of the key principles in MSA is the term "micro," which refers to dividing a task into small subtasks and executing them efficiently in an independent manner with a service. This concept can extend to multiple application components within an enterprise software system. This includes software components such as

- Business services

- Integrations

- API management

- Front-end applications

- Security components

Let us discuss how we can build these components in a "micro"-architecture so that we can build a cloud-native enterprise platform.

Business Services

These are the core business applications that process the business transactions and store and retrieve data from data sources. These applications can come in different flavors such as COTS applications purchased from third-party vendors, SaaS applications purchased from third-party vendors, and in-house applications developed by internal IT teams. In the case of COTS or SaaS-based applications, we don't have much flexibility in terms of the development and deployment choices. We have to live with the models supported by the vendor. But in case of in-house applications, we can design them in a manner which can utilize the benefits offered by the cloud. We can design these business applications adhering to microservice architecture. Once we do that, it is easier to deploy them in cloud-based infrastructure as well as container-based infrastructure without any problem.

Integrations

Integrations are another important part of an enterprise software system which is typically deployed as a centralized component that connects with different types of applications and systems. Instead of deploying the integration component as a centralized, monolithic application, we can deploy that as a set of integration microservices to make it more cloud-native. There are many integration tools developed by third-party vendors that support this kind of deployment model. In case if you build the integration layer by yourself with the usage of some libraries, you can easily adopt this model since each integration is already developed as separate services in that case.

API Management

API gateways allow external and internal consumers to access the business data via a secured and managed interface. Typically, these gateways are deployed as centralized components that hold all the API proxies. These centralized gateways are horizontally scaled as per the requirements of the consumer demand. The drawback of this sort of deployment is that a failure of a single API or a set of APIs can cause the entire server to be down, and hence, the consumers will not be able to access the business services. On the other hand, if we need to scale only a few APIs, we need to scale the entire server rather than scaling the required APIs. Hence, it makes more sense to deploy the API gateways in a manner where APIs are segregated into groups and deployed in separate gateways or even deploy gateways per API so that we have the full flexibility in scaling the APIs. Additionally, this sort of approach will reduce the impact a particular API has on other APIs. In addition to the API gateways, a typical API management platform provides additional components such as developer portal, security component (key manager), and API design tool (publisher), which can be deployed in a centralized manner since those components do not need the same level of scalability. We call these components as "control plane" as a whole, and the API gateways are called "data plane."

Front-End Applications

The business functionality exposed by the API gateways is consumed by customer-facing, front-end applications such as mobile and web applications. These applications have been evolving over the years, and the latest development in front-end applications is the usage of microservice architecture–related concepts in developing these applications. The approach of using MSA for front-end applications is called "micro frontends" where the front-end application (e.g., web application) is designed, developed, and deployed as a set of microservices. Instead of having a monolithic web application with all the components deployed together, this approach allows developing progressive web applications in an efficient manner. As an example, let's say we are designing a web application for an online store where people can browse through the available products and purchase them through the website itself. Our web application will have options to discover the products (browse), recommended products (based on AI), and a checkout option to make the purchase. We can design each of these capabilities as separate micro frontends and let different teams manage these components separately. Once the user accesses the web application using a browser, we can integrate these micro frontends and offer a unified experience.

Security Components

Securing different applications and systems is a key requirement of an enterprise software system. In a zero trust architecture, every system needs to be verified before granting access to another system. The role of a security component is highly critical in such architectures. For microservices, we can use an agent-based security where each microservice has a security agent running alongside the service itself. Then we can have a separate control plane to change and enforce the security policies on these sidecars (security agent) as and when required. In addition to this, there needs to be a secure token service (STS) that does the user authentication and token management so that the clients can generate these tokens and use them for validation by security agents, individual microservices, or authentication services.

With that understanding, let's put all these ideas together and design a "micro-architecture" using these concepts so that we can gain the maximum benefits from a cloud computing platform.

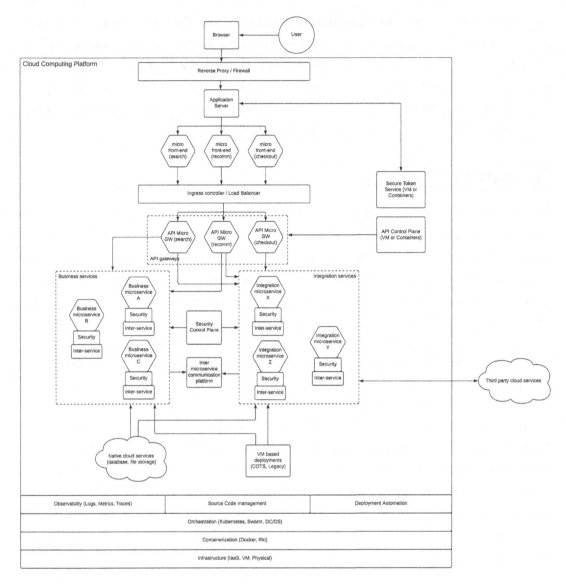

Figure 8-5. *Micro-architecture pattern for an enterprise*

Figure 8-5 depicts a solution architecture that is designed with the usage of micro-architecture where all the software components that are suitable to implement as microservices are designed in that manner. At the top, we have the user who needs to access a business service via a web browser (client). Once the user types in a URL in the web browser, the web browser will reach the web server that hosts the website that is related to the URL. There will be an entry-level component such as a proxy server and/or a firewall to block malicious access attempts and hide the internal details.

The application server hosts the web application that aggregates several front-end microservices that have their own functional domains to execute on. In our sample, we have three front-end microservices called search, recomm, and checkout. These components will be responsible for the respective functionalities of the website. Any improvement to one of those aspects (e.g., search) will be done by the team who is responsible for that specific front-end microservice.

Then we have the entry point to the enterprise platform where we have the backend systems. The front-end microservices need to connect with the backend systems to fetch data and update the data that is captured from the user. To do that, they will connect with service-specific API gateways, which we can call as microgateways. There are three microgateways for each front-end microservice to access the backend systems. Before reaching the gateways, the requests will go through the ingress controller or load balancer component to distribute traffic among replicas of the microgateways. The API microgateways are deployed in a manner where APIs are partitioned across them and each set of APIs related to the specific functionality (e.g., checkout) can run independently and scale independently. If you need to go beyond this level of partitioning, you can even have one API microgateway for each API in the system. Then each API can scale independently from other APIs. It is a viable option that you need to select based on the requirements. These microgateways can be deployed as containers in a containerized environment such as Docker or Kubernetes. In support of the microgateways, we have the API control plane that contains certain functionalities such as API development (publisher), API discovery (developer portal), throttling and rate limiting (traffic manager), and optionally security. This control plane can be deployed in containers or VMs based on the requirement. This component does not need the same level of scalability when compared with the microgateways.

There is a separate component to handle the user management, authentication management, and token management related to the security of the platform. We can use an identity provider that can act as a secure token server (STS) that can issue tokens after authenticating the users via strong authentication using multifactor authentication as well as other modern authentication mechanisms. This component can be deployed as a monolithic component or we can even utilize an identity-as-a-service (IDaaS) platform to implement security functionality.

Then we have the microservices layer where we have implemented both business services and integration service following MSA. There we use two sidecar components that run alongside each microservice to provide security validation and interservice communication. We can use a mechanism such as Open Policy Agent (OPA) to implement security policies at each service level, and there will be a separate control plane that is used to configure the security policies that are stored with the security agent. For interservice communication, we can use a proxy-based approach where each microservice has a sidecar proxy running alongside the microservice to act as the data plane of a service mesh. In this approach, the data plane will take care of routing, load balancing, service discovery, and error handling. There will be a separate service mesh control plane to configure the policies on the sidecar proxies for interservice communication. As an alternative approach for interservice communication, we can also use a messaging platform such as Kafka or NATS so that services can communicate with one another in an asynchronous manner. With this approach, we do not need the sidecar proxy for interservice communication, and instead, each service should implement the client side of the communication with the message broker.

Integration microservices will connect with various internal systems such as COTS applications and legacy applications. In addition to that, these integration microservices will also connect with SaaS services offered by external cloud vendors. Also, there will be interactions with databases that will be utilized from the underlying cloud service provider if that is possible. Business microservices will also connect with the databases to store and retrieve data on behalf of the user requests that are coming from the front-end applications.

Next, we have the core business systems that act as the source of truth or data sources for the applications that we described before. There will be requirements for different types of databases based on the data that are stored in the system and the consumption pattern of the data. As an example, for checkout front-end microservice, a relational database would be sufficient, and we can utilize a managed database service offered by the cloud service provider. But for the recommendation engine, we might need to use a NoSQL sort of database to implement various machine learning and artificial intelligence–related data processing. In addition to the databases, we also have COTS applications, which might have been there for decades within the enterprise platform. Some high-performance applications such as hotel booking systems, airline reservation systems, and enterprise resource planning (ERP) systems need dedicated hardware to run these components. This sort of applications is not suitable for running as microservices in containers. Hence, we can run these applications in VMs with high-profile hardware resources. Most of the cloud providers offer this sort of infrastructure to run this sort of applications. Additionally, there can be some legacy, in-house applications that might have been developed by internal IT teams in the past but have never been updated. Such systems also need to run in VM-based deployments until the functionality is migrated to more modern microservice-based applications.

Running these different software components within a cloud computing platform or a container platform is not sufficient to make the platform cloud-native. We need to make sure that the required supportive functionalities are also implemented properly. One key aspect of an enterprise platform is the observability where we should be able to derive the internal state of the system by looking at the external outputs. Having a proper observability solution using the cloud vendor-provided technologies or other open source/commercial tools is extremely important. These observability solutions consist of data agents who publish observability data, data collectors, data processors, and then various visualization and presentation tools and notification tools that we discussed in Chapter 7, "Implementing Observability for Enterprise Software Systems." Except the data publishing agents that run alongside each microservice and application, other components are typically deployed as centralized components with sufficient computing resources. Hence, running them on VM-based deployments would be sufficient. In case you use the vendor-provided observability solutions, you don't need to worry about setting up these components and just use the service.

Another supportive functionality that is required by an enterprise platform is the source code management. Most of the cloud providers can easily integrate with existing SaaS-based SCM tools such as GitHub, Bitbucket, or GitLab. Utilizing such a solution makes it easier for the teams to collaborate with one another and deliver the software in time. Deployment automation is another critical capability required to build a true cloud-native enterprise architecture. Once the applications are designed and implemented by the development team, these applications (code) need to be built and deployed into different environments (e.g., dev, UAT, prod) with proper testing. If we do this manually, there can be delays in releases due to various challenges that may occur in finding the right people to do the job at the right time. Due to the friction between teams, releases can take more time than expected, and the quality of the final deliverable can also be affected. Hence, it is important to automate the process of building the source, deploying into environments, running the tests, and finally promoting the build to the production system with minimal human interaction. This allows us to release new services more often than not. As an example, it took several months in the past to release a given service, while now we have teams who do multiple service releases within a given day through automation. If you are using a cloud solution such as a PaaS, you will get all the automation tools and pipelines preconfigured in the environment for you, and you just need to provide the required parameters to execute the build pipelines. But if you are using an IaaS platform, you need to build the automation pipelines for software delivery using tools such as continuous integration tools (e.g., Jenkins, CircleCI), testing tools (Newman, JMeter) and build tools (Spinnaker, Packer) on top of the underlying infrastructure.

At the bottom of Figure 8-5, we have the infrastructure layer of the solution. Depending on where you need to build the solution, you have to either manage these components or you can just use these components as a service from the cloud service provider. Utilizing a container orchestration solution such as Kubernetes, let us forget about the underlying infrastructure management and just consider the entire infrastructure as a single computer where we can run our applications as Kubernetes components such as pods, deployments, services, namespaces, and many more. There are many cloud service providers who offer managed Kubernetes services that we can just utilize. In case if you decide to run the solution on self-hosted data center, you can run the Kubernetes cluster on top of physical servers or virtual machines. Kubernetes utilizes a container platform to run the containers that run inside the pods. We can use Docker or any other compatible container runtime that is supported by the cloud platform. If you are running the infrastructure by yourself, you can easily run Docker as the containerization platform. If you only need to use containers, but not Kubernetes due to some reason, there are cloud providers who offer their own container orchestration services such as Amazon ECS (Elastic Container Service) or Azure Container Service (ACS). These services use their own mechanisms to manage the deployment of containers within the infrastructure and manage the state and the life cycle of containers.

Finally, we have the infrastructure layer where computing resources are set up, installed, and managed in a physical location such as data center. If you are utilizing the bare minimum of a cloud computing infrastructure, you will be only using this layer, which is the IaaS layer. At this layer, you have the choice of either using the bare-metal servers or virtual machines as your infrastructure choice. Choosing VM-based infrastructure is the popular choice since it allows a higher-level interface to work with the infrastructure rather than worrying about hardware and operating system–level details.

That concludes our micro-architecture pattern that can be used to build a true cloud-native enterprise software system that can reap many benefits offered by the cloud computing technology. We can use the options such as multiple availability zones, regions, and automated scalability to expand the solution to global scale with proper placement of the components based on the needs. If the performance is critical for a given application, we can select the infrastructure location that is closer to the userbase. Similarly, these cloud service providers offer various additional services to improve the overall experience that we deliver to the users. If we are building this kind of architecture by ourselves from scratch (starting with infrastructure), it will require a significant amount of engineering effort. But you can make the choice on which level of cloud services you need to utilize, and the rest of the components can be developed and managed by yourself so that you have the best of both flexibility and ease of infrastructure management.

Kubernetes-Based Deployment Pattern

Designing a cloud-native enterprise software system requires the workloads (software applications) to run as independent components. Container platforms such as Docker allow to achieve this requirement. But running a considerable number of workloads across multiple nodes (computers) in a reliable manner requires a mechanism to keep track of individual workloads and their states. A container orchestration platform such as Kubernetes allows you to achieve this goal. Some major advantages of Kubernetes include the following:

- Run workloads (software applications) in containers

- Self-healing

- Automated scale-up and scale-down

- Service discovery at runtime

- Load balancing

- Automated rollouts and rollbacks

- Storage orchestration

Kubernetes allows users to run their distributed systems in a resilient manner with the aforementioned advantages. Features such as self-healing, automated scaling, and automated rollouts and rollbacks make life easier for the operations team who otherwise spends long days and nights executing these operations manually. Let us first take a look at Kubernetes architecture in a bit more detail.

Kubernetes Architecture

Kubernetes typically runs on a cluster of computers (nodes). There are two main components in the cluster:

- Control plane

- Workers (nodes)

These components are responsible for running the applications (workloads) in a cluster of nodes. Figure 8-6 depicts the architecture of Kubernetes platform.

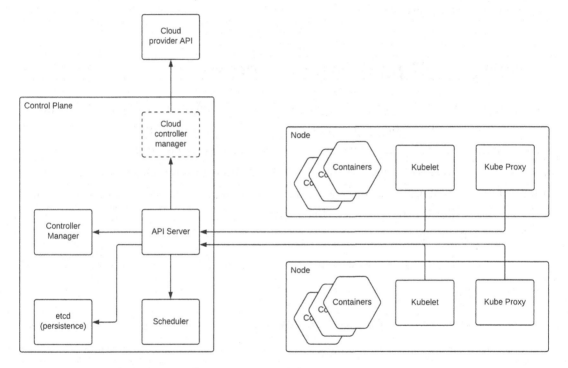

Figure 8-6. *Kubernetes architecture*

As depicted in the figure, the control plane runs separately from the workers (nodes) that actually host the applications as containers (pods). The control plane consists of the components that are responsible for running the containers (pods) in a cluster of nodes. It has an API server that acts as the interface of the control plane. The entire Kubernetes cluster can be controlled through the APIs exposed by the API server. As an example, a CLI tool such as kubectl can call the API server and run the workloads in pods within the workers. The scheduler component is responsible for assigning newly created pods to the respective nodes to run based on certain conditions that are set by the user.

There is a persistence data storage component called etcd, which allows the cluster to store the configurations as key/value pairs. The controller manager component is there to manage various controller processes that keep an eye on the nodes, jobs, endpoints, and security controllers. Also, there is an optional component that comes with cloud service provider–specific Kubernetes platforms called cloud controller manager that runs the cloud vendor–specific controllers by calling the API provided by the vendor.

The workers or nodes are the instances that run the application workloads as containers in pods. They have a component called kubelet that runs as an agent on each node to make that application workloads are running as containers in pods. It takes a specification (PodSpec) and makes sure the containers specified in that specification are running and healthy. There is another component that runs on each node, called the kube-proxy, which provides a Kubernetes-specific network layer. It defines network rules to access the pods from within the node as well as from outside the node. Additionally, we also have the container runtime in each node to run the containers as pods within the Kubernetes environment.

With this basic understanding of Kubernetes, let's discuss a bit more about the objects that we defined via configuration files. These objects represent the state of the Kubernetes cluster. We need to identify several main objects in order to understand the deployment architecture on top of Kubernetes. Those objects are

- Namespace

- Deployment

- Pod

- Service

- Ingress controller

Namespaces are used to group applications and components in Kubernetes into an independently manageable unit without interfering with the other applications and components. As an example, different teams within an organization can utilize the same Kubernetes cluster by having their own namespaces to make sure they don't interfere with one another. Namespaces separate various Kubernetes objects logically.

A deployment defines a declarative configuration for pods and replica sets and makes sure the state of these objects is maintained consistently. It allows users to group related Kubernetes objects (pods and replica sets) together and configure them as a single unit. Pods are the smallest unit of work within Kubernetes that can run one or more containers with shared network and storage resource with its own IP address. A single pod can run more than one container in case those containers are tightly coupled with one another for the application (microservice).

A service allows multiple pods running the same workload (application) as a network endpoint for the consumers. The service will balance the load across different pods (replicas). The service gets its own IP called a "cluster IP" through which the consumers can access the service. If we are exposing these services outside of the Kubernetes cluster, we need to use an "Ingress" to do so. It provides an externally reachable endpoint to the service and provides capabilities such as load balancing, SSL termination, and name-based virtual hosting. The ingress controllers are the implementation of Ingress, and there are multiple ingress controllers available to deploy along with Kubernetes.

Deployment Architecture

Let us design a deployment architecture pattern to run a cloud-native enterprise software system in a Kubernetes environment with the knowledge that we gained in the preceding sections. We can run different types of workloads in Kubernetes such as business microservices, integration microservices, API microgateways, and even front-end microservices that we discussed in a previous section. Additionally, we can isolate the different teams or environments using the namespaces of Kubernetes. Figure 8-7 depicts a solution architecture that utilizes cloud-native architecture within a Kubernetes environment.

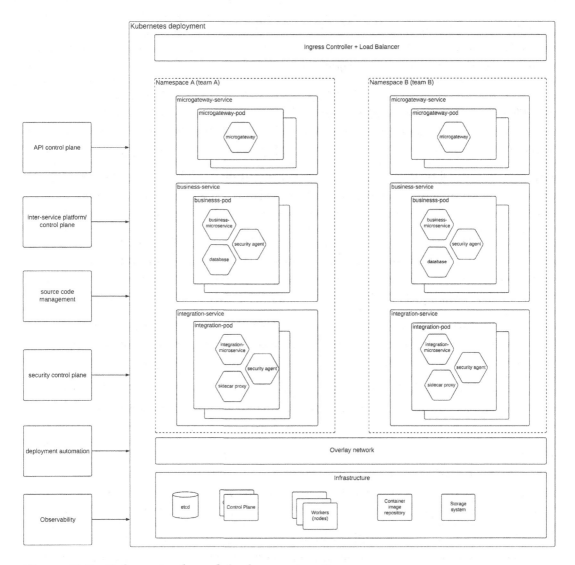

Figure 8-7. *Kubernetes-based deployment pattern*

The figure depicts a deployment architecture that we can utilize to run a cloud-native enterprise software system in Kubernetes. This deployment can be run in self-hosted or vendor-managed Kubernetes environments alike. At the top of the diagram, we have the main entry point to the deployment, which is the ingress controller along with the load balancer. It routes the incoming requests (ingress) to the Kubernetes deployment by identifying the correct service endpoints. Then we have two separate namespaces defined in Kubernetes to represent two different teams who deploy their workloads (applications) on a given deployment. This can simply be two different

295

environments (e.g., prod, pre-prod) managed by the same team as well. The advantage of defining namespaces is that we can make sure that other teams or other environments do not impact a given set of workloads.

Then we have the services defined for each of the components, gateway, business service, and integration service. Each of these services runs one or more pods depending on the capacity and scalability requirements of the platform. We can have dynamic scalability with minimum and maximum number of replicas to make sure that only the required amount of resources is utilized at a given time and the deployment can scale up if there is more demand. The definition of pod and a scale set can be defined within a deployment object for easier maintenance. Inside the pod, we have the containers required for that specific application. In our sample deployment, the gateway pod has one container, which is the microgateway that is capable of handling the security and routing requirements along with other functionalities such as rate limiting. This microgateway interacts with the API control plane for various tasks such as updating and configuring the microgateway. The business pod is somewhat different from the gateway pod. Since the business pod's main goal is to execute the business logic, it has a container that runs the business logic. In addition to that, it has two more containers running in the same pod for providing security functionality and data storage (database) for storing application-specific data. Then we have the integration pod, which also consists of three containers for integration logic, security, and interservice communication (sidecar proxy). These three example pods – gateway pod, business pod, and integration pod – show different approaches to run pods within an enterprise platform. These pods will communicate with control plane components such as security control plane and interservice control plane (service mesh control plane) or message broker, which may or may not run within the Kubernetes deployment itself.

There are other supportive components used by the Kubernetes deployment such as source code management, deployment automation, and observability solutions that run outside of the Kubernetes deployment and used as services by Kubernetes. Underneath the runtime components, we have the infrastructure layer that consists of the networking layer and the computing infrastructure. As depicted in the figure, there is an overlay network that is implemented by Kubernetes to manage the network traffic within the Kubernetes deployment as well as to/from outside the deployment. At the infrastructure level, we have the Kubernetes control plane and nodes (workers) running on separate servers or machines. We can also use a dedicated etcd server for persisting the configurations of the Kubernetes deployment. Also, we need a private container registry to store the container images that are deployed into the Kubernetes pods. We also need a storage system to keep the application data in a persistent manner.

The deployment pattern depicted in the figure is a template that you can use to design your enterprise applications to run on Kubernetes platform. Kubernetes is a versatile platform with many advanced features such domain name system (DNS), web UI, and container resource monitoring and logging that you can utilize on top of this deployment to reap the full benefits offered by the platform.

Multi-cloud Deployment Pattern

Cloud service providers are offering unique services through their platforms, and sometimes, enterprises have to deal with multiple such vendors to fulfill their IT and business requirements. One cloud provider may offer better pricing and features for database services, while another cloud provider may offer similar benefits for infrastructure services. As an IT organization, we need to make sure that our platform has enough flexibility when it comes to switching cloud vendors rather than locking into one vendor. Using multiple cloud providers within your enterprise software system is called multi-cloud deployment, and it is becoming a common approach among enterprises. There are several benefits that we can gain from having a multi-cloud deployment model:

- Provides better availability for the platform – Since the applications are running across multiple cloud platforms, the unavailability of one cloud platform will not bring down your entire platform. Rather, it will function with some degradation.

- Provides flexibility to switch vendors – Having a single cloud vendor for all your services will lock you into that platform unnecessarily. With the multi-cloud approach, you can become free from vendor lock-in.

- Allows to use the best-fit technology – Instead of using a limited set of services from one cloud vendor, you have the freedom to select from multiple vendors and go for the best-fit option in terms of technology and price.

- Provides better performance to the customers – It is possible to select the data centers that are closer to the customers from the respective cloud vendors to offer better experience to the customers in terms of latency.

- Allows procurement teams to strike better deals – Due to the competitive nature of the services that we are utilizing, we can negotiate better deals from the cloud vendors with a multi-cloud option.

These benefits and several other aspects make the multi-cloud deployment an interesting approach to design enterprise software systems.

While using different services from different cloud providers, there will be certain software components such as API gateways that need to be deployed along with each of these services to provide a unified experience to the end users. Most of the cloud vendors provide their own API gateways to expose the internal business services to external consumers. Due to this, we can identify two main approaches to design an enterprise software system.

1. Vendor-specific gateway and a common API marketplace

2. Single API gateway vendor with a marketplace

Let us discuss these two options in detail.

Vendor-Specific API Gateway with Common API Marketplace

Having a multi-cloud architecture allows us to utilize the vendor-native components for better performance and easier integration. API gateway is a component that we use to expose the business services to internal and external consumers in a secured, monitored, and metered manner. Hence, it is becoming a commodity software component such as a load balancer. Due to this higher adoption and ubiquity of API gateways, most of the cloud vendors provide their own versions of API gateways. Utilizing these API gateways reduces the overall cost while providing easier configuration and better performance. This approach will lead us to having separate API gateways for each cloud platform. While it is okay to have vendor-specific API gateways for better runtime performance, one challenge with this approach is that we cannot use the

API marketplace that is offered by the vendors to publish different APIs from different gateways. Hence, we need to use a common API marketplace software component that can publish the APIs from different cloud-specific API gateways. Figure 8-8 depicts this architecture.

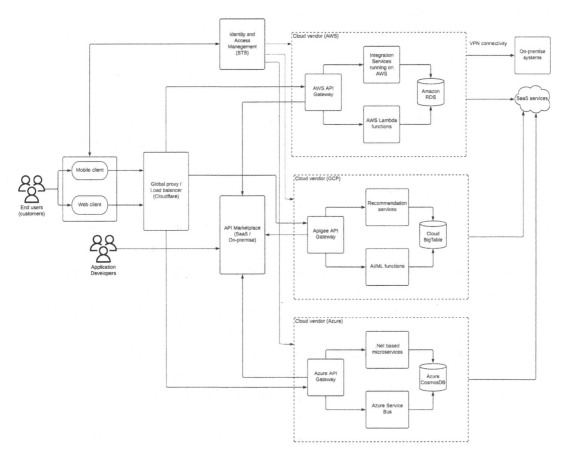

Figure 8-8. *Multi-cloud deployment pattern with vendor-specific API gateways*

The figure depicts a multi-cloud deployment pattern in which we have used three different cloud vendors (AWS, Google, and Azure) for different functional requirements. In the AWS deployment, we have the AWS API gateway along with the AWS lambda-based services for business functionality and an integration platform running on AWS, which connects with on-premise systems via a VPN connection. It also uses Amazon RDS as the relational database for storing data. We also have a deployment on Google Cloud Platform (GCP), which has Apigee API Gateway along with a few business-specific services for recommendation and AI/ML-related functionalities. This deployment uses

Google Cloud Bigtable as the NoSQL database, which can perform well for the analytics and recommendation system use cases. This deployment will also connect with other SaaS software that is required for the business operations such as CRM software. We also have another deployment on Azure that is focusing on developing in-house applications using .NET Framework in a microservice environment and utilizing the Azure service bus for asynchronous communication between services. This deployment is fronted by the Azure API Gateway. We use Azure Cosmos DB for this use case, which is a highly versatile database that can perform well for many types of applications with an easy to use interface (API) to interact with.

Having APIs running on different cloud platforms provides many benefits. One challenge that we need to address in this design is to put all these different APIs into a common marketplace so that application developers can easily find out these APIs and create awesome experiences to the users. That is why we have used an API marketplace software component to publish all the APIs deployed in different gateways. This can be a SaaS product or an on-premise application. This component allows application developers to browse, comment, rate, and try out APIs without worrying about the actual infrastructure that the APIs are running on. We also have a common IAM platform to handle all the authentication, authorization, and user management tasks. We can utilize Azure AD as the IAM solution if required or we can go with a different vendor. In either case, all the API gateways will keep a trust relationship with the IAM platform, and these gateways will accept the tokens issued by the IAM component for access requests.

One other important component that we need in a multi-cloud deployment is a global load balancer that can share traffic among multiple clouds in a cloud-agnostic manner. There are several vendors that provide this sort of capability. Cloudflare is a sample vendor that offers multi-cloud load balancing. In addition to these basic components, we can utilize the cloud-provided tools for source code management, deployment automation, observability, and monitoring functionality. In case you need to have a common observability solution for all the cloud deployments, you can use a dedicated deployment of the ELK stack or Grafana stack in one of the cloud environments or utilize the SaaS version of these tools to connect from different cloud platforms.

Single API Gateway Vendor with a Marketplace

Having different vendors for the same functionality (API gateway) can be challenging in some cases if those vendors behave differently and the developers need to put a lot of effort to learn different technologies to deal with such a deployment model. Instead, we can use a single vendor that is cloud-agnostic to provide the API gateway functionality and utilize the built-in API marketplace to build a smooth experience for the application developers. This model allows us to control the entire API gateway deployment with a single control plane component. Figure 8-9 depicts this deployment model.

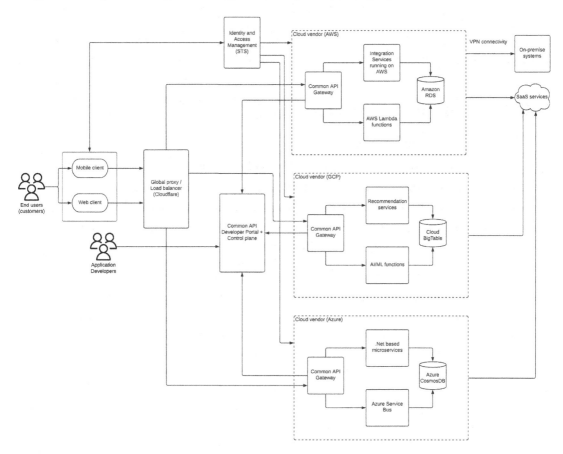

Figure 8-9. *Multi-cloud deployment with a common API gateway*

As depicted in the figure, we are using the same API gateway component deployed in different cloud platforms to interface the services with external and internal client applications. It is important to select an API vendor that can run on any cloud platform in a cloud-agnostic fashion while controlling each deployment with a single control plane. Additionally, the figure depicts the usage of the common API marketplace (developer portal) that comes with the same API vendor so that the integration becomes much easier and simpler.

In this deployment model also, we are using a dedicated IAM platform to provide the security functionality and act as an STS server. The API platform builds a trust relationship with this IAM component to allow requests that come with a token issued by the STS to grant access to the business services. Here also, we need a global load balancer to route traffic in a shared manner across multiple cloud platforms.

Highly Available Multi-cloud Deployment

In both the aforementioned approaches, we assumed that APIs are partitioned into separate groups and deployed into different cloud platforms, which is a good assumption to make since each cloud platform can have its own scalability and availability features. But there can be some extreme use cases where we need to deploy the same set of APIs across multiple cloud platforms for the sake of better availability. We can support such an architecture with a primary deployment that has a control plane and a primary data source that will synchronize with other secondary data sources in other deployments. Figure 8-10 depicts this deployment model.

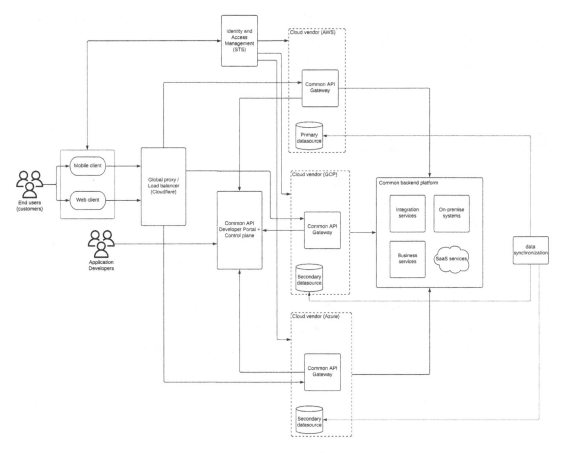

Figure 8-10. *Multi-cloud deployment with high availability and common API gateway*

The figure depicts how we can deploy an API gateway in a multi-cloud deployment model with the purpose of high availability. In this model, all the APIs deployed in one cloud platform are replicated into the other cloud platforms for higher availability. In case one cloud platform goes off, still other cloud platforms can serve the traffic. Also, it allows us to balance the load among different cloud platforms and sometimes bind certain applications to specific cloud platforms for better performance. Instead of having different backend systems and use cases on each cloud platform, this model connects to the same backend platform from all the API gateways since those APIs are identical in functionality. One key aspect of this architecture is that at any given time, all three deployments should be identical in terms of the APIs exposed. This requires proper data synchronization across cloud platforms via a dedicated data synchronization mechanism. We can achieve this by using the same database in all three cloud platforms for storing API-specific data. Also, it is recommended to use one deployment as the primary deployment and make all the necessary changes via that deployment instead of doing changes in multiple cloud platforms. By doing so, we can avoid data inconsistency issues.

Cloud Migration Pattern

Designing and implementing an application or a software system from scratch on a cloud platform is comparatively easier than moving an already-existing application or software system from on-premise to a cloud platform. Hence, cloud migration is considered one of the most complex yet essential requirements of modern enterprise IT ecosystem. Hence, it is important to understand the complexity of the process from the beginning and plan the migration properly. Different cloud vendors provide their own migration strategies and services to get customers into their respective cloud platform. But it is important that as the enterprise architect or developer, you need to understand the overall process properly. We can identify three main phases of cloud migration regardless of the cloud platform:

1. Assessment

2. Preparation

3. Migration and modernization

Let us discuss these points in detail.

Assessment

Since cloud migration is a complicated process that takes a considerable amount of time and resources, it is essential to identify the business need for such a move and the immediate and future benefits gained by migrating. As part of this assessment, we need to identify the state of the organization in terms of cloud readiness and which components need to be migrated as it is (lift and shift), which components need to rearchitected, and which components need to be dropped and purchased.

Preparation

Once we have a proper idea on the software components and their future state along with the business backing both from organizational level and investment level, we can start preparing the migration by formulating the required teams and building the necessary skills to do the actual migration. We can also work on the timelines for migration and identify the order of the migration and the success criteria for each component.

Migration and Modernization

The final phase of the migration is actually doing the migration and modernization as per the planning we did at the initial stages. It is important to get the support from the cloud vendor during this phase for performing the migration tasks. As part of the migration, we might need to rearchitect the solutions from scratch and use better methodologies to improve the existing implementations. At the same time, there can be certain software components we need to let go and build the functionality in-house from scratch. There can be other applications that can be easily replaced with SaaS products that are readily available. While migrating, it is important to learn from your mistakes and iterate the good practices to make it more efficient.

Let us take an example use case and discuss how we can migrate an existing brownfield enterprise platform to cloud.

Sample Cloud Migration Use Case

Let us take a medium-sized organization that has an SOA-based enterprise software system that is running in an on-premise data center. This system consists of several COTS applications for business operations (e.g., CRM, ERP, HR), a relational database, a number of in-house applications built as SOAP/REST-based applications, some legacy applications that were developed a long time ago, and an ESB to integrate all these applications. There is a web application that is based on JSP (Java Server Pages) that provides access to the business services via an accessibility layer that consists of a load balancer and a firewall. Figure 8-11 depicts the existing architecture.

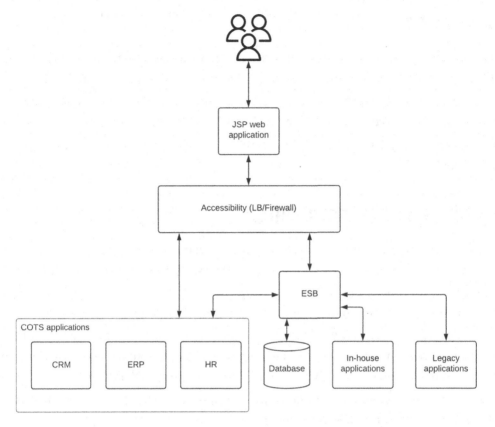

Figure 8-11. *Brown-field, on-premise enterprise platform example*

Let's go through the phased approach for cloud migration of this architecture.

Assessment

During a recent conversation with the business leadership team, it is identified that there are several drawbacks in the current system when it comes to catering the future demands of the company. The executive team asked several questions on the existing platform.

- How scalable this architecture is if we are to expand business operations globally?

- What happens if one of the components fails? What happens if the entire data center fails?

- How long does it take to roll out a new service?

- What is the update cycle for this platform?

Based on these discussion points, the architecture team gathered and decided that migrating to a cloud platform can solve most of these challenges of the current platform and also it helps align with the organizational goal of globalizing the business operations. With a cloud platform, we can scale the deployment to global scale with minimum effort. Also, we can distribute the components across physically distributed locations of the cloud platform to make sure applications are available even during a data center failure. With the availability of resources at the fingertips, we could release new services pretty quickly. Based on the type of application and cloud service that we select, the upgrades will also become easier and sometimes become completely transparent to the users. This assessment provides enough information to convince business leaders on the cloud migration approach. The next step is to iron out the plan for the migration and prepare the teams to embrace the migration.

Preparation

During the preparation phase, we need to come up with an overall effort estimation for the cloud migration and a detailed breakdown of the timelines for migrating each component or the set of related components. As an example, we can identify the following approaches for the migration of the software components in our sample architecture:

- Turn in-house applications into microservices.

- Utilize a cloud-provided database for an existing database.

- Use a modern hybrid integration platform in place of existing ESB.

- Purchase SaaS products for COTS applications as much as possible.

- Run remaining COTS applications on VMs.

- Move legacy application functionality to microservices.

- Run remaining legacy applications as VMs.

With these details identified and put into a timeline with proper success criteria, we can kick start the migration process.

Migration and Modernization

As we have identified in the preparation stage, we can start working on several aspects in parallel such as moving data from on-premise DB to cloud database, breaking down in-house applications into microservices, and looking for SaaS alternatives to COTS applications as well for ESB. If we have enough resources, we can even start working on legacy application modernization as well. While doing all these changes, we need to make sure that the existing users do not get impacted by these internal changes that we carried out. To do that, we can use the "strangler pattern" and introduce an intermediate layer to hide the internal details from the external customers. We can use an API gateway as the intermediate component as depicted in Figure 8-12.

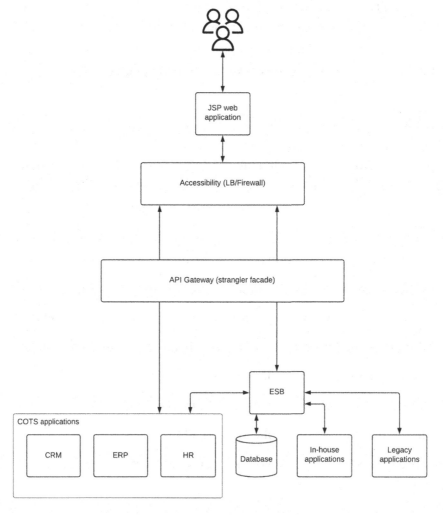

Figure 8-12. *Using API gateway as strangler facade for cloud migration*

As depicted in the figure, the API gateway hides the details of internal systems and applications that were directly connected to the web application before. We need to make some changes to the web application as part of this process. But it is a one-time task, and it will allow us to make necessary changes in the backend side without impacting the customers.

Once we have the API gateway in place and the required changes are done on the web application side to accommodate that change, we can start rolling out new changes in small fractions by changing the API gateway layer to point to the new services in place of old endpoints in a graceful manner. Figure 8-13 depicts a state where half of the systems are migrated toward cloud-native architecture.

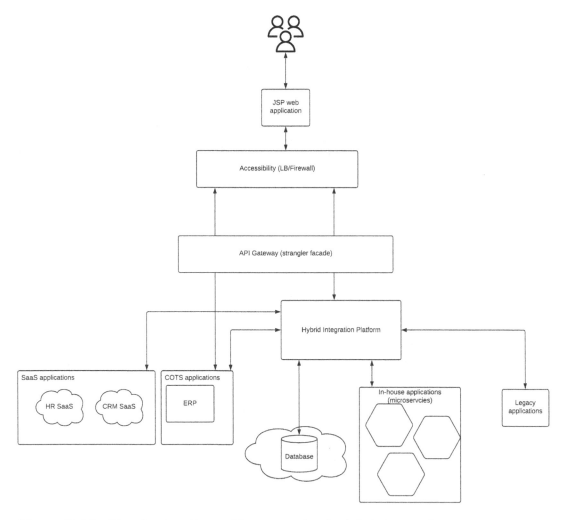

Figure 8-13. *Cloud migration with a strangler facade intermediate state*

As depicted in the figure, at this point in time, the migration is half done, and the applications are either rearchitected (in-house applications), repurchased (database, CRM, HR), or replatformed (ESB). All of these components can run on a cloud platform either on top of IaaS or PaaS. The final phase of the migration is to migrate the legacy applications and remaining COTS applications by rehosting (lift and shift) on the cloud platform. Figure 8-14 depicts the final architecture where all the components are migrated to cloud.

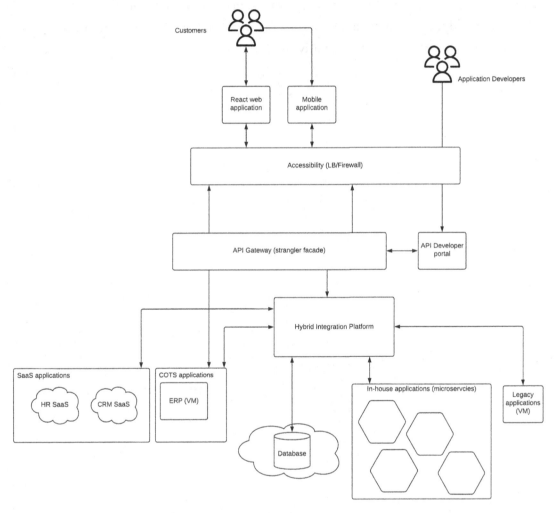

Figure 8-14. *Cloud migration with a strangler facade final architecture*

As depicted in the figure, the final architecture consists of components that can be run on top of any cloud platform. The remaining components of legacy application functionality and any COTS applications will run as VMs on the cloud platform. Additionally, we have also added a mobile application to provide improved experience to the users by utilizing the API gateway. Also, a developer portal is added to expand the business to third-party application developers who can take the business to new customer bases.

Once the migration is done, we can measure certain metrics such as performance improvements, usage improvements, and sales improvements to validate the decision we took at the beginning of the migration. That would make it a complete task with results to go with.

Summary

In this chapter, we looked at building cloud-native enterprise platforms by utilizing the benefits offered by cloud computing. We started the chapter with an introduction to cloud computing and cloud-native concepts and discussed two key technologies in containers and Kubernetes. Then we designed a solution architecture using microservice architecture principles to reap the benefits of cloud computing platforms. There we discussed different types of enterprise applications and converted them into cloud-native applications using the MSA concepts. Then we discussed Kubernetes and building a cloud-native enterprise platform using it. Next, we discussed about multi-cloud deployment model and different types of options we have when deploying enterprise software systems across different cloud platforms. Finally, we discussed in brief about migrating an existing enterprise software system to a cloud platform using the strangler pattern.

CHAPTER 9

Industry-Specific Architecture Patterns

Every business domain has its own set of problems that need to be addressed with an enterprise software system. There are many industry-specific use cases, and software vendors have developed special software to cater to those use cases. As an architect, it is important to have a knowledge of the domain when designing software systems for a given enterprise. We have discussed many common architecture patterns in this book that can be utilized by enterprises regardless of their business domain.

In this chapter, we are going to focus on the specific software components that are used in certain industries and come up with a set of industry-specific solution architecture patterns that can fulfill the needs of the respective industries. We will discuss the unique challenges that a particular business domain has and the solutions that we can provide using the technology. The solutions that we discuss in this chapter can be reused by enterprises across the globe when they operate on that particular domain.

In this chapter, we are going to discuss the solution architecture patterns for the following industry domains:

- Transportation industry

- Telecommunications industry

- Retail industry

- Education industry

- Automotive industry

- Healthcare industry

- Power and energy industry

- Hospitality industry

© Chanaka Fernando 2023
C. Fernando, *Solution Architecture Patterns for Enterprise*, https://doi.org/10.1007/978-1-4842-8948-8_9

Having prior knowledge of certain industries would help you to gain the best out of this chapter. But we have tried to provide some foundational information on each industry within the chapter for a novice reader.

Transportation Industry

Transportation is one of most important industries out there. It allows people to go from place to place and fulfill their needs. There are three main types of transportation we can identify:

- Ground transportation

- Air transportation

- Water transportation

In any of these transportation mediums, technology is utilized to not only manufacture the transportation vehicles but also to coordinate the transportation. If we think about air and water transportation, those are comparatively less congested given the vast space we have in those mediums. If we think about the ground transportation, it is much complicated due to the limited space that we use to transport vehicles on the ground. On the other hand, the most used and busiest transportation mechanism is the ground transportation. In this section, we are going to design an enterprise software solution to cater to the needs of the ground transportation.

Congestion or "traffic jam" is the main challenge we face in designing a solution for ground transportation. It is an inevitable part of the ground transportation. There are many attempts made by the governments, vehicle manufacturers, and technology companies alike to resolve this congestion problem. Some solutions are

- Promoting public transportation to reduce the number of vehicles on the road

- Developing self-driving cars to efficiently utilize the roads

- Building technology-driven platforms such as Uber and Lyft to reduce the private vehicles on the road

These solutions and many other creative ideas help reduce the congestion problem to a certain extent. Let us discuss how we can help this problem from the technology perspective.

Understanding the Ecosystem

In a typical ground transportation ecosystem, we can identify three main components that interact with each other:

- Humans (passengers, drivers, pedestrians, police officers, road workers, road designers)

- Infrastructure (roads, signalling systems, sensors, control centers)

- Vehicles (private vehicles, self-driving cars, taxies, public transportation)

Let us try to understand how these different stakeholders use the ground transportation ecosystem in a bit more detail.

- Passengers – Individuals who travel as commuters of vehicles. These users are interested in reaching their destination in a more convenient and time-efficient manner. They would like to get information about traffic conditions, vehicle locations, capacities, and vehicle conditions.

- Drivers – Individuals who drive vehicles and share the infrastructure with each other. Their responsibility is to move passengers from the starting point to the destination in a safe, timely manner. They are interested in traffic conditions, traffic light system, passenger capacities, roadside maintenance activities, events happening in that area, etc.

- Pedestrians – Individuals who use the roads by travelling on foot and walking around the city. They are interested in knowing about air pollution, crowded areas, and efficient routes (shortcuts).

- Vehicles (including self-driving) – The physical unit that drivers are using to carry passengers around. Vehicles have sensors to capture data about the surroundings and actuators to act upon receiving the data. Self-driving vehicles are solely driven by these two types of data, while other vehicles use those data points to improve driver efficiency, eventually contributing to the overall efficiency improvement of the system.

- Sensors – Tiny hardware units that can be used to improve the overall system efficiency by capturing the details in the vicinity. There are different types of sensors used in a ground transportation system:

  - Traffic sensors – These sensors can be installed in the road near junctions (e.g., SCOOT). They will capture raw events about how many vehicles passed through the sensors. That can be used to derive the traffic flow of a particular direction within a junction and eventually communicated to the traffic control system so that the overall traffic lighting system can be improved.

  - Platform gate sensors – These sensors can be used to measure the capacity at a given platform of a railway station, and based on that, users can be distributed to different sections of the platform to have a uniform distribution of load to the compartments.

  - Air pollution sensors – By measuring the air quality of an area, pedestrians can select healthy areas to take a walk, and vehicles can be moved away from roads that are heavily used by pedestrians.

  - Vehicle-mounted sensors – These are the units installed within the vehicle such as parking assist sensors, reverse sensors, auto-break sensors, and many other types of modern sensors found in vehicles.

- Traffic management system – This is the central control system of the color light system within a given area. Adaptive signal light systems can take feedback from roadside sensors and change the durations of green light and control the traffic flows as a whole, and based on the day of the week and the time, it can decide on the timing of lights across the entire system. Traffic police can also receive this information through a control center so that they can take decisions on changing the system based on practical situations such as accidents.

- Infrastructure maintenance – Road maintenance is a common task that is carried out in a ground transportation system. Providing this information ahead of time allows people to manage their trips properly without facing unwanted congestions.

- Stations (bus, railway, tram) – Places where public transportation users gather around, and having regular, up-to-date information from these points helps a massive portion of the users. Showing details about schedule, current running vehicles and their locations, and time to reach the destination helps passengers immensely. With the usage of sensors on vehicles, more detailed information like capacity of each compartment, locations of buses, and predicted time can be communicated to the users through public communication mechanisms available in these stations.

- Taxi services have a huge impact on the traffic condition since it reduces the number of personal vehicles entering the city through ride sharing with professional drivers with advanced devices. These drivers can make smart decisions and be more effective on the roads with quality information and experience.

- Transportation authorities – Most of the public transportation is controlled by these authorities. They can impose rules for better transportation system and run buses, trains, and trams within cities.

With that understanding of the ecosystem, let us try to understand the technical requirements of an effective ground transportation system.

Technical Requirements

Based on what we have discussed in the preceding section, we can identify the following high-level requirements for our transportation system:

- Collect – Capture the information coming from various sensors and other sources.

- Store – Store the information for later referral and processing.

- Process – Analyze the information and derive valuable insights.

- Publish – Communicate the valuable insights with the consumers.

- Act – Take actions based on certain information.

The next step in designing the solution is to identify the technical components that we can use to cater to these requirements. The following is a list of components that we need to implement a solution:

- Real-time data processing component – This component is used to collect the information in real time and apply various processing techniques.

- Data storage component – This is required to store the processed information so that they can be referred by other systems later.

- Integration component – This is required to connect the transportation data with other systems that store data about population, vehicles, and maintenance.

- API component – When users need to access information about schedules, locations, and capacities from their mobile devices or via web applications, API gateway is required to expose this information securely.

- Security component – Needed to implement security at each layer of the system.

- Message broker component – This is used to connect data publishers with data consumers in an asynchronous manner.

With this information, we can now design a solution architecture to improve the experience of a user who is involved in ground transportation.

Solution Architecture

Figure 9-1 depicts a solution architecture that we can use to build an effective ground transportation system.

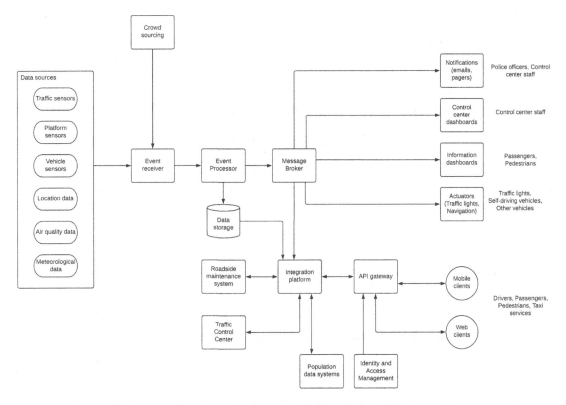

Figure 9-1. *Solution architecture for ground transportation system*

As depicted in the figure, various sensors capture information about transportation system and its behavior. These events can be pre-processed if required on the source side before pushing them into the event receiver. As an example, air quality data can be aggregated from multiple sensors and sent as a single event for a given location instead of sending data from each and every sensor. These events are then received by the event receiver, which is capable of connecting to various event sources such as MQTT, HTTP, TCP, and other protocols. The event processor then applies various real-time processing techniques such as filtering, cleansing, aggregation, and correlation and makes valuable insights of these events. It will store certain insights such as summary information in the database while publishing real-time statistics and notifications to the message broker.

The message broker is there to decouple the data sources from the data subscribers. It publishes valuable information through topics so that relevant subscribers can receive information in real time in an asynchronous manner. Some examples are

- Police officers receiving notifications on certain conditions such as excessive congestion or meteorological warnings

- Control center staff receiving notifications related to failures of traffic lights and unexpected people gatherings

- Passengers receiving real-time statistics and information through dashboards about whereabouts of the buses and trains and their estimated arrivals and departures

- Sending actions to traffic lights and navigational systems based on certain traffic conditions to improve the overall system performance

There will be several other systems that hold information related to transportation-related activities such as roadside maintenance activities, population data, geographic information systems (GIS), and police department data that need to be integrated into the solution to provide a better experience. There is the integration component that connects these systems together as well as the message broker to bridge the real-time data with the static data. It will also connect with the data storage systems that store the processed information from the real-time events. Then we have the API gateway that is used to expose the information related to the transportation system in a synchronous manner for consumption by mobile and web applications. The Identity and Access Management system is used to provide security capabilities to the platform. Even though the diagram only shows a connection between API gateway and IAM component, there can be many other systems that utilize the IAM platform in addition to the API gateway.

This solution architecture can be realized with many open source and commercial applications available in the market.

Telecommunications Industry

Sending a message from one place to another has been crucial for not only humans but also for all the living species. Humans have gone through leaps and bounds to find new ways to communicate among themselves no matter how distant they are from each other. Telecommunication is the technology that enables humans to communicate with one another regardless of the location. It helped people to save lives, win wars, make peace, and many other things. Alexander Graham Bell made it possible to send a message over a wire, and that opened the door for revolutionary innovations such as over-the-air communication (wireless), and finally, we are in the age of satellite-based communication (thanks to Sir Arthur C. Clarke), which made it possible to connect people in far corners of the world within a whisker. Now we are in a world where we have more mobile phones than the human population.

Telecommunication (specifically mobile) technology has gone through several iterations (e.g., 2G, 3G, 4G, 5G), and the main focus point of that was to improve how information is exchanged across the network. As any other technology, telecommunication has gone beyond the need of voice message exchanges to data communications to video conferencing to shopping to financing and many more. You can absolutely do anything with the device (mobile phone) that was used to send messages in the past using your fingertips. The organizations who bring this technology to the end user are called the Mobile Network Operator (MNO). Even though they deal with these technical advancements continuously, their main focus point is their customer base, which they refer to as subscribers. It is their responsibility to provide value to their subscribers on top of the telecommunication capability that they offer through technology.

Understanding the Ecosystem

Let's start with a simple use case where you make a phone call to your friend. For this event to happen successfully, you should have a mobile phone with a sim card that has a subscription from a mobile network operator (MNO) who provides network services within that region. Once you dial the phone number, it will be communicated via the access network that connects your phone with the closest telecommunication tower through signalling network and find out the subscriber related to that number. Once the mobile network identifies the subscriber and their network, it will make a connection with that network over the telecommunication backbone. If the callee is from a different MNO, then that network will check the status of the subscriber, and if it is valid, the call will be connected to the callee using the access network. This process looks like a complicated task, and in reality, it is more complicated than what is described here. In reality, all of these tasks execute within a few seconds, and the caller is able to make a call to the callee.

There is one key principle in the telecommunication industry to secure the network and provide access to the users. This concept is called AAA, which stands for Authentication, Authorization, and Accounting.

- Authentication is the step where the user identity is verified based on the credentials provided by the user.

- Authorization step checks which policies apply to the user and provides access to different services and resources based on these policies.

- Accounting step is used to charge the user for the services that the user has consumed. It can be a data access or phone call or any other value-added service.

AAA provides a secured network with proper charging so that the telecommunications network can be maintained and continuous service levels can be achieved, which is a crucial aspect of any telecommunication infrastructure.

In a typical telecommunication ecosystem, we can identify several key stakeholders:

- Mobile network operator

- Subscriber

- Device manufacturers

- Internet service providers

- Third-party businesses

- Regulators

Let us discuss each of the stakeholders in detail.

A Mobile Network Operator (MNO) is an organization (enterprise) that maintains a telecommunication network and offers services to its subscribers. The MNO is responsible for acquiring the frequencies, setting up the infrastructure (signalling towers, base stations, switches, antennas, etc.), designing the network based on capacities, testing the signal strengths, and finally marketing and selling the service to the end users.

Subscribers are the end users who are using the network, which is built and maintained by the MNO, and pay for the subscription. These users can purchase value-added services through the mobile operator such as data communications, video conferencing, financial services, healthcare services, and insurance services to name a few.

Device manufacturers are the vendors who do research on technological advancements and build the equipments (phones, antennas, routers, switches, servers, etc.) that provide the infrastructure layer for message exchanges. These devices need to be built according to a given standard so that different components in the ecosystem can communicate with each other.

Internet Service Providers (ISP) are the organizations that maintain the connectivity between the MNO-maintained network and the public Internet as well as other MNOs. Normally, they maintain the backbone of the mobile network by setting up advanced infrastructure that requires significant investments. They provide connectivity between countries and continents as well.

Third-party businesses provide additional services to mobile subscribers by partnering with the MNOs. Services such as taxi services, e-channeling, payment services (banks), location-based services, and many other types of services are offered through either mobile network over signalling channels (SMS and USSD) or data network through Internet.

Regulators also play a key role in establishing a given MNO within a region. A telecommunication regulatory commission or a similar authority has the power to regulate the frequencies and create competition in the market so that subscribers get the best-valued service from the MNOs.

Technical Requirements

With that understanding of the ecosystem, let us focus on the technical requirements that we have in the telecommunications industry. One important thing to note is that we have two key technology areas within a telecommunication ecosystem:

- Telecommunication network

- IT system

Let us discuss these two systems in a bit more detail.

Telecommunication Network

Telecommunication network is the core networking infrastructure that provides the networking infrastructure to connect a phone call or data access request with the target phone number or a website. This network consists of components such as

- Mobile device

- Access network

- Telecommunication tower

- Base station

- Core network

- Internet

These components work together to offer the basic functionality of the mobile network, which is to make a phone call or access a website. In addition to these core networking components, we need to utilize a connected IT infrastructure to perform tasks such as billing, metering, value-added services, subscriber management, and many other customer-centric operations. That is the component that we focus in this section of the book.

IT System

In the telecommunication industry, both the networking infrastructure and the subscribers are equally important to the business. The main purpose of the IT system is to maintain the systems and their interactions where subscriber-related information and value-added services reside. Functionalities such as billing, charging, value-added services, subscriber information, and service subscriptions are stored in these systems. There will be purpose-built software to store these types of information, which will either be built in-house or purchased from external vendors. On the other hand, these systems can be deployed as on-premise, cloud, or hybrid applications in the IT infrastructure.

Solution Architecture (Single Operator)

Once we have these kinds of disparate systems within an IT system, integration platforms become a necessity. In addition to that, more and more services are offered through omni-channel experiences to the subscribers such as mobile, web, and phone channels. Having a secured API gateway also becomes a requirement for IT system. Figure 9-2 depicts a solution architecture that we can utilize to build an IT system for a telecommunication-based enterprise.

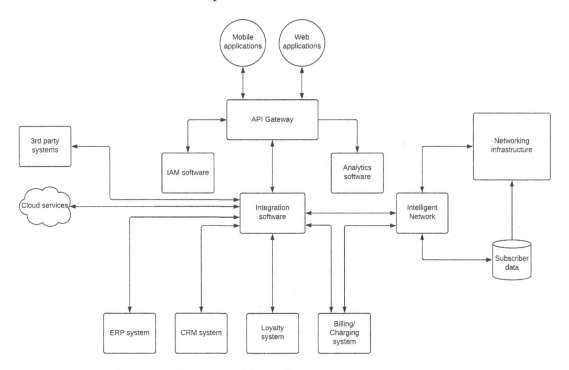

Figure 9-2. *Solution architecture for a telecommunication IT system*

The figure depicts a solution architecture with the key components used in a telecommunication ecosystem. The diagram depicts the networking infrastructure that takes care of making the connections between subscribers and Internet services as a separate component to make the diagram less complicated. This networking component is connected to the IT system via the intelligent network component that handles the subscribers and their usage information. The intelligent network also connects with the subscriber database, which stores information about the mobile subscribers.

We can also identify that there are other systems such as billing and charging software, loyalty software, CRM software, and ERP software used in the IT system. Some of these systems such as billing and charging systems use telecommunication-specific protocols such as Diameter that need to be supported in this solution. These software components are integrated via an integration software component. Additionally, this integration software also connects with cloud services that are utilized by the organization such as payment gateways and SaaS services along with the intelligent network. Internet of Things or IoT devices are becoming a major user of telecommunication infrastructure in which case it is required to integrate with protocols such as MQTT into this solution. With the introduction of value-added services via third-party business integrations, there will be requirements to connect with the systems that are maintained by these third parties. Some examples are e-channeling systems and ride-sharing systems. The integration that happens at this layer will be a B2B integration.

The integrated services will be exposed to the subscribers via mobile applications as well as web applications. We need to use an API gateway to expose the internal services and data to the external subscribers. Additionally, we also need a security component that is capable of providing IAM capabilities. Analytics software is also used in the telecommunication industry to identify the usage patterns of the subscribers and offer more creative, customized experiences to the subscribers. It can play a big role in providing differentiated services to the subscribers in a highly competitive market.

A new trend that we see in the telecom industry is the usage of common APIs to create interoperability between MNOs to provide much better and flexible services to the subscribers. As an example, if I'm using a subscription from operator (MNO) X and move into an area that only has coverage from operator (MNO) Y, I should be able to use the mobile network with an extra cost, which will be shared across two operators. For the subscribers, it is a value-added service since they have to use two subscriptions and two sim cards. Let's discuss how this can be achieved with a simple improvement to our solution architecture.

Solution Architecture (Multiple Operators)

MNOs have their own strengths and weaknesses when it comes to the network capabilities and other service offerings to their subscribers. MNOs want to expand their strong capabilities to subscribers in other networks, while subscribers want to get the best possible service no matter who the operator is. The telecommunication industry has introduced a mechanism to share the subscriber data between operators using a set of standard APIs. This standard is called GSMA OneAPI. In simple terms, it is a mechanism to expose set of capabilities within MNOs through a standard set of APIs so that everyone can build applications on top of those APIs and allows interoperability across different MNOs (like they do for roaming) for services that they offer.

If we think about roaming capabilities, there should be an agreement between your local MNO and the visiting MNO so that you can use the same SIM card in that visiting country or region. With the OneAPI specification, this interoperability brings the service to the next level where users can use services and applications that are offered by the visiting MNO. Figure 9-3 depicts a solution architecture that we can use to implement this OneAPI concept across multiple MNOs.

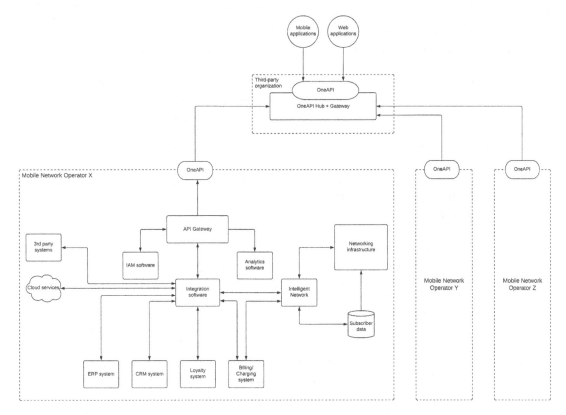

Figure 9-3. *Solution architecture for the telecommunications industry with OneAPI*

The figure depicts a solution architecture that utilizes the OneAPI concept to share services to subscribers from different MNOs. As depicted in the figure, each operator will expose a standard set of APIs called OneAPI to expose various services such as location services, charging services, SMS services, and MMS services. There is a hub and a gateway that expose various services to application developers so that they can provide value-added services on top of these APIs to the subscribers. At the same time, the operators will work with one another via the hub operator to strike business deals when sharing networking services over the OneAPI gateway. This architecture allows multiple operators within a country, region, or even a continent to work together and provide seamless experiences to the subscribers with a single subscription.

Retail Industry

No matter how rich you are, you purchase goods and services from a retail store in most cases. These stores are closer to you in one way or another. In the recent past, the retail industry has gone through major changes in terms of customer experience, delivery models, and operation models. A few of them are as follows:

- Physical stores vs. online stores – With the advancement of mobile devices and the ubiquitous nature of online shopping, more and more people are spending their money on online stores rather than physical stores.

- Omni-channel experiences – More and more retailers are providing users with options to do the shopping through multiple channels such as order online and pick up from nearest stores so that they can spend less time on finding items.

- Improved delivery experiences – With more and more technology-driven retailers, same-day delivery for fresh items such as vegetables and fruits makes life easier for customers.

- Unique customer experiences – With online shopping, customers get recommendations, similar products, and many other advanced features that were not possible with physical stores. Additionally, customized deals and payment terms can also entice customers to do more shopping than they actually need.

With these changes, the retail industry needs to step up the innovation process and build robust enterprise software systems to cater to these demands.

Understanding the Ecosystem

Regardless of the size of the retailer, there are some common components that we can identify in a typical retail software system. Those components include the following:

- Warehousing systems

- Inventory management systems

- Finance management systems

- Supplier sourcing systems

- HR management systems

In addition to these systems, if you are operating a medium to large-scale retail chain with online stores and in-store self-service options, you will have more systems such as

- Point of sales (POS)/kiosk systems

- Self-checkout systems

- Price checking points

- Mobile shopping applications

- E-commerce web applications

- Delivery systems or partner integrations

The enterprise software solution that we design needs to integrate with these components and provide differentiated experience to the customers coming into your retail experience.

Technical Requirements

Given the number of different systems required to run the operations in a retail business, it is quite common to use an integration platform to connect systems in a given store as well as other stores and main control centers that provide online shopping experience to the users. Given the fact that customers are using different channels to purchase products and make payments, having an API gateway with proper security is also critical for the success of the retail business. If providing an online store, having a message broker system is also crucial to accept the orders from the customers and process them asynchronously. Having a proper analytics system can also become handy when providing unique experiences to the customers through online stores such as recommendations and special offers.

Solution Architecture

The goal of building a solution architecture for the retail industry is to provide great experiences to the customers while allowing the business to achieve growth and acquire more customers by overcoming the challenges posed by the competition. In a typical retail platform, there are software components used by individual stores as well as software components used by central stores that provide online shopping experience to the customers. Figure 9-4 depicts a solution architecture that can be used to build a modern retail platform.

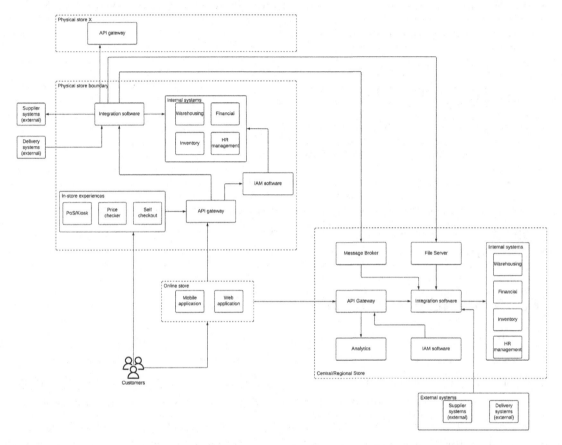

Figure 9-4. *Retail industry software system solution architecture*

The figure depicts a solution architecture that can be used to build a software system for a retail company that integrates software components in a physical store, an online store, and a regional store to offer unique experiences to the shoppers (customers). In the physical store, we have internal systems that are there to keep track of sales, operations, HR management, and stocks. These systems are integrated with third-party software systems for sourcing purposes and delivery purposes. These integrated services are exposed to internal and external clients using the API gateway. In this particular case, we have internal clients in the form of in-store devices such as PoS/kiosk machines, price checker devices, and self-checkout counters. There is an IAM software component to provide the required security for the platform. In case the online shopping experience allows shopping at a given physical store (e.g., in-store pickup), those external clients also connect to the internal systems through the API gateway. In case this particular store needs to connect with another store, we can use the integration platform to make that integration to the API gateway of the secondary store.

The online store provides two channels for the users to shop: through the mobile application or the web application. The requests coming through the online store are served through a central or regional store, which may act as an online-only store in some cases. If someone needs, they can use the same physical store that we discussed in the previous section to fulfill the online requests as well. But assuming that there is a separate store to cater to the online purchases, we have designed the solution architecture here. This central store also uses the same set of internal systems to keep track of business and stocks data. It also uses an integration platform to connect these systems. An API gateway is used to expose different types of online services to the mobile and web applications. The API gateway will also use an analytics engine to understand the customer behavior so that we can provide more customized user experience to the customers. The IAM component is also there to provide the security features to the platform such as SSO, MFA, social logins, and consent management.

This central store has a message broker to process the online purchases in an asynchronous manner. Given that online purchases take time to process these requests, using an asynchronous model is the correct approach. Additionally, there is a file server in the centralized store that is used to collect various reports from the physical stores for bookkeeping purposes. The central store also integrates with sourcing partners as well as delivery partners for supplies and delivery, respectively.

Education Industry

Education is one of the most influential ways to change the world order. It simply changes the way people understand the world and lets them explore what they could not have done before. Even though education institutions are the ones who produce innovators who advance the technology, sometimes, the same institutions are not using the technological advancements to their benefit.

Understanding the Ecosystem

This has changed a lot in the recent past with more and more universities opening up their courses to wider audiences through the usage of online technology. From online course materials such as PDFs and source code to learning management systems to virtual classrooms to online degrees, the usage of technology within the education industry has increased. These online platforms allow students and teachers to perform certain activities in a much easier and manageable manner. Some of these activities are

- Assignment submissions
- Discussions
- Collaborations
- Exams
- Libraries
- Alumni

In addition to the benefits offered to the inmates of the institution, it also allows it to offer the educational services to a wider student base across the globe using their own LMS or some education platforms such as Coursera, edX, or Udemy.

A typical education software system consists of the following software components:

- Learning Management System (LMS) – This is the core application used by the students, teachers, and authorities to move the educational programs forward with continuous interactions.

- Student portal – A portal for students to perform certain tasks such as payments, registrations, and other related activities.

- File server – To keep various types of files associated with the courses

- Video conferencing platform – Provides the ability to perform online classes.

- User store – To keep various user information including students, teachers, and administrators.

- In-house applications – There can be many applications developed by students to implement certain improvements to the overall experience of the platform.

- Databases – There will be databases to store various information such as events, schedules, and research data.

- Cloud applications – There can be SaaS applications used for certain use cases within the education platform.

- Library system – This system will allow students to borrow books from physical libraries as well as digital libraries.

Technical Requirements

The main technical requirements that we can identify in an education software system are

- Integrating disparate systems that are built in isolation

- Managing users across platforms

- Expanding to wider audiences

- Competing with the online learning platforms

- Supporting hybrid learning models

To support these requirements, we can use the following software components:

- Integration software for connecting disparate systems

- Identity and Access Management software for managing users across systems

- API gateway for expanding the services to wider audiences

- API gateway for complementing learning platforms

- Video conferencing tools to support hybrid learning models

With these options in mind, let us design a solution architecture for an education IT system.

Solution Architecture

The main focus of our solution is to provide a unified experience for the users based on the type of user who is accessing the system. There can be certain information that is only visible to students and certain other information that is only visible to teachers and administrators. Additionally, there will be public information about course details, events, and other information that can be shared with the general public. We can design our front-end applications to reflect these different use cases and permission models with the help of backend systems such as API gateways. Figure 9-5 depicts a solution architecture that we can use to build a modern enterprise software system for an educational institution.

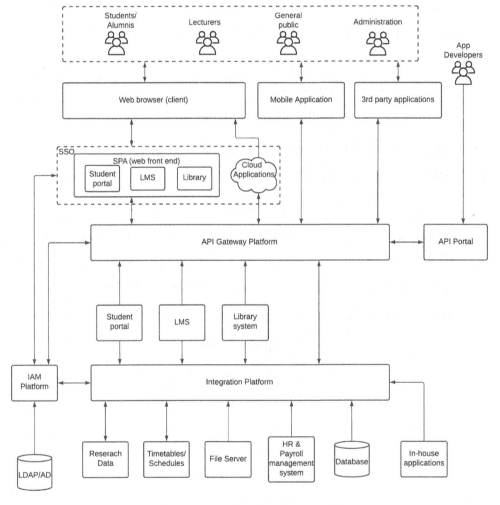

Figure 9-5. *Solution architecture for the education industry*

As depicted in the figure, we can design a solution architecture for the education industry using the components included there. At the top level, we have different types of users who interact with the system via different channels including mobile applications, web applications, and third-party platforms such as Coursera. The web application is designed in such a way that it can load different information from different backend systems in a seamless manner without full page refresh for better user experience. Also, these different application components such as student portal, LMS, and library applications are enabled with SSO so that login into one application allows the users to log into the other applications automatically.

API gateway is used to expose the internal systems and backend to the internal users (students) as well as external users who are coming through third-party applications. The integration platform connects various systems depicted in the figure based on the requirements of the user. An API portal can be used to expose certain functionalities to external application developers so that they can build innovative applications such as Coursera or Udemy.

The IAM platform is used to provide users with modern security features such as SSO, MFA, social logins, and consent management to name a few. It connects with a single user store and acts as the centralized IAM platform for all the different applications in the system. The API gateway also utilizes the IAM platform to authenticate users based on the tokens issued by the IAM platform.

Automotive Industry

Building self-driving cars or autonomous vehicles has been a dream of automobile manufacturers for some time. Even though some manufacturers are coming closer to developing such vehicles, there are still doubts about the technology and its accuracy and the ethical nature. On the other hand, modern vehicles have become so smart that with the interaction between the vehicles and the human, we can complete a much better vehicle than a self-driving car. Some features available in the modern vehicles include

- Making/answering phone calls
- Playing media (songs, movies)
- Navigation systems (routes, gas stations, malls)
- Automatic parking/brake assistance/cruise control
- Weather alerts

We can design a better platform for the automotive industry using the capabilities provided by these modern vehicles along with the enterprise software tools.

Understanding the Ecosystem

Vehicles are moving objects that travel from point A to point B without colliding with other objects on the way. Some objects are living beings, some are similar vehicles, and others are stationary objects. The driver of the vehicle (forget about the self-driving cars for the moment) is the one who is assigned with this task. In modern vehicles, there are a ton of sensors and actuators installed on the vehicle to help the driver execute this task of moving from A to B. The sensory data coming from these devices need to be processed, analyzed, and converted into actionable information using a system that consists of an in-vehicle component as well as components sitting outside the vehicle. The need for an external system comes with the advanced nature of the information that is provided to the driver. As an example, taking the inputs from all the cameras and placing them on a display is a simple task that can be performed by the in-vehicle computing platform. But providing the fastest route from A to B requires connecting to external services like traffic services and integrating that information with location data that is coming from a GPS unit installed on the vehicle. Another example would be automatically booking a vehicle service based on the distance traveled since the last service requires calling external services.

Technical Requirements

Let us think about a scenario where a modern vehicle is moving along the road. We have various components inside the vehicle as well as outside the vehicle that are interacting with one another during this process. There are certain things that we can identify to improve this experience:

- The vehicle has a variety of sensors to capture details of the surroundings. This information needs to be processed and displayed to the user effectively.

- The driver and the passengers (optional) who sit inside the vehicle should be able to do certain activities based on the information.

- External services (restaurants, vehicle services, shopping, payments, etc.) need to be utilized to provide additional information in the dashboard by connecting over a WAN.

- Some vehicle-specific data need to be sent over to the enterprise side (car manufacturer, dealer, services company) to process and provide actionable information in a timely manner.

- Vehicle owners should be able to access the vehicle-specific information and historical and analytical data through off-vehicle applications (mobile app, website).

We can categorize these technical requirements into two main components depending on where the computing happens:

- Edge computing – These are the computing resources available in the vehicle, and we call this "edge" since it is closer to the end user. The computing power and the resources are limited in the edge due to various factors such as power consumption, mobility, and network accessibility.

- Enterprise computing – This is the section where most of the heavyweight computing operations are carried out. This is a typical enterprise IT deployment with all the required computing resources to execute various complex computing tasks that are required to provide the best possible experience to the users.

The link between edge computing and enterprise computing components is the "access network," which is typically a mobile network. The advancements in the telecommunications industry like 5G connectivity help largely to provide a seamless user experience in the near future.

Solution Architecture

Let us design a solution architecture based on the technical requirements that we discussed in the preceding section. We identified two main types of computing needs in an automotive enterprise software system. Let us discuss the technical components we need to implement a solution on each of those types.

Edge Computing Components

At the edge, we have the vehicle with network connectivity. In the vehicle, there are various types of sensors that receive data from the surroundings and pass it back to the central computing platform within the vehicle. In most cases, it is a low-end computing device with a small processor and memory. This will have a display with a touchscreen or with physical buttons that can execute simple tasks like changing the display mode, changing across sensors in the display, and controlling actuators like temperature, lighting, entertainment system, etc. All these functionalities can be done offline without connectivity to the external system over the network.

In addition to these traditional in-vehicle capabilities, modern vehicles come with a number of useful features in the form of "applications" that can be utilized while in the vehicle. These applications require connectivity to external systems to execute their tasks. Some examples of such applications are Navigation, Shopping, Restaurants, and Weather. In addition to these applications, there is a feature called driving assistance that relies on external systems to provide better insights into the driver on road conditions, traffic conditions, vehicle maintenance, and many other useful information.

Enterprise Computing Components

As we discussed in the previous section, certain applications installed in the vehicle require additional information and computing resources to carry out those functions. This is the task of the enterprise computing component of the platform. It requires certain components that are essential to support the edge computing resources. The following is a list of high-level functionalities required on the enterprise side:

- Gateway – This is required to connect with external systems over a standard and secured channel from the in-vehicle applications. It allows the enterprise platform operators to offer different classes of services to the users with required access controls.

- Event broker and analysis – This component is needed to process real-time events coming from various sensors within the vehicle that require near real-time processing and are sent back to the vehicle as actionable information. At the backend of these events, various AI and ML models can be executed for predictive analysis and provide user experiences such as ahead-of-time notifications on sensor replacements, vehicle part replacements, vehicle services, traveling patterns, effective routes with better air quality, etc.

- Integration – Providing an experience that involves multiple systems requires an integration component that understands those different systems. That is the role of integration in this solution. As an example, to provide an integrated food-ordering application in the vehicle requires connecting to restaurants, payment services, and location services.

- Data store – This is required to provide various short-term and long-term analytics on driving patterns, vehicle conditions, predictive analysis, and many other aspects of the overall experience that relies on historical data.

- Other applications – There can be many other applications that support the overall experience of the driver and the passengers that operate outside of the "edge." Some examples are weather services, location services, enterprise applications, and cloud services.

- User (off-vehicle) applications – These applications provide the users with the capability to review and analyze the various metrics of the vehicle and driving patterns through a mobile application or a website from an off-vehicle device like a mobile computing device (e.g., phone, laptop, tab).

With the understanding of the main components that are involved in the automotive IT platform, let's build a solution architecture that can be realized with the technologies available in the market. Figure 9-6 depicts a solution architecture that is designed to cater to these requirements.

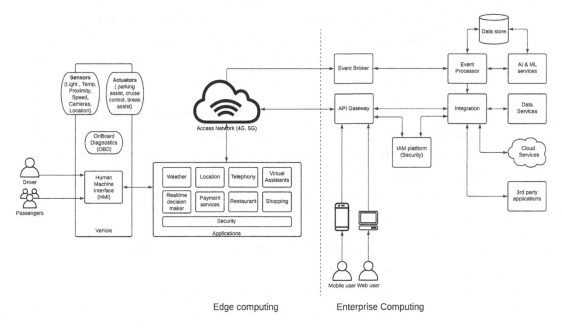

Figure 9-6. *Solution architecture for an automotive industry IT system*

The figure depicts a solution architecture that uses in-vehicle computing capabilities and enterprise computing capabilities to design a comprehensive solution for automotive industry. The diagram depicts the vehicle along with some of the common sensors found in modern vehicles. In addition to that, the built-in dashboard or touchscreen is depicted as the Human-Machine-Interface (HMI), which is a common term used for such interfaces. This interface consists of multiple applications that help the driver achieve their task of moving from A to B while providing additional mobility as a service function. These applications come with security requirements like authentication and authorization for doing certain tasks like payments. These applications rely on the enterprise computing backbone that does the heavy lifting of these applications.

API gateway acts as the interface between edge computing and enterprise computing components and provides quality-of-service (QoS) capabilities such as security, rate limiting, analytics, and different classes of services (e.g., free, monetized). It connects with various business systems and applications as the backend possibly through an integration layer that interconnects all these heterogeneous systems. There is an Identity and Access Management (IAM) platform that provides the necessary security features to the platform.

The real-time events and sensor data captured in the vehicle are sent to the event broker via a simple messaging protocol like MQTT to reduce the overhead added by a protocol like HTTP. These events are captured and processed in real time by an event processor or a stream processor and generate actionable insights and store them for further analysis by AI and ML services. These processed and analyzed information are then stored in data stores and exposed as data services to the edge applications over HTTP interfaces. At the same time, real-time notifications and insights are sent via the event broker in a publish-subscribe model. The applications running on the edge consume these processed and analyzed information within the HMI so that drivers can take benefit from that. In addition to that, these enterprise systems provide predictions on certain events and automatically generate events such as vehicle services, part replacements, and traffic conditions.

The same API gateway is used to expose certain details about the vehicle, driving patterns, service schedules, and maintenance activities via a mobile phone or a web application. It can also provide information such as the location of the vehicle and any movements even if the user is not within the vehicle.

Healthcare Industry

The importance of the healthcare industry grew rapidly during the COVID-19 pandemic that spans across several years starting in 2019. The usage of technology to provide healthcare services has become increasingly popular with this pandemic. Even before that incident, the healthcare industry has been utilizing technology in many areas within the domain to provide improved experiences to the healthcare users.

Understanding the Ecosystem

In a typical healthcare environment, we can identify several key stakeholders that interact with and make use of the environment:

- Healthcare facilities – These are the hospitals, laboratories, care centers, and other types of facilities that provide healthcare services. This can be a government-managed one or a private facility managed by a company.

- Internal users – These are the medical officers (doctors), nursing officers, technicians, patients, and many other professionals working within these hospital facilities.

- Governing bodies – Institutions that set the standards and govern the healthcare system quality so that the users receive quality healthcare regardless of where they are getting the service from. Health ministries, universities, research institutes, and unions comprise this segment.

- External users – Police officers, healthcare business owners, and the general public are some of these external users who interact with the ecosystem on a daily basis.

- Healthcare business/service – There is a huge external ecosystem built around the main healthcare stakeholders mentioned previously. These are various businesses like pharmacies, healthcare equipment, insurance companies, public services like police, emergency and ambulance services, etc.

With that understanding, let us try to identify the key units within a healthcare facility such as a hospital so that we can figure out the technical requirements for the solution that we are building using the IT resources. Figure 9-7 depicts some of the common units we can find within a hospital.

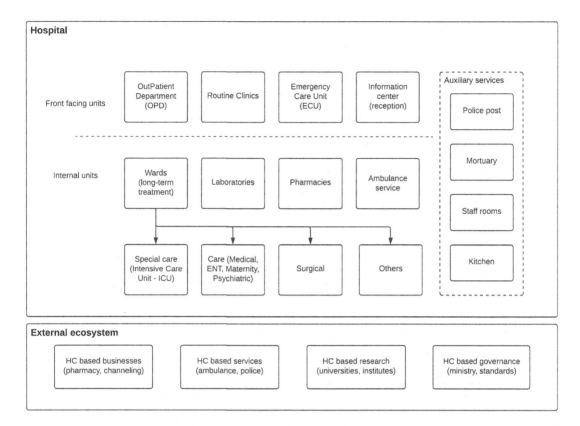

Figure 9-7. *Main units of a hospital and external ecosystem*

The figure depicts the main units within a hospital and the external ecosystem that interacts with a hospital. As depicted in the figure, units that interact with external people directly can be called as front-facing units. These units are as follows:

- Information center (reception) – This is where people get information about which unit they wanted to go once they enter a hospital facility.

- Outpatient Department (OPD) – This is the unit where people come and see doctors to get regular medication and consultancy.

- Emergency Care Unit (ECU) – If there are emergency situations like accidents, poisoning, or general emergency situations, this is the unit that handles those people (patients).

- Clinics – There are many routine clinics happening at the hospital where people with long-term health issues attend.

There are intermediate units that are accessible only by authorized personnel. These units provide services to patients who are getting long-term treatments.

- Wards – Once the doctors from OPD or ECU decide that a patient needs to get a long-term treatment, that patient will be admitted to the wards. There are different wards for different types of treatments needed by the patient.

- Laboratories – All the internal testing of various patient conditions is done in these laboratories and they are heavily interacting with medical staff, and the accuracy of these results defines the quality of the service provided by the hospital.

- Pharmacies – The people who are signing out from the wards, OPD patients, and clinical patients get their medicines from the hospital pharmacy.

There are special internal facilities that are only accessible by authorized personnel. These special units provide critical services to the patients.

- Intensive Care Unit (ICU) – When patients require consistent, intense care due to a special situation, those patients are treated in isolated areas that can only be accessed by authorized personnel.

- Surgical wards – These are the wards that actually carry out major surgeries of patients and can only be accessed by authorized personnel.

Now we have a better understanding of a typical healthcare ecosystem and different units that operate within a given healthcare facility. Let us try to understand the technical requirements for this ecosystem.

Technical Requirements

Most of the decisions made within the process of healthcare services are based on the various reports that are captured from the information related to a patient. These reports need to be shared as soon as possible with the respective parties so that decisions can be made soon, which will eventually help in providing the medicine at the right time.

On the other hand, this information needs to be protected against unauthorized access since healthcare-related information is highly sensitive. The key requirements of a healthcare information system include the following:

- Storing data in an efficient manner

- Sharing data quickly

- Consuming required information from external sources

- Providing interfaces to external people so that they have access to critical information

To strengthen our understanding of the requirements, let us discuss some of the common data points shared within a healthcare information system:

- Clinic schedules – These are valuable information for the general public, and the data are mostly static.

- Public health notification – Valuable information for the general public, and the data are mostly static.

- Patient report card – Highly dynamic, highly sensitive data collected on each and every patient.

- Lab results – Highly sensitive, highly verified information.

- Drug reports – Cumulative, less-dynamic details on available drugs and the requirements for each and every ward/unit.

- Staffing/patient reports – Numbers required for planning of operations.

- External reports – Police reports and birth/death certificates interact with external parties.

- Static data repositories – Information about profiles of certain users of the system are stored in static repositories.

In a typical healthcare system, these types of data need to be stored, shared, and utilized in a secure and effective manner. Doctors need to access patient report cards and lab reports as soon as those are available. Administration teams need to understand the capacities of the units and allocate healthcare staff members accordingly. Third parties need to access various kinds of reports in an easier manner without wasting their time. Let us design a solution architecture to cater to these requirements.

Solution Architecture

One common use case that occurs within the wards is doctors (consultants) visiting each and every patient (called as ward round). When they do that, they go through the patient's historical data that is mentioned in the patient report card. This is a real-time information exchange scenario where the user (doctor) needs access to patient data at that moment. Unless you have historical data stored somewhere (previous admissions, surgeries, etc.), the doctor has to rely only on the current report card related to that particular admission. Imagine a situation where the doctor has access to all the patient's data and it provides an analysis of patient health conditions, the decisions that doctor makes become much better.

Another use case is that the patients are sent to laboratories to get various tests done. Once these tests are done, laboratories send over the reports to the wards. This is a perfect example of asynchronous data exchange. Instead of getting the reports in batch mode (someone collects reports at a fixed time), we can build an event-based system that immediately sends the reports to the wards through events.

Security is another key aspect of a healthcare system where we need to protect personal health information from malicious access. Figure 9-8 depicts a solution architecture that can improve the experience of the overall healthcare ecosystem.

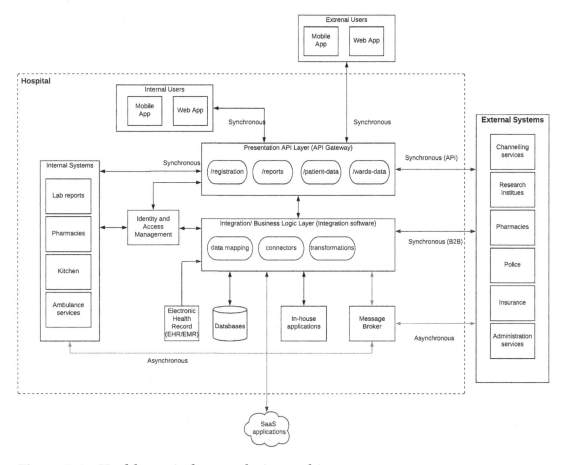

Figure 9-8. *Healthcare industry solution architecture*

As depicted in the figure, the solution architecture is designed based on two principles:

1. Messaging based – Synchronous vs. asynchronous

2. API driven – Information exchanges (synchronous) happen through APIs.

Let's start from the top layer where users (internal and external) interact with the system through client applications. These applications can be mobile or web applications installed on a laptop/desktop/tablet or even mobile phones. This layer is supported by the presentation API layer, which exposes data that needs to be accessed in a synchronous manner. Example APIs are

- Patient registration

- Patient report card

- Lab reports of a patient

- Ward statistics

There is an additional component called the Identity and Access Management component that takes care of the sensitive nature of data and how people access that data. The aforementioned information will be accessed by human users as well as other applications and systems that are internal.

Underneath this presentation API layer, there is a layer that does the actual heavy lifting and the processing of the data and orchestrates between multiple raw data systems to produce results that are consumable through presentation APIs. This layer integrates healthcare data from different EHR/EMR systems such as Epic or Cerner and other in-house and cloud applications as well as databases. It also integrates with other internal systems such as laboratory systems, pharmacy systems, and administration systems.

There is another major component within this architecture that is the "message broker," which will be used as the reliable messaging layer for asynchronous information exchanges. Some examples are

- Releasing lab results

- Police reports

- Birth/death reports

- Research data

- Drug reports

By using the message broker and an asynchronous communication approach, we can reduce the latency and manual interventions when sharing different types of reports with the recipients.

With the relevant access controls in place, the external healthcare ecosystem can be integrated with the hospital system through the message broker for asynchronous communication scenarios like lab reports, equipment, and drugs. Additionally, these systems can access the data in a synchronous manner using the APIs exposed at the API gateway. Also, there will be integrations between external systems and healthcare platform in cases such as research data integrations.

Benefits of the Solution

Having this sort of platform opens up a lot of advantages to the entire community. Here are some of the high-level advantages:

- Healthcare professionals get access to real-time data as well as historical data and analysis of the same data, which will increase the accuracy of their decisions significantly.

- Administration people can monitor the operations within a hospital as well as interactions with external parties and improve the overall operational efficiency of their service.

- The general public get the advantage of knowing their health conditions better and act responsibly.

- A notification system can be utilized to build awareness among the general public when there are certain medical conditions breaking out in certain areas and give people warnings and instructions as and when happens with much more transparency and trust.

- The medical research activities will get access to a lot of quality real data points to improve the quality of their medical research.

- Connecting this platform with healthcare-related businesses (e.g., pharmacies, healthcare equipment manufacturers, channeling centers, etc.) opens up a big market to those people as well as allows the general public to get better quality service at competitive prices.

Power and Energy Industry

The demand for energy has increased significantly in the recent years due to the developments in consumer electronics, mobile devices, as well as other equipments and machinery. Nowadays, you can find an electronics device for almost all the things that you did manually in the past. But this growing demand can cause challenges to the power and energy industry due to the effort required to cater to this demand and the resulting impact on the environment due to various power and energy generation activities.

Understanding the Ecosystem

The energy industry needs to deal with not only an increase in energy demand but also the technology and consumer advancements around it. With the innovations happening around electric vehicles, battery systems, renewable energy sources, and consumer expectations, having the technology backbone supporting these advancements is a critical step to achieve success in the energy industry. This means that the dynamics around the energy industry is shaping into a common model that is similar to industries like financial services and the automotive industry with specific aspects like markets, operations, and third-party service providers that are involved in the energy industry.

Figure 9-9 depicts a model of the energy industry along with its interaction with the market, operations, and service providers. It is a conceptual model that explains the interconnection of the traditional energy life cycle of generation, transmission, distribution through distributed energy resources (DERs), and consumption with the energy market, continuous operations, and involvement of third-party service providers and energy companies. It does show that these interconnections (or integrations) are critical to providing a quality service to the customers.

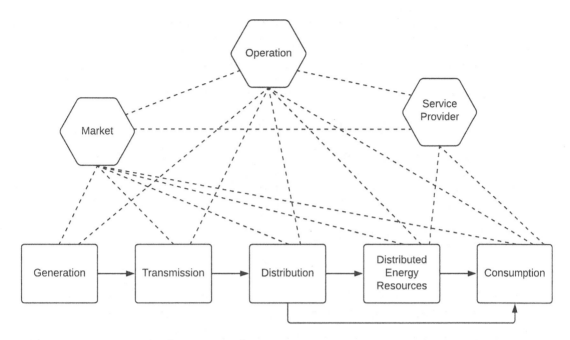

Figure 9-9. *Power and energy industry ecosystem*

Technical Requirements

From the perspective of the energy industry, the high-level requirements that we need to fulfill with a technical solution are as follows:

- Support the growing energy demand.

- Measure the impact on the environment and control it.

- Provide customers with the freedom to control their energy consumption.

- Provide customers with a continuous energy supply with minimum disruption.

- Improve the overall efficiency of generation, distribution, and delivery.

Most of the power and energy enterprises are finding it harder to fulfill these requirements due to the legacy nature of their existing IT infrastructure. The major challenges most of these enterprises face include the following:

- Legacy applications are used to store data.

- Higher cost for point-to-point integrations.

- Integrating with business partners requires a lot of manual work.

- Customer services are provided through traditional channels such as phone and in-person.

- Not enough information on what is happening on the grid.

- Could not make real-time decisions due to lack of data.

We need to design a solution that can cater to these challenges and provide the support to fulfill the requirements mentioned in the previous section.

The high-level capabilities that we need to design a solution for these requirements and challenges can be identified as follows:

- Integrating multiple systems through a common platform

- Exposing data through secured APIs so that partners and third parties can integrate instantly

- Improving the efficiency of energy generation and distribution through integrated systems and real-time decision-making

- IoT-enabled devices to monitor, collect, and act on data

- Mobile apps to manage the usage of energy, partner interactions, and internal employees through APIs (omni-channel customer service)

- Integrating and optimizing assets, devices, networks, servers, applications, and data across the enterprise and energy companies can drive business agility and more intelligent networks.

Solution Architecture

A solution that we design needs to be able to integrate disparate systems while exposing the required services in a secure manner through different channels. At the same time, smart devices and event processing need to be supported to monitor the system continuously and avoid failures and recover from failures. Figure 9-10 depicts a solution architecture that can offer these capabilities.

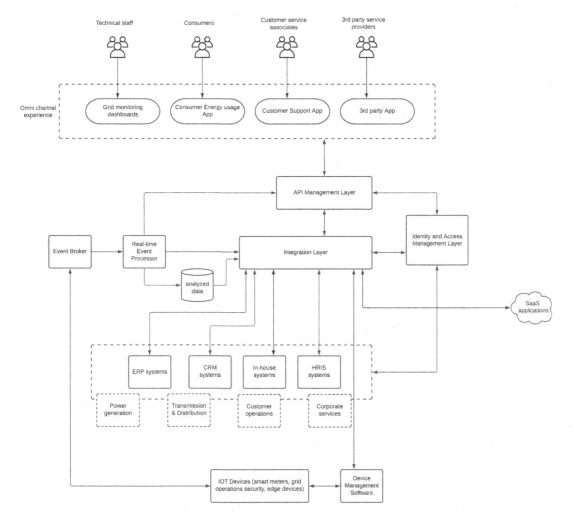

Figure 9-10. *Solution architecture for energy industry*

As depicted in the figure, "Integration Layer" is the main component that integrates disparate systems. It makes sure that systems are well integrated through data and necessary insights are generated to take key business decisions. It also helps to improve business efficiency and customer experience through timely access to data. In certain cases, we might need to implement long-running business processes for use cases such as providing a new connection and provisioning a new power plant. In that case, we can use a business process management (BPM) software component alongside the integration component.

The "API Management Layer" exposes the data that needs to exposed to internal and external users with security and control. These users can use different channels to interact with data through this layer. As an example, the operations center of the organization will use their interactive website to connect through WebSockets to listen to real-time notifications about system failures, while energy consumers will use their mobile applications to check the current month's energy usage. It also helps when interacting with various regulatory, compliance bodies and makes sure that processes are well integrated and maintained with the necessary access and auditing capabilities.

The "Identity and Access Management" layer is responsible for securing the data from fraudulent access and also makes life easier for the internal users to access multiple systems with a single login using Single Sign-On capabilities. In addition to that, it also helps to implement advanced security for consumer access with multifactor authentication (MFA) schemes.

One of the critical aspects of providing a continuous service is to keep monitoring every aspect of the energy generation, transmission, and distribution with proper tools. In addition to that, the consumer side also needs to be monitored. That is the functionality of various devices used in different locations within the grid, and those devices generate millions of events every minute. These events need to be collected and processed in real time to identify any abnormal behaviors in the grid and the distribution network. That is the task of the event broker and the real-time event processing components that are mentioned in the figure.

The preceding architecture can be expanded to support modern requirements like artificial intelligence, machine learning, and cloud computing with the usage of appropriate technologies. As an example, AI and ML-related functionalities can be integrated with the event broker and real-time event processing components easily. All the required integration points are available for such improvements to the system. Given this architecture is independent of any particular vendor or specific technology, users can use their preferred cloud vendor that offers these basic functional components with their offering. The good news for such users is that most of the major public cloud vendors provide these functional capabilities as cloud services.

Hospitality Industry

The hospitality industry spans across a wide range of products and services including hotels, restaurants, and spas to name a few. It is a blend of nature, culture, history, and technology. In recent years, technology played a major role in transforming the hospitality industry. More and more people started to become part of this industry, thanks to platforms such as Airbnb and other travel and booking websites and applications.

Understanding the Ecosystem

There are four main stakeholders that we can identify within the hospitality ecosystem:

- Guests (customers)
- Facilities
- Services
- Staff

Guests are the people who come to experience the hospitality provided by a hospitality provider such as a hotel. These guests use facilities such as rooms, restaurants, pools, and spas while experiencing the hospitality. In addition to these physical facilities, guests will also use services such as events, gaming, travel, and dining services offered by the provider. These services might be provided directly from the hotel or through the partners that are associated with the hotel. Then we have the staff who provide the human touch to the overall experience of the guests.

Technical Requirements

At a high level, a guest should be able to make a reservation of a facility and/or a service through multiple channels including mobile, web, global distribution systems (GDS), phone, and in-person. To offer such a capability, we need to have an API gateway that could hide the internal details of the system and provide a unified interface to these different clients. Then these reservations need to be checked against the systems such as reservations systems, royalty systems, event management systems, and internal databases. We need a component that can orchestrate these systems and provide a consumable data to the clients. An Integration component can fulfill this requirement.

Then we also need to have security enabled for clients to make sure that our system is accessed only by valid customers (not machines). Some common systems that we find in hospitality platform include the following:

- Central reservation system – Keeps track of all the property details and their availability

- Guest profile management system – Keeps track of guest information to provide better experience

- Loyalty management system – Keeps details about the loyalty programs

- Meeting/events inventory – Stores information about events that are organized within the premises

- Infrastructure management system – Stores information on devices, sensors, and their status

- Database – Stores application-specific data that are stored outside of the respective applications for reliability

Depending on the application type, different types of information need to be exposed through the system as APIs. Some APIs are only exposed to internal applications, while others are exposed to external applications. This requires proper segregation of APIs into different categories and exposes them with required security measures at the gateway layer. At the same time, internal applications need to be integrated to provide a seamless user experience like Single Sign-On.

Scalability and Performance Requirements

Providing multiple options for customers to make a booking improves the customer experience significantly. At the same time, one of the important aspects of these different channels is the average success rate of these channels. Not all the channels provide the same success rate, and these channels utilize different amount of resources in the system. It is the task of the system architects to design the system so that it can provide the best possible experience to the customers while maintaining a healthy information system performance without affecting other channels.

Based on the data captured by one of the largest hospitality providers, here are the success rates for these channels (Lookup-to-Book ratio):

- Direct bookings – 3:1
- Call center – 15:1
- Mobile/web apps by the provider – 60:1
- GDS systems – 120:1
- Third-party apps – 400:1

The preceding statistic clearly shows that different channels have different success rates. At the same time, another important statistic is the percentage of bookings for each channel.

- Direct bookings – 45%
- Call center – 9%
- Mobile/web apps by the provider – 25%
- GDS systems – 13%
- Third-party apps – 8%

If we consider both these statistics together, it is clear that we need to architect the system in a way that it provides the best possible experience to the channel with best conversation rate and booking ratio. At the same time, other less successful channels can be provided with somewhat lower performance while maintaining the system stability and the overall cost of the system. The method to achieve this type of segregation is to have microgateways that are specific to a certain client channel and scale them based on the needs of individual channels rather than putting all the APIs into one common gateway and scaling that monolithic gateway.

Solution Architecture

Based on the requirements we discussed in the preceding section, we can come up with a solution architecture consisting of API microgateways, integration, IAM, and other components as depicted in Figure 9-11.

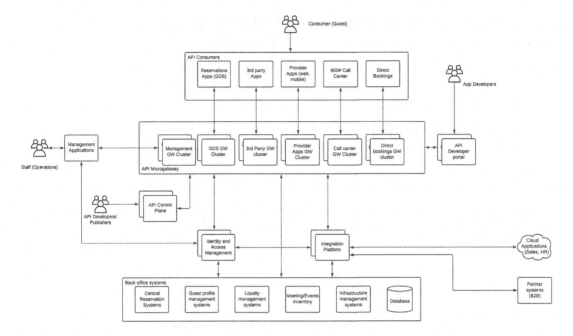

Figure 9-11. *Solution architecture for a scalable hospitality platform*

As depicted in Figure 9-11, APIs are deployed independently within API microgateway runtimes so that they can be managed and maintained separately without impacting the performance of the other APIs. This is a key aspect given the statistics we showed earlier where third-party apps can eat up a lot of resources with minimum success if we put all the APIs into the same gateway. In addition to that, the API control plane is deployed as a separate scalable component as well as the developer portal.

In addition to the gateway component, there is an integration component and IAM component that would provide the integration and security capabilities to the platform. Supporting legacy integration protocols is a crucial requirement in hospitality systems. Modern security requirements such as social logins, MFA, and multioption login also can be good-to-have features in the IAM platform. B2B integrations can also play a key role in this solution since the hospitality provider may work closely with business partners to operate the business.

This solution can be improved by adding analytics capabilities to identify unique customer usage patterns and provide recommendations for customers based on their historical travel and leisure habits. With the usage of AI/ML technologies, we can provide unique experiences to the users.

Summary

In this last chapter of the book, we discussed a set of solution architecture patterns that can be reused when designing and implementing enterprise platforms for certain industries. We discussed the transportation, telecommunications, retail, education, automotive, healthcare, power and energy, and hospitality industry–specific solution architecture patterns. Under each of these industries, we first went through the ecosystem identification, technical requirements gathering, and solution architecture design in each of the sections. We covered certain industry-specific use cases, systems, technologies, and performance requirements and designed the solution accordingly.

Index

A

ABAC model, 79
Accessibility software components, 250
Active Directory (AD), 77
Adaptability, 17
Adaptive authentication, 40, 186, 200, 201,
    212, 214
Air pollution sensors, 24, 316
Amazon ECS (Elastic Container
    Service), 290
Amazon Web Services (AWS), 116, 239,
    243, 269, 299
Analytics software, 326
Apache Camel, 86
Apache Synapse (XML), 66, 86
API definitions, 16, 90
API developer portal, 90–92, 124, 125,
    131, 177
API ecosystems, 230
API gateways, 48, 58, 74, 84, 85, 88, 89, 124,
    125, 142, 158–161, 175–177,
    217–224, 251, 254, 257, 280, 284,
    298–302, 308, 309, 320, 331
API governance, 123–125, 137
API key-based authentication, 219, 220
API-led connectivity architecture
    applications, 126
    business processing, 131
    common protocols, 130
    complex protocols, 129
    consumer-facing applications, 129
    enterprise-controlled components, 129

    industry-specific protocol, 130
    interoperability, 128, 130
    layered architecture, 127, 128
    standards, 128
    system-of-records applications, 131
    systems, 129
    technical approaches, 132
API life cycle management (LCM), 90, 106,
    107, 134
API management, 119, 121
    business insights, 124
    business leaders, 122
    capabilities, 136
    hypothetical organization, 122
    KPIs, 122, 123
    technical leaders/developers, 122
    ZZZ company's vision, 123
API management control plane, 136
API management platform, 16, 106, 107,
    136, 284
API manager deployment, 88
API microgateways, 34, 287, 294, 357, 358
API monetization, 124, 125
API platform components, 125, 126
API reusability, 106, 123
API security, 124, 125, 218–220
API security pattern
    API gateway, 217
    API key-based authentication, 219, 220
    basic authentication, 218
    delegated authentication with OAuth2,
    220, 221
    standards, 217

361

© Chanaka Fernando 2023
C. Fernando, *Solution Architecture Patterns for Enterprise*, https://doi.org/10.1007/978-1-4842-8948-8

Printed in the United States
by Baker & Taylor Publisher Services